The C
Name Book

Written by: Sheri Knight

Edits and Consultation by:
Dana Hollenbeck
&
Carrie Barnes

Special Thanks:
Michael DeMetro, for your support

Drew & Scout, for the inspiration

A

Abel - Hebrew. "Breath"; "son"; "breathing spirit"; in the *Old Testament* of *The Bible*, Abel was the son of Adam and Eve and was killed by his brother Cain in a fit of jealousy

Abelia - Shrub with small flowers of the honeysuckle family named in 1818 after French botanist Clarke Abel

Abellio - Celtic god of apple trees

Abelot - The Middle English masculine of Abeloth

Abeloth - A family name in Britain and Ireland in the Middle Ages, most commonly given to a girl; a fictional character on the dark side of the Force in the *Star Wars* universe

Abilene - Hebrew. "Grass"

Abitha - Aramaic. "Gazelle"; Notable Bearers: a fictional character in *Grandpa's Little Girls and Miss Abitha* (1928) by Alice Turner Curtis; Indian film actress Abitha goes by just her first name

Abner - Hebrew. "Father of light"

Abnoba - Celtic. "Goddess of the hunt"

Aboshan - *Magic: The Gathering* legendary creature

Abott/Abbott - Late Latin, Greek from Aramaic. "Father"; a man who is the head of a monastery; father superior

Abra - Hebrew. "Mother of many"; in *The Bible*, Abra was King Solomon's favorite wife

Abraham - Hebrew. "Father of many"; Notable Bearer: Abraham Lincoln (1809-1865) led the Union during the Civil War, brought about the emancipation of slaves and served as 16th President of the USA

Abram - Hebrew. "Father is exalted"; in *The Bible*, the first patriarch and ancestor of the Hebrews

Abraxas - An ancient charm composed of Greek letters inscribed on amulets, originally believed to have magical powers

Absalom - Latin, Hebrew. "The father is peace"; in *The Bible*, David's favorite son

Absinthe - A narcotic spirit which originated in the 17th century

Abzu - In Sumerian and Akkadian mythology, Abzu referred to the primeval sea below the void space of the underworld (Kur) and the earth (Ma) above

Acamarchi - A mountain in the Andes

Acheron - Greek, Latin. "River of sorrow or woe"; in Greco-Roman mythology, a river in Hades over which Charon ferried the souls of the dead

Achille/Achilles - Greek, Latin. In Homer's *The Iliad*, Achilles was the Greek hero of the Trojan War who killed Hector and was killed by Paris with a fatal arrow shot to the heel, his only vulnerable spot

Achsah - Biblical. "Adorned"; "bursting the veil"; in *The Bible*, Achsah was the daughter of Caleb, prince of the tribe of Judah

Acquario - French. "Aquarius"

Acrux - Latin. "A cross"; the star Alpha Crucis is the brightest star in the southern constellation Crux and the twelfth brightest in the sky

Ada - French. "Nobility"; a form of Old German Adalheidis

Adalbert - German. "Noble bright"; "noble shining"

Adalberta - German. "Noble and bright"

Adamaro - *Magic: The Gathering* rare legendary spirit

Adela - Latin. "Of the nobility"; Saint Adela was a 7th century Frankish princess who founded a monastery in Pfazel, France

Adelaide - Capital of South Australia, named after Queen Adelaide, consort to King William IV

Adeliza - English/Irish wife of Richard Trench, 4th Earl of Clan Carty; Italian countess and vampire siren figure

Adhara - Arabic. "Maidens"; the second brightest star after Sirius in the constellation Canis Major

Aditi - Sanskrit. "Limitless"; in *The Vedas*, Aditi is mother of the gods and all 12 zodiac spirits from whose cosmic matrix, the heavenly bodies, were born

Adkin - Old English from Hebrew. "Red-earth" (possibly referring to the earth from which God formed the first man in the *Old Testament* of *The Bible*)

Adlard/Allard - Norman English. "Noble"; "brave"; "strong"

Adler - German. "Eagle"; in Christian iconography, the eagle is the symbol of John the Evangelist, and as such a stylized eagle was commonly used as a house sign/totem in German-speaking areas

Admentus - Latin, Greek. "Wild"; "unbroken"; in Greek legend, a king of Thessaly whose wife, Alcestis, sacrificed her life for him but was brought back from Hades by Hercules

Admiral - Middle English, Old French, Arabic. "Ruler of"; a naval officer of the highest rank; any of various colorful butterflies with very small forelegs

Admiranda - English, Indian. "Worthy of admiration"

Adolph/Adolf/Adulf - Old High German, Latin. "Noble wolf"

Adonis - Latin, Greek, Phoenician. "Lord"; a very handsome young man; in Greek mythology, a young man loved by Aphrodite because he was so very handsome

Aed - Celtic. "Fire"

Aegir - Norse god of the sea

Aegis - Latin, Greek. "Goat skin"; "a protection; sponsorship; auspices"; in Greek mythology, a shield or breastplate used by Zeus and later by his daughter Athena

Aegisthus - Latin, Greek. In Greek legend, the son of Thyestes and lover of Clytemnestra; he helped her to kill her husband, Agamemnon

Aegyptus - In Greek legend, a king of Egypt whose 50 sons married the 50 daughters of his brother Danaus

Aeliana - Latin. "Noble and gracious"

Aelfthryth - Old English. "Strength"; Notable Bearer: Queen Aelfthryth (945-1000) was the first queen of England

Aelthered - Old English. "Noble-counseled"; Æthelred the Unready (986-1016) was King of the English; he was the son of King Edgar the Peaceful and Queen Ælfthryth

Aeneas - A Trojan hero in Greco-Roman mythology, the son of the prince Anchises and the goddess Venus

Aeolus - Latin, Greek. In Greek mythology, the god of the winds; a king of Thessaly, the Aeolians' forefather

Aernus - A Celtic god entrusted with protecting the Zoelae, an ancient Celtic tribe of Gallaecia

Aesa/Asa - Hebrew. "Physician"; King of Judah in *The Bible*; the name was revived by Puritans in the 17th century

Aeschines - Athenian orator from 389-314 BCE, a rival of Demos Thenes

Aeschylus - Greek writer of tragedies, lived 525-426 BCE

Aesclepius - In Greek mythology, the God of healing and medicine, corresponding to the Roman Aesculapius

Aesculapius - In Roman mythology, the God of medicine and healing, son of Apollo; associated with the Greek Asclepius

Aesir - In Norse mythology, a group of warrior gods led by Odin

Aesop - Master of fables, Aesop was a Greek storyteller in the 6th century BCE; he lived as a slave on the island of Samos

Aethelryth - Anglo-Saxon. "Noble"; "might"; "strength"

Aetheria - In Roman mythology, the daughter of Heliades; the original name for Ethiopia

Aetherius - Latin. "Of or pertaining to heaven"; "celestial"; "heavenly"; "sent by heaven"; "divine"

Aethewulf - Old English. "Noble Wolf"; Æthelwulf was King of Wessex from 839 to 858

Agamemnon - In Greek legend, king of the Mycenae and commander-in-chief of the Greek army in the Trojan War

Agatha - Greek. "Good"; Saint Agatha was 3rd century Christian martyr; the name was popular in the Middle Ages; Notable Bearer: Agatha Christie is a British writer

Agathocles - Tyrant of ancient Syracuse, lived 361-289 BCE

Agent - Latin. "To do; act"; Greek. "To drive"; a person or thing that performs actions or is able to on behalf of others; an active force or substance producing an effect

Aggi - Old Greek. "Kind; good"; "pure; chaste"; Celtic. "Hunger"; "lamb"; "one"

Aglaia/Aglaea - Greek. "Splendor"; "beauty"; in Greek mythology, she was one of the Graces and the goddess of beauty, splendor, glory and adornment

Agnella - Greek. "Pure"

Agnes - Greek. "Poor"; a popular name until the 16th century, again revived in the 19th century; Notable Bearer: Saint Agnes (291-304) was a Christian virgin martyr

Agni - Sanskrit. "Fire"; the Vedic fire god of Hinduism; Agni also refers to one of the guardian deities of direction, who is typically found in southeast corners of Hindu temples

Agniya - Russian. "Pure"

Agnu/Agnew - Gaelic. "Action"; "activity"; "descendant of Gníomh"

Agrafena - Russian. "Born feet-first"

Agragan - Surname in 17th century England

Agrona - Welsh goddess of war and slaughter

Agrus - *Magic: The Gathering* rare legendary human soldier

Ague - Middle English. "Old fashioned"

Agusta - Latin. "Majestic; grand"; originally given to female relatives of Roman emperors

Agustin - Latin. "Deserving of respect"

Agustus/Augustus - Latin. "To increase"; "great"; "venerable"; Augustus was the title given to Octavian, the first Roman emperor; he was the adopted son of Julius Caesar who rose to power through a combination of military skill and political prowess

Ahasuerus - Persian. In *The Bible*, either of the two kings of the Medes and Persians, especially the one who took Esther as his wife

Ahir/Aheer - An Indian ethnic group

Ahmose - Egyptian. "Born of Iah"; this was the name of the first pharaoh of the 18th dynasty; he defeated the Hyksos and drove them from Egypt

Ai - Japanese. 愛 "Love, affection"; 藍 "indigo"

Aias - Greek. "Mourner"; "of the Earth"

Aikman - Old English. "Oak man"; the ancestors of the Aikman family were part of an ancient Scottish tribe called the Picts who lived in Lanarkshire; Notable Bearer: Troy Kenneth Aikman is a former American football quarterback

Aiko - Japanese. "Loving child; affectionate child"

Ailwin/Aylwin - English. "Wise friend"

Aisling - Irish. "Dream; vision"; 17th/18th century genre of poetry; was not used as a name until the 20th century

Aitne - One of the moons of Jupiter; in Greek mythology, Aitne (or Aetna) was a nymph who was seduced by Zeus; the name of the Sicilian volcano Mount Etna derives from this name

Ajani - Nigerian. "He fights for possession"; *Magic: The Gathering* mythic rare planeswalker

Ajax - The name is borne in Greek mythology by two heroes renowned for their valor and prowess

Ajomies - Finnish. "Constellation"

Akako - Japanese. "Red child"

Akemi - Japanese. "Bright"; "beautiful"

Aker - Norse, Swedish. "Plowed field"; Egyptian god of Earth and the horizon

Akhenaten/Akhenaton/Echnaton/Ikhnaton/Khuenaten - Egyptian. "Effective for Aten", Greek. "Amun is satisfied". Ancient Egyptian pharaoh of the 18th Dynasty especially noted for abandoning traditional Egyptian polytheism and introducing worship centered on the Aten

Akhtang - Volcano in Japan

Akio - Japanese. "Bright or luminous man"

Akilina - Russian. "Eagle"

Akiko - Japanese. "Sparkle; bright"; "autumn" + "child"

Akira - Japanese. 明 "Bright"; "intelligent"; "clear"; Sanskrit. "Graceful strength"

Akroma - *Magic: The Gathering* legendary angel

Alabama - Yellow hammer/cotton state, "Heart of Dixie", the 22nd of the United States

Alabaster - A compact and fine-grained variety of gypsum often carved into ornaments

Aladdin - A chinese boy in *The Arabian Nights* (1706) who found a magic lamp and ring

Alamak - A Malay expression of dismay, surprise or alarm that has long been rumoured to mean "Allah's mother" but more likely means "God be with you" or "God forgive you"

Alamo - A poplar or cottonwood tree native to the southwest area of the USA

Alaric - King of the Visigoths who conquered Rome in 410

Alarica - Teutonic. "Universal ruler"

Alaska - Aleut. "The great land"; "the mainland"; "the object toward which the action of the sea is directed"

Alaunus - Celtic god of healing and prophecy

Alban - Saint Alban was a 3rd century British martyr

Albania - Country of Southeast Europe's Balkan Peninsula rich in castles and archaeological sites

Alas - Latin. "Weary"

Albany - Latin. "Of Alba"

Albion - A poetic or literary term for Britain or England (often used in referring to ancient or historical times)

Albedra - Arabic. "Reunion of broken parts"

Albray - Surname in 1840 England

Alceone/Alcyone - Latin from Greek. "King Fisher"

Alcestis - A princess in Greek mythology known for her love of her husband; *Alcestis* is an Athenian tragedy by the ancient Greek playwright Euripides; it was first produced at the City Dionysia festival in 438 BCE

Alcina - Opera seria by George Frederic Handel; he used the libretto of *L'isola di Alcina,* an opera that was set in 1728 Rome by Ricardo Broschi

Alcmene - In Greek mythology, the mother of Hercules

Alcor - Mizar and Alcor form a naked eye double star in the handle of the Big Dipper (or Plough) in the constellation of Ursa Major; Mizar is the second star from the end of the Big Dipper's handle, and Alcor its faint companion

Alcott - English. "From the old cottage"

Alden - Old English. "Old friend"; "wise friend"; "from the old manor"; a common name in the Middle Ages

Alder - A widely distributed tree of the birch family that has toothed leaves and bears male catkins and woody female cones

Alderon /Alderaan - A fictional planet in the *Star Wars* universe, called "the planet of beauty, nature, poetry, philosophy, art, couture and cuisine"

Aldith - Medieval English form of Ealdgyd; a character in the *Pokemon* universe

Aldred - Old English. "Old counsel"; "wise or red-haired man"; Aldred was common before the Norman Conquest and was revived in the 19th century

Aleaeus - Greek lyric poet from 620-580 BCE

Aleita/Alida - English, Greek, Spanish, Hungarian, Dutch, German, Italian. "Truthful"

Aleksei/Aleksey - Russian. "Defender"

Aleksandru - Medieval Slavic. "Defender of men"

Alexiane/Alexein - Greek. "To defend"; "to help"

Alfa/Alpha - The first letter of the Greek alphabet; the first star in a constellation

Alfredo - Anglo-Saxon. "Elf-counsel"; "wise counselor"

Alfwin - Ancient German. "Elf friend"

Algeria - Republic in Northwest Africa; the region was settled in 2000 BCE by Berber-speaking people

Algernon - French. "With a mustache"; *Flowers for Algernon* (1958) is a science fiction story by Daniel Keyes

Alhammarret - *Magic: The Gathering* rare legendary sphinx

Alias - Latin. "Introducing distortion or error"; a false or assumed identity

Alief - In philosophy and psychology, an automatic or habitual belief-like attitude, particularly one that is in tension with a person's explicit beliefs

Alioth - A variable star of the first magnitude that is seen in the handle of the Big Dipper

Alistair - Scottish, Gaelic from Greek. "Defender of man"

Allegany - Allegewi. "Lovely; beautiful"

Allis - Teutonic. "Noble humor"

Alloy - Old French. The relative purity of gold or silver; a metal that is a mixture of two or more metals

Ally - Middle English, Old French, Latin. "To bind"; "to unite or associate for a specific purpose"; "an associate, helper, or auxiliary"

Almolonga - Volcano in Guatemala

Almond - The edible, nut-like seed of a fruit resembling the peach, or the small, pink-flowered tree that this fruit grows on

Almus - Ancient Roman. "Nourishing"

Almyra/Elmira - Arabic. "Lucky number"

Alodia - Gothic. "Other; foreign"; "riches, wealth"; Saint Alodia was a 9th century Spanish martyr along with her sister Nunilo

Aloisa - German. "Famous warrior"

Alonzo - Teutonic. "Eager for war"

Aloysius - German. "Fame in war"

Alpharetta - Suburb of Atlanta, Georgia

Alpheus - In Greek mythology, a river God who pursued Arethusa until she was changed into a stream by Artemis

Alphina - Scottish. "Blonde"

Alphonsine - French. "Eager, noble warrior"

Alsea - Tillamook. "Flatheads"; the name applied to the Alsea tribe by their neighbors, the Tillamook and Coos peoples

Altair - Arabic. "The bird"; a star of the first magnitude in the constellation Aquila

Althaea/Althea - Greek. "Wholesome"

Alto - Italian, Latin. "High" (in music); the range of the lowest female voice (contralto) or the highest male voice

Alttari - Finnish. "Altar"

Alucard - One of the main protagonists in the *Hellsing* series

Alula - Latin. "Winglet"; Arabic. "First-born"

Alva - Hebrew. Often associated with the Latin Albus (white)

Alwain/Alwyn - German. "Noble friend"

Alysonne - German, French. "Noble"; "kind"

Amabel - Latin. "Beautiful"; "loving"; "lovable"; the name was used frequently during the Middle Ages and briefly in the 19th century, but has been largely replaced by the diminutive Mabel

Amadeus - Greek. "Love of God"; Latin. "To love God"; Notable Bearer: Austrian composer Wolfgang Amadeus Mozart (1756-1791) was actually born Wolfgang Theophilus Mozart but preferred the Latin translation of his Greek middle name

Amadis - Spanish. "Love of God"; the hero of several medieval romances in Spanish, French and English literature

Amador - Latin. "Lover of God"; it was particularly popular in the 16th century, having been borne by various saints

Amaethon - Welsh. "Laborer; ploughman"; in Welsh mythology, Amaethon was the god of agriculture

Amalthea - Latin, Greek. In Greek and Roman mythology, the goat that nursed Zeus (Jupiter); one of its horns was called the "horn of plenty" because it would become full of whatever its owner desired

Amaranth/Amarantha - Any plant of genus Amaranthus; an imaginary flower that never fades

Amarillo - Spanish. "Yellow"; Arabic. "Amber-colored"; a name given to several species of American arbors

Amaryllis - A bulbous plant with white, pink, or red flowers and straplike leaves

Amaterasu - Japanese 天照大神 "Great goddess"; "great spirit who shines in the heavens"; a deity of the Japanese myth cycle and also a major deity of the Shinto religion; she is seen as the goddess of the sun and universe

Ambersene - Popular baby name in Lithuania; the surname of a fallen family of Missouri pioneers in the 1840's

Ambisagrus - Celtic god of thunder, lightning, wind, rain and hail

Ambra - Italian. "Amber colored"

Ambre - French. "Jewel"

Ambrose - Latin, Greek. "Anything that smells or tastes delicious"

Ambrosia - Latin from Greek. "Immortal"; in Greco-Roman mythology, it is the food of the gods and immortals

Amelia - Old German. "Diligent"

Amenhotep - Egyptian. "Peace of Amon"; this was the name of four pharaohs of the New Kingdom, including Amenhotep the Magnificent, who ruled over Egypt during a time of great prosperity

Amethyst - A purple or violet variety of quartz used in jewelry; the ancient Greeks thought amethyst prevented intoxication

Amethystine - Made of or like amethyst

Ametrine - A naturally occurring variety of quartz which is a mixture of amethyst and citrine with zones of purple and yellow or orange

Amia - French. "Beloved; dearly loved"

Amicia - Old French. "Loved"; Latin. "Friend"

Amicus - Latin. "Friend of the court"

Amina - Turkish from Arabic. "Justice"; used in Victorian England; Notable Bearer: English aristocrat Almina, Countess of Carnarvon (1876-1969)

Amity - Old French, Latin. "Friendly"; "friendship"; "peaceful relations" (as in between nations)

Ammit - An Egyptian goddess who devoured condemned souls

Amnesty - French, Latin, Greek. "A forgetting"; "a deliberate overlooking of an offense"; "to pardon"

Amoret - An infant cupid, especially common in Italian art of the 16th century

Amoretta - Latin. "Little love"

Amphion - In Greek mythology, the son of Zeus and Antiope; with a lyre that Hermes gave him, he built a wall around Thebes by charming the stones into place

Amphitrite - In Greek mythology, one of the Nereids, a goddess of the sea and wife of Poseidon

Amphitryon - In Greek legend, a king of Thebes; Amphitryon's wife, Alcmene, became the mother of Hercules by Zeus, who seduced her by appearing in the likeness of Amphitryon

Amulet - French, Latin. "A charm"; something worn, often around the neck, as protection against injury or evil

Amun - Egyptian god of mystery

Amunet/Amaunet/Amonet - Egyptian. "The female hidden one"; a primordial goddess in ancient Egyptian religion; she was a member of the Ogdoad and the consort of Amun

Amus/Amos - Hebrew. "Born by God"; a Hebrew prophet of the 8th century BCE

Anabel/Annabel/Annabelle - English form of Latin Amabel. Edgar Allan Poe's poem *Annabel Lee* (1849) made this name popular throughout the English-speaking world

Anafenza - *Magic: The Gathering* legendary human soldier

Anaheim - Old German. "Ana's home"

Anahita - Avestan. "Kindness"; "being personable"; Iranian Water Goddess

Anakin - Anakin Skywalker is the antagonist in the *Star Wars* franchise; the name's meaning is unknown but is thought to be an homage to a friend of George Lucas

Ananke - Greek. "Force"; "constraint"; "necessity"; in Greek mythology, Ananke is the personification of inevitability, compulsion and necessity; she is often depicted as holding a spindle

Anala - Sanskrit. "Fire"; in Hinduism, one of the Vasus (gods of the material world); he is equated with Agni

Anaoero - Nauruan. "I go to the beach"

Anastasia - Greek. "Of the resurrection"; the feminine of Anastasius, emperor of the Eastern Roman Empire (491-518)

Anat - Syrian goddess of war and fertility who was adopted by the Egyptians

Anatole/Anatoli/Anatoly - French, Greek. Russian. "Sunrise"

Anaxagoras - Greek philosopher and geometrician who taught in Athens in the 5th century BCE

Anaximander - Greek philosopher in the 6th century BCE

Anbay - Qataban. "Of command and decision"; Anbay was a pre-Islamic deity of justice and an oracle in attendance to the moon deity Amm

Ancamna - A Celtic protector goddess of the Treveri, a tribe from the Moselle River area in Germany

Anchises - In Roman legend, the father of Aeneas

Anchor - Moor (a ship) to the sea bottom with a weight

Anchorage - The name of the city came from the name of a hardwood store operated from a boat, and refers to a place where a ship can lay anchor

Andalusia - A large autonomous region of hills, rivers and farmland bordering Spain's southern coast

Andalusite - A silicate of aluminum, from Andalusia where it was discovered, found in rhombic crystals in different colors

Anders - Scandinavian. "Manly"; in Sweden, Anders has been one of the most common names for many centuries

Anderson - English, Norse. "Son of Anders or Andrew"

Andora/Andorra - A town in Italy

Andradite - A variety of iron garnet containing calcium ranging from light green to black in color

Andraste - [on-DRAH-stay] In Celtic mythology, the goddess of war and victory; she was also the patron goddess of the Iceni tribe

Andrena - Commonly called the mining bee, the largest genus in the family Andrenidae is nearly worldwide in distribution

Andrion - Latin. "Man from Hadria"; "dark one"

Androclus/Androcles - A Roman slave who, according to legend, escaped death when thrown into the arena with a lion because the lion recognized him as the man who once extracted a thorn from his foot

Andromeda - Greek. "To be mindful of man"; in Greek mythology Andromeda was an Ethiopian princess rescued from sacrifice by the hero Perseus; a constellation in the northern sky which contains the Andromeda Galaxy

Andrusha - Russian. "Manly"

Andvari - In Norse mythology, a dwarf from whom Loki stole gold and a magic ring

Angeles - Latin. "Angels"; from a short form of the Marian personal name María de los Ángeles (Mary of the Angels)

Angeline/Angelina - Greek. "Messenger of gods"; Notable Bearer: Angelina Jolie Voight is an American actress

Angelous/Angelus - Latin. "Angel"; in the Roman Catholic Church, a prayer that is said at morning, noon and night in observance of the Annunciation

Angkor - Anglo-Saxon, Latin, Greek. "A device that holds something else secure, keeps it from giving way"

Angola - A Portuguese colony on the Southwest coast of Africa

Anguilla - Anglicized Latin. "Eel"; the place was formerly known as "Snake" or "Snake Island"

Angus/Aengus - In Celtic mythology, the god of love

Anhur - Egyptian god of war and hunting

Anila - In Hinduism, one of the gods of the elements of the cosmos; he is equated with the wind god Vāyu among the Vasus

Anise - French, Greek. A plant of the carrot family with small white or yellow flowers; the seeds are used in cooking and in medicines

Anita - Hebrew. "Grace"; "graceful"; in Avestan, Anita is the short form for Anahita, the Iranian Water Goddess

Anjali - Sanskrit. "Divine offering"; the name given to the greeting between Hindus, Buddhists and other Indian religions

Anjana - Indian. "Mother of lord Hanuman"

Anjar - Arabic عنجر Armenian, French. "Unresolved or running river"

Anju - In Indic languages, Anju is a diminutive form of the female given names Anjali and Anjana; in Japanese 杏樹 it is a feminine name meaning "apricot tree"

Ankaizina - Volcano in Madagascar

Ankh - ☥ Egyptian. "Life"; "soul"; a cross with a loop at the top; an ancient Egyptian symbol for life

Ankou - In Celtic mythology, Ankou is the personification of death who comes to collect the souls of passed-over humans

Annapolis - Mixture of Anna (grace) and Apollos (destroyed; ended)

Anneliese/Annaliese - German, Hebrew. Derived from a compound of Anna (grace) and Liesa, a German diminutive of Elizabeth (God is bountiful)

Anneth - Hebrew. "God was gracious"; "God has shown favor"; Arabic. "Friendly"

Annetta - French. "Little Ann"

Annika - Sanskrit name used commonly by Hindu followers

Annis - Greek. "Poor, pure, or chaste"; Black Annis, also known as Black Agnes, is a bogeyman figure in English folklore; she is imagined as a blue-faced crone with iron claws and a taste for humans (especially children)

Annora - Hebrew. "Grace"; Latin. "Honor"; one of the most common forms of the name Honor in the Middle Ages in England

Anowon - *Magic: The Gathering* rare legendary vampire shaman

Anput - Egyptian goddess of the dead and mummification

Ansel/Anselm - Latin, German. "Follower of a nobleman"; "god's helmet"

Anselma - Feminine of Anselm, for Saint Anselm, archbishop of Canterbury (1093-1109)

Anselmus - Latin, German. "God's defender"

Ansgar/Ansgard - German, Swedish. "God spear"; Saint Ansgar was a 9th century missionary who tried to convert the Danes and Norwegians

Anshar - Babylonian. "Whole heaven"; the primordial god of the sky and of male principle in Mesopotamian mythology; his consort is Kishar

Antaeus - In Greek mythology, a giant wrestler who was invincible as long as he was touching his mother, the Earth

Antares - Greek. "Mars"; a large red star, the brightest in the constellation Scorpio

Anthea/Antheia - Greek. "Flower; blossom"; this was an epithet of the Greek goddess Hera

Antica - "Antique"; used in names of restaurants and various artisan shops to recall the quality of the past; sometimes a reference to the foundation date, other times to the working process

Antigone - In Greek legend, the daughter of Oedipus and Jocasta; she defied her uncle, Creon, by performing funeral rites for her brother Polynices

Antigonus - Antigonus Cyclops (382-301 BCE) was the Macedonian general of Alexander the Great

Antje - [ONT-ya, on-TEE-yuh] Frisian, Dutch and German diminutive of Anna

Anton - English. "Highly praiseworthy"

Antonetta - Swedish. "Priceless"; Latin. "Praiseworthy"

Antosha - Russian. "Inestimable"

Anu - Sumerian. "Sky; heaven"; the Mesopotamian god of the sky known as "Sky Father, King of the Gods, Lord of the Constellations"

Anubis/Anuba - In Egyptian religion, a god with the head of a jackal, who led the dead to judgement; identified with the Greek Hermes

Anuket - The goddess of Egypt's southern frontier regions

Anumati - Sanskrit. अनुमति "Divine favor"; also known as Chandrama, Anumati is a lunar deity and goddess of wealth, intellect, children, spirituality, and prosperity in the Hindu religion

Anya/Ania - Russian. "Gracious"; "bringing goodness"; Hungarian. "Mother"; Berber. "Graceful rhythm"

Anzoy - Russian. "Sword of God"

Anzu - Japanese. 杏子, あんず "Apricot"

Aodh - Scottish, Irish, Gaelic. "Fire"; the Celtic sun god

Aoi - Japanese. 葵 "Hollyhock"; "althea"

Apamea - On the right bank of the Orontes River in Syria, the site of a treasure city of the Seleucid kings

Aparah - Sanskrit. "Latter; later; successor"

Aphra/Aphrah - Hebrew. "Dust"; the biblical house of Aphrah means "house of dust"; Notable Bearer: 17th century British dramatist and novelist Aphra Behn

Aphrodite - Greek. "The foam-born"; in Greek mythology the goddess of love and beauty who was said to have sprung from the sea; identified with Venus by the Romans; a type of butterfly

Apkallu - The seven Mesopotamian demigods who are said to have been created by the god Enki to establish culture and give civilization to mankind

Apollo - Greek. "To destroy"; Latin. "A handsome young man"; in Greek mythology Apollo was the son of Zeus and Leto and the twin of Artemis; he was the god of prophecy, medicine, music, art, law, beauty, and wisdom

Apollonia - Biblical. "Perdition; destruction"

Apollyon - Greek. "Destroying"; "ruining"; "the angel of the bottomless pit"; "the devil"; "satan"; an evil spirit subdued by the hero, Christian, in John Bunyan's *Pilgrim's Progress* (1678)

Appia - Feminine variant of a popular name used by the Claudia family in the 3rd century BCE; a common nickname is Ap or App

Appius - Used predominantly by the Claudia family; Appius Claudius Caecus was a Roman statesman of the 3rd century BCE and was responsible for the first Roman aqueduct

April - Middle English. "Avril"; Sanskrit. "Latter; later; successor"; Gothic. "Afar"

Apus - Greek. "No feet"; a small constellation in the southern sky representing a bird-of-paradise which was once wrongly believed to lack feet; a sacred bull worshipped by ancient Egyptians because of a supposed connection with the God Ptah

Aquarius - Latin. "The water carrier"; a large central constellation representing a man pouring water from a container; the 11th sign of the zodiac

Aquilla/Aquila - Latin. "Eagle"; a northern constellation in the Milky Way galaxy outlining an eagle

Ara - Latin. "An altar"; a constellation in the southern sky

Arabella - Old German. "Beautiful eagle"

Arabesque - French, Italian. "Fantastic and elaborate"; a ballet pose; a musical composition in rondo form; a complex and elaborate design of intertwined flowers, foliage, or geometric patterns painted or carved in low relief

Arabia - Biblical. "Evening"; "desert"; "ravens"

Arachne - In Greek mythology, a girl who was turned into a spider by Athena for challenging the goddess to a weaving contest

Aragon - A local surname for someone who once lived, held land, or was born in the beautiful region of Spain

Araminta - English "Prayer and protection"; Notable Bearers: abolitionist Harriet Tubman (1822-1913) was born into slavery as Araminta "Minty" Ross, but changed her name when she escaped; Araminta Estelle "Minta" Durfee (1889-1975) was an American silent film actress

Aranea - A spider-like creature from the *Dungeons & Dragons* fantasy role-playing game

Aranyani - In Hindu religion, a goddess of the forests and the animals that dwell within them; Aranyani has the distinction of having one of the most descriptive hymns in the *Rigveda* dedicated to her, in which she is described as being elusive, fond of quiet glades in the jungle, and fearless of remote places

Arashi - Japanese. "Storm"

Arausio - A local Celtic water god who gave his name to the town of Arausio (Orange) in southern Gaul, as touted by ancient inscriptions

Arawn - In Welsh mythology, Arawn was the king of the otherworld realm of Annwn, a world of delights and eternal youth where disease is absent and food is ever-abundant

Arbiter - Latin. "A person authorized to judge or decide"

Arbor - Middle English, Latin, Old French. "Tree; family tree"

Arc - The apparent curved path of a star or planet

Arcade - French, Latin. "Bow, arch"; an avenue of trees

Arcadia - Greek. "Pastoral simplicity and happiness"

Arcane - Old English. "Understood by few"; "mysterious or secret"

Arcanis - Latin. "Faithful in secret"

Arche - Greek. "Beginning"; "origin"; "source of action"

Archer - A person who shoots with a bow and arrows, especially at a target for sport; the constellation Sagittarius

Archibald - Old German. "Genuine"; "precious"; "bold"

Archimedes - Greek mathematician and physicist in the 3rd century BCE; he discovered principles of the lever and of specific gravity

Arcturus - Latin, Greek. "A bear"; "a guard"; the brightest star in the constellation Bootes

Ardel - English. "From the hare's dell"

Arden - A wooded district in Warwickshire, England, the site of a former forest made famous by William Shakespeare in *As You Like It* (1623); a land of romance

Ardis - Irish, Scottish. "Fervent"

Ardley - English. "From the home lover's meadow"

Ardra - Sanskrit. "Green"; "the moist one"; a nákṣatra in Hindu astrology; in Hindu religion, a goddess associated with Taraka, an asura who is granted invulnerability by Brahma

Ares - The Greek god of war; he is one of the Twelve Olympians, the son of Zeus and Hera and brother of Athena; he often represents the physical and untamed aspect of war

Aretha - The Greek version of Athena; Notable Bearer: Aretha Franklin is an American musician and singer-songwriter

Arethusa - Latin, Greek. In Greek mythology, a woodland nymph, changed into a stream by Artemis so that she might escape her pursuer, the river god Alpheus; a variety of orchid with one long, slender leaf and one rose-purple flower

Argentina - Latin. "Silver"

Argo - Latin, Greek. In Greek legend, the ship on which Jason sailed to find the Golden Fleece; a large, southern constellation between Canis Major and the Southern Cross

Argus - Latin. "Vigilant"; "keenly observant"; Greek. "Bright"; in Greek mythology, a giant with 100 eyes ordered by Hera to watch Io; after Argus was killed by Hermes, his eyes were put into the tail of the peacock

Argyle - A pattern composed of diamonds of various colors on a plain background

Arjuna - Sanskrit. "Bright"; "silver"; the third of the Pandavas, the sons and princes of Pandu, who is considered to be the hero of the Hindu epic *Mahabharata*

Aria - Italian from Latin. An air or melody in an opera, cantata or oratorio, especially for solo voice with instrumental accompaniment

Ariadne - In Greek legend, King Minos' daughter who gave Theseus the thread by which he found his way out of the minotaur's labyrinth

Aries - Greek. "The ram"; a constellation in the northern sky

Ariete/Arietta - Italian. "Little aria"; German. "Eagle"

Arion - A Greek poet and musician; a mythical magic talking horse born to Poseidon and Demeter

Aristarchus - Greek astronomer who discovered the precession of the equinoxes in the 3rd century BCE

Aristotle - Greek philosopher (384-322 BCE); a pupil of Plato, the tutor of Alexander the Great, and the author of many scientific works

Arizona - A southwest state bordering Mexico, nicknamed the "Sunset State"

Arkansas - French. "Land of downriver people"; Sioux. "People of the south wind"; the Kansa tribe of Native Americans are closely associated with the Sioux tribes of the Great Plains

Arlo - Old English. "Army; fortified troops" + "war"

Armani - African. "From the house of Armand"; an Italian fashion house founded by Giorgio Armani

Armilda - Teutonic. "Armored battle maiden"

Armistice - An agreement made by opposing sides in a war to stop fighting for a certain time; a truce

Armstrong - Scottish from Middle English. "Man with strong arms"

Arnemetia - The goddess of water in Celtic mythology

Arnott/Arnot/Arnoth - Scottish, English. Habitational name from a place called Arnot, near Kinross

Arrah - Irish. Used to express surprise or excitement

Arrakis - A fictional desert planet featured in the *Dune* series of novels by Frank Herbert

Arrow - Anglo-Saxon, Latin, Gothic. "Belonging to the bow"

Artaxerxes - [ar-tah-ZIRK-cees] Old Persian. "Whose reign is through truth"; Notable Bearer: King of Persia from 404 BCE until his death in 358 BCE; he was a son of Darius II and Parysatis

Artelia - Latin, English. "Attentive"

Artemesia/Artemisia - Greek. "Gift from Artemis"; "of Artemis"; the Greek counterpart of the Roman goddess Diana; Notable Bearer: 4th Century Queen of Caria who was responsible for the Mausoleum of Halicarnassus, one of the Seven Wonders of the World

Artemis - In Greek mythology, the goddess of the moon, wild animals and hunting; Apollo's twin sister and daughter of Zeus; she is identified with the Roman goddess Diana

Arthurina/Arthur - Latin. "Noble, courageous"; Notable Bearer: Legendary 6th century King Arthur of Britain and his Knights of the Round Table

Artio - [AR-show] The Celtic goddess of wildlife, transformation, and abundance

Aruna - In Hinduism, the personification of the reddish glow of the rising sun, which is believed to have spiritual powers; the presence of Aruṇá, the coming of day, is invoked in Brahmin prayers to Surya

Arvernus - In Gallo-Roman religion, Arvernus was the tribal god of the Arverni and an epithet of the Gaulish Mercury

Arvilla - Latin, Old German. "Fertile"

Arya - Persian. آریا "Goddess"; Sanskrit. आर्य "Of nobility and honor"; "great"; "truthful"; in Old World countries it is a masculine name but is usually used as a feminine name on the Western side of the globe

Asbjorn - Old Norse. "Divine bear"

Asbury - Old English. "Fortified manor"; a city on the New Jersey shore

Asgard - In Norse mythology, the home of the gods and slain heroes

Ash/Ashe - Hebrew. "Happy"; in Egyptian lore, the god of the Libyan desert and of the oases of west Egypt

Ashadha - A month of the Hindu calendar that corresponds to June/July in the Gregorian calendar

Ashaya - *Magic: The Gathering* legendary elemental creature

Ashberry - An Asiatic evergreen shrub (Mahonia japonica) with handsome foliage and yellow flowers

Asher/Ashur - Hebrew. "Happy, fortunate, blessed"; in Assyrian mythology, the god of war and empire; in the *Old Testament* of *The Bible*, Asher was the eighth son of Jacob and the second son of Zilpah

Ashford - English. "Lives by the ash tree ford"

Ashildr - Old Norse. "God battle"; a fictional character in the *Doctor Who* franchise

Ashiok - *Magic: The Gathering* planeswalker

Ashlesha - Sanskrit. One of the 27 nakshatras in Hindu astrology; Ashlesha is also known as the Clinging Star, Nāga or Hydra

Ashling - Irish. "A vision"; "a dream"; a popular poetic genre from the 17th and 18th centuries in which Ireland is personified as a beautiful woman in peril

Ashta - Indian. अष्टलक्ष्मी "Eight Lakshmis", a group of eight Hindu goddesses

Ashtaroth/Ashtoreth - Syrian goddess of love and fertility

Ashvini - The first nakshatra (lunar mansion) in Hindu astrology, corresponding to the head of Aries

Asira - A local god worshipped in pre-Islamic northern Arabia; he was revered at Taima and was strongly influenced by Egyptian culture

Ascella - Another name for Zeta Sagittarii, a binary star in the constellation of Sagittarius

Aslan - Turkish. "Lion"; the name of the lion in C.S. Lewis's fantasy book series *The Chronicles of Narnia*

Asmodeus - Latin, Greek, Hebrew. "Chief demon"; an evil spirit in Jewish demonology

Aspasia - Ancient Greek. "Welcome embrace"; Aspasia was an influential immigrant to Classical-era Athens who was the lover and partner of the statesman Pericles

Asphodel - An immortal flower said to grow in the Elysian fields; Homer describes it as covering the great meadow and it is mentioned by several poets in connection with mythology

Astara/Astra - Latin. "Of the stars"

Astaroth/Astarot/Asteroth - In demonology, the Great Duke of Hell, he is part of the evil trinity along with Beelzebub and Lucifer; Astaroth is named after the Mesopotamian goddess Ishtar

Astarte - In Phoenician mythology, the goddess of the moon, fertility and sexual love; also known as Ishtar or Ashtoreth

Aster/Astor - Greek. "Star"; denoting relationship to a star

Asteroid - Greek. "Starlike"; shaped like a star or starfish; in astronomy, any of the small planets with orbits between those of Mars and Jupiter; a planetoid; in Zoology, a starfish

Astrid - Scandinavian. "Godly strength"; German. "Divine strength"; "divine beauty"; Astrid has been used by Norway's royal families for hundreds of years

Astyanax - In Greek legend, the young son of Hector and Andromache; he was killed when thrown from the walls of Troy by the Greek conquerors

Asura - Sanskrit. असुर A class of divine beings or power-seeking deities related to the more benevolent devas (also known as suras) in Hindu mythology; Asuras are sometimes considered nature spirits and they battle constantly with the devas

Aswiniis - Hindu. "Harnessing horses"; the first nakshatra (lunar mansion) in Hindu astrology, corresponding to the head of Aries; this name was popular in the 6th century

Atahualpa - Last Inca king of Peru, lived 1500-1533

Atalanta - Latin. In Greek legend, a beautiful, swift-footed maiden who offered to marry any man able to defeat her in a race, death being the penalty for failure; Hippomenes won by dropping three golden apples in the path, which Atalanta stopped to pick up along the way

Atalya - Spanish. "Guard tower"

Atari - American video game company founded in 1972 which was primarily responsible for the video arcade and the modern video game industry

Aten/Aton - The disk of the sun in ancient Egyptian mythology, originally an aspect of the god Ra

Athena - In Greek mythology, the goddess of wisdom, skills and warfare; identified by Romans as Minerva

Athreos - *Magic: The Gathering* mythic rare legendary enchantment god

Atlantis - Ancient Greek. "Island of Atlas"; a fictional island mentioned in Plato's works *Timaeus* and *Critias* representing his embodiment of an ideal state; a fabled lost city

Atlas - Latin, Greek, Indo-European. "To bear"; in Greek legend, a giant compelled to support the heavens on his shoulders; any person carrying a great burden

Atlaua - A water god in Aztec mythology who was the protector of fishermen and archers

Atli - Old Norse name for Attila the Hun; in Norse mythology, the King of the Huns, killed by his wife because he had killed her brothers for the treasure of Sigurd

Atreus - In Greek legend, a king of Mycenae, son of Pelops and father of Agamemnon Menelaus; to avenge the treachery of his brother Thyestes, who seduced his wife and planned his murder, Atreus killed Thyestes' sons and served their flesh to him at a banquet

Atreyu/Atreju - Originally found in the German fantasy novel, *The Neverending Story* by Michael Ende (1979); in the book, the character Atreyu's parents are killed when he is a baby and the village raises him, therefore the name means "son of all"

Atria - Form of atrium, a chamber or cavity, especially an auricle of the heart

Atropos - Latin, Greek. "Not to be turned"; in Greek mythology, one of the three Fates who is represented as cutting the thread of life

Attica - Greek. "Shore"; "maritime place"

Atticus - Latin. "Man of Attica"; dating back to antiquity, Attica is the region in Greece which surrounds Athens; Atticus Finch is the protagonist of Harper Lee's 1960 novel *To Kill a Mockingbird*

Attila - Gothic. "Little father"; Notable Bearer: Attila the Hun (5th century) was so named by the Visigoths who were dominated for a time by the Huns

Auberee - Middle French. "Hut"; "to lodge"; East German. "To shelter an armed force"

Auburn - Middle Eastern. "White" + "brown"

Auden - English. "Old friend"

August - Latin. "Inspiring awe and reverence"; "imposing and magnificent"; "dignified and majestic"; "from high position or rank"

Augustine - Latin. "Of August"; Notable Bearers: 1st Century Roman monk who went to spread Christianity to the English; first archbishop of Canterbury

Aura - Latin, Greek. "Air"; "breeze"; an invisible emanation or vapor, as the aroma of flowers; an invisible atmosphere emanating from and surrounding a person or thing; electricity

Aurelia - Latin. "Golden"

Aureliana - Feminine of Roman emperor and militarist Aurelianus (212-275)

Auriga - Latin. "Wagoner"

Aurora - In Roman mythology, the goddess of dawn, associated in Greek mythology with Eos; luminous bands of light appearing in the night sky at the Earth's poles as Borealis (north) and Australis (south)

Auster - Latin. A poetic personification of the south wind

Austrina - An appealing southeast cactus, especially when in flower or with ripe fruit

Avalon - Welsh. "Apple"; "island of apples"; Old English. "Island of paradise"; deeply rooted in Arthurian legend, Avalon is said to be the resting place of King Arthur

Avatar - Sanskrit. अवतार "Descent"; a concept in Hinduism that refers to the material appearance or incarnation of a deity on earth

Avel - Russian. "Gentle breath"

Avelina/Aveline - Variant of medieval given name Avis (bird)

Aventine - Latin. "Hill"; one of the seven hills on which Rome was built

Averil - Anglo-Saxon. "Born in April"

Averroes - Arabic. "Good judgement"; a medieval Andalusian polymath

Aveta/Evita - In Gallo-Roman religion, a mother goddess associated with fresh water; Aveta is known mainly from clay figurines depicting the goddess with infants at the breast, small lap dogs, or baskets of fruit

Aveza - Latin. "Desired"

Avis - Latin. "Bird"; the Normans introduced this name to England and it became moderately common during the Middle Ages

Axel/Axl - Swedish. "Supporter"; Notable Bearer: William Bruce "Axl" Rose is an American musician

Axis - An agreement or alliance between two or more countries that forms a center for an eventual larger grouping of nations

Axton - English. "Swordsman's stone"

Aya/Aja - In Akkadian mythology Aya (or Aja) was a mother goddess, consort of the sun god Shamash; she developed from the Sumerian goddess Sherida, consort of Utu

Aykroyd - Anglo-Saxon. "Oak clearing"; Notable Bearer: Daniel Edward Aykroyd is a Canadian American actor

Ayumi - Japanese. "Step or walk"; "walker"

Ayyappan - A Hindu deity worshiped in a number of shrines across India; Ayyappan is believed to be an incarnation of Dharma Sasta, who is the offspring of Shiva and Vishnu and is generally depicted in a yogic posture

Azalea - A deciduous flowering shrub of the heath family with clusters of brightly colored, sometimes fragrant flowers

Azami - Japanese, Persian. "Thistle flower"; "greatest"

Azara - Persian. "Scarlet"; Hebrew. "Help"

Azazel/Azazael - Hebrew. "For the complete removal"; appears in *The Bible* in association with the scapegoat rite; in some traditions of Judaism and Christianity, it is the name for a fallen angel

Azimua - A goddess in Sumerian mythology, one of the eight deities born to relieve the illness of Enki

Azizos - In ancient Levantine mythology, Azizos or Aziz is the Palmyran god of the morning star; he is usually portrayed as riding a camel with his twin brother Arsu

Azlee - Old English. "Lives in the ash tree grove"

Azorite/Azurite - A mineral that occurs as blue prisms or crystal masses, often with malachite

Azrael - Aramaic, Hebrew. "Help of God"; the angel who, according to ancient Jewish and Muslim belief, parts the soul from the body in death

Azura/Azure - Old French. "Bright blue in color"; like a cloudless sky

Azusa - Arabic. "Lily"

B

Baal - In Egyptian lore, the god of the sky and storms

Baalbek - Ancient Phoenician city located in what is now Lebanon

Babbette - Greek from Hebrew. "Oath of God"; "God is satisfaction"

Babel - Hebrew, Assyrian, Babylonian. "Gate of god"; "a confusion of voices, languages"; "a place of such confusion"

Babrius/Babrias - The author of a collection of Greek fables, many of which are known today as *Aesop's Fables*

Babylon - Latin, Greek, Hebrew. Capital of Babylonia, an ancient city on the Euphrates River famous for wealth, luxury and vice

Babylonia - Latin, Greek. An ancient empire of southwest Asia which flourished from 2700-538 BCE

Baccari - Swahili. "Noble promise"

Bacchus - An ancient Roman god of wine and revelry; earlier called Dionysus by the Greeks

Bach - Middle High German. "Stream"; Notable Bearer: Johann Sebastian Bach (1685-1750) was a German composer and musician of the Baroque period

Badge - Middle Eastern. A distinctive mark or sign worn to show one's rank, belief, membership, etc.

Bahama/Bahamas - A state of the Lucayan Archipelago consisting of more than 700 islands, cays, and islets

Bahrain - Arabic. "Two seas"; a nation in the Arabian Gulf consisting of 30 islands

Bailey - Old English. "Bailiff"; "the outer wall of a castle"

Baja - Spanish. "Lower"

Bakugan - Japanese. "Exploding sphere"

Balaam - In *The Bible*, a prophet hired to curse the Israelites; when he beat his donkey, the animal rebuked him

Baldas - Phoenician. "Baal protects the king"; a reduced form of Balthazar

Balder - Old Norse. "Bold hero"; in Norse mythology, the god of light, peace, virtue and wisdom

Baldric - Middle Eastern, Old French, Old High German. A belt worn over one shoulder and across the chest to support a sword, trumpet, etc.

Baldwin - Old French, Middle High German. "Old friend"

Bale - Middle English. A poetic description of evil, sorrow, disaster or harm

Balefire/Baelfire - Old English. "A large fire in the open air"; "bonfire"; Baelfire, also known as Bae, is a fictional character in the fantasy series *Once Upon A Time*

Balena - Italian. "Good luck"

Bali - Hindi. "Soldier"; in Hindu mythology, Bali is the monkey king who can weaken enemies with a wish

Ballad - French. "Dancing song"; Latin. "Ball" (dance); a romantic or sentimental song with the same melody for each stanza

Ballard - Old English. "White spot"; "bald head"

Ballas - Italian. "Bullet"; "cannonball"

Balor/Balar - In Irish mythology, Balor was king of the Fomorians, a group of supernatural beings; he has been interpreted as personification of drought and blight

Baltazar/Balthazar - Phoenician. "Baal protects the king"; the name is commonly attributed to one of the three wise men in *The Bible*

Balthier - Hebrew. "God protect the king"

Balthor - Diminutive of Balthazar; *Magic: The Gathering* legendary zombie dwarf

Baltimore - From the title of the English Barons of Baltimore, borne by members of the Calvert family, who were Lord Proprietors of the colony of Maryland in the 17th century and for whom the state capital was named

Bane - Hawaiian. "Long-awaited child"; a fictional supervillain in the *DC Comics* universe

Banjo - Yoruba. "Dance for me"; a string instrument

Banquo - A fictional character in William Shakespeare's tragedy *MacBeth* (1606)

Banshee - Irish. "Woman"; "fairy"; in Irish and Scottish folklore, a female spirit believed to wail outside a house as a warning that a death will soon occur in the family

Baptista - Greek, Middle English. "Immerse"; "Baptise"; Latin. "Baptist"; a unisex name in the Middle Ages

Barack/Barak - African. "Blessed"; a variant of the Hebrew name Baruch and the Arabic name Mubarak, both meaning "blessed"; Notable Bearer: Barack Obama was the 44th President of the USA

Baraka/Barakah/Berakhah - In Judaism, a blessing usually recited during a ceremony; in Islam, the force from God that flows through the physical and spiritual spheres

Barbarella - A 1968 science fiction film based on the comic book of the same name

Barbarossa - Italian. "Red beard"; Notable Bearers: Barbarossa (1123-1190) was the Holy Roman Emperor who conceded supremacy to the pope and drowned leading the Third Crusade; Frederick Barbarossa was a 16th century pirate

Barclay - English, Scottish. "Where birches grow"

Bard - Gaelic, Irish. An ancient Celtic poet, composer and singer who usually sang to the music of a harp

Bardan - English. "One who lives near the boar's den"; "barley valley"

Bardolph - Old German. "Bright wolf"; a fictional character who appears in four plays by William Shakespeare

Barinthus - The god of sea and weather in Irish mythology

Barkley - Old English. "Birch valley"; "birch tree meadow"

Barley - Old English. "Wild boar"; "woodland clearing"

Barlow - Old English. "Lives on the bare hill"

Barnabas - Latin, Greek, Aramaic. "Son of exhortation"

Barnett - Old English. "Place cleared by burning"; from a medieval personal name

Baron - Middle English, Old French, German. "Man"; Indo-European. "To carry; to bring"; in the Middle Ages, a feudal tenant of the king or any other high-ranking lord; a nobleman

Baroness - Middle English, Old French. A baron's wife, widow or, in some countries, daughter; a lady with a barony in her own right

Barony - Old English. "The rank and estates of a baron"; Irish. "A division of a county"; Scottish. "A large manor or estate"

Baroque - Relating to or denoting a style of European architecture, music, and art of the 17th and 18th centuries that is characterized by ornate detail

Barret - Norman English. "Bear power"; introduced to Britain during the Norman Conquest

Barringer/Berengier - Norman English. "Bear spear"

Barsheba - Biblical. "Seventh well"; "well of the oath"

Bartel - Aramaic. "Ploughman"

Bartlett - A Hebrew pet form of Middle English Bartholomew (having many furrows)

Barton - English. "An outlying grange"

Baru - Indonesian. "Fresh, original, striking, strange, eccentric or fantastic"

Basandra - *Magic: The Gathering* rare legendary angel

Bashir/Basheer - Arabic. بشير "The one who brings good news"

Basilea - Old Greek. "Royal or kingly"

Basilica/Basillica - Latin. "Royal palace"

Bass - A voice, instrument, or sound of the lowest range

Bast - An Egyptian goddess linked with protection from evil; she is represented as a cat or lioness

Bateman - Anglo-Saxon. "Boat man"

Bathsheba - Hebrew. "Oath"; "voluptuous"; Bathsheba Everdene is a fictional character in Thomas Hardy's novel *Far from the Madding Crowd* (1874); King David's wife in the *Old Testament* of *The Bible* bears this name

Battle - Middle English, Old French from Latin. "Military or gladiatorial exercises"

Bau - Akkadian goddess of healing

Baudouin - Son of Leopold III, King of the Belgians

Baxter/Bakster - Anglo-Saxon, Scottish. The feminine version of the occupational surname meaning "baker"

Bay - Late Middle English. A broad inlet of the sea where the land curves inward

Bayard - A French soldier hero known as a fearless and irreproachable knight; a magic bay horse in legends renowned for his spirit

Baynard - Old German. "Brave or strong"; the name was introduced into England in the forms Baignard, Bangiard and Baniard

Bazel/Basil - Latin, Greek. "Kingly"

Bazman - Stratovolcano in a remote desert in southeastern Iran

Beach - Old English. "Brook"; "pebbly river valley"

Bear - A large mammal with thick fur and a very short tail; bears are related to the dog family, but most species are omnivorous

Beatrice - Italian form of Beatrix. Notable Bearer: Beatrice Portinari (1266-1290) was the woman who was loved by the Italian poet Dante Alighieri and serves as a character in his epic poem *The Divine Comedy* (1321); a fictional character in William Shakespeare's comedy *Much Ado About Nothing* (1599)

Beatrix/Beatriz - Latin. "She who makes happy"

Beau/Bo - French from Latin. "Handsome"; "a fashionable young man"

Beaufort - A scale of wind speed based on a visual estimation of the wind's effects

Beaumont - French. "Beautiful mountain"

Beauregard - French. "Respected; regarded highly"; "beautiful or handsome gaze"

Beauty - Latin. "Beautiful; fine"; a fictional character in the fairy tale *Beauty and the Beast* (1740) by Gabrielle-Suzanne de Villeneuve

Beauvoir - Norman French. "A place with a fine view"; Notable Bearer: Simone de Beauvoir (1908-1986) was a French writer

Beck - Old Norse. "Brook or stream"; Notable Bearer: Beck Hansen is an American singer, songwriter, rapper, record producer, and multi-instrumentalist

Beckett - Middle English. "Stream; brook; Notable Bearer: Samuel Barclay Beckett was an Irish avant-garde novelist, playwright, theatre director, poet, and literary translator (1906-1989)

Becrux - Chinese. 十字架 "Cross"

Bedelia - Irish. "High one"; "strength"

Bedford - English. "Bede's ford"

Bedivere - In Arthurian legend, the loyal knight who was with the dying king Arthur and saw him go away to Avalon

Beebee - Old English. "Bee settlement"

Beelzebub - Latin, Greek, Hebrew. "God of insects"; the chief devil; Satan

Beethoven - Old German. "Better meadows"; Notable Bearer: Ludwig van Beethoven was a German composer and pianist (1770-1827)

Begonia - Latin. An herbaceous plant of warm climates, the bright flowers of which have brightly colored sepals but no petals

Belenus - Irish. "The fair shining god"; "the shining one"; the god of the sun in Celtic mythology

Beliminah/Bellamina - French. "Beautiful love"

Belinda - Old High German. "Bright serpent"; "bright linden tree"

Belisarius - A general of the eastern Roman empire in the 6th century

Belladonna - Italian. "Beautiful lady"; a deadly nightshade plant with bell-shaped flowers

Bellamy - English, Irish, French. "Fine friend"

Bellatrix - Latin. "Female warrior"; this is the name of the star that marks the left shoulder of the constellation Orion

Belle - French. "Beautiful"; Notable Bearer: Belle Starr was an outlaw of the American west (1848-1889)

Bellerophon - In Greek mythology, the hero who killed the monster chimera, aided by Pegasus

Bellerose - French. "Beautiful rose"

Bellevue - French. "Beautiful view"

Bellezza - Italian. "Beauty; loveliness"

Bellflower - A plant with bell-shaped flowers that are usually blue, purple, pink, or white; a popular name in the Victorian era

Bellona - In Roman mythology, the goddess of war and the sister of Mars

Beloved - Late Middle English. "Be pleasing"; "love"

Belshazzar - Hebrew. "May Bel protect the King"; in *The Bible*, the last king of Babylon, who was warned of defeat by the handwriting on the wall

Beltane - Gaelic, Scottish. May 1st, the ancient Celtic May Day

Belvadere/Belvedere - Italian. "Beautiful to look at"

Benecia/Benicia - Latin. "Blessed one"

Benedetta - Italian. "The blessed"

Benedict - Latin. "Blessed"; Notable Bearer: 6th century Italian Saint Benedict of Nursia founded the Benedictine order of monks and nuns

Benitoite - A rare blue barium titanium silicate mineral found in hydrothermally altered serpentine

Bennett - A form of Latin Benedict (blessed)

Bennu - An Egyptian solar and creator deity, often depicted as a bird

Benoit - [ben-WAH] Old Catholic French. "Blessed"; equivalent to the Latin name Benedict

Benson - Old English. "Son of Ben"

Bentley - Old English. "From the bent grass meadow"

Beornwulf - King of Mercia in the 9th century

Beowulf - Old English. "Bee wolf"; "bear"; the titular character in the anonymous 8th century epic poem *Beowulf*

Beran - Old English. "Brave, strong or hardy"

Berbentina - A very small place in the region of the Marches in Italy

Berengaria - Latinized Old German. "Spear-bearer maiden"; Notable Bearer: medieval queen of England, the wife of King Richard of the Jimenez dynasty

Berenger - Old German. "Bear spear"

Bergamot - An arbor that bears a variety of Seville Orange, from the rind of which bergamot oil is extracted

Berislav/Berislava - Slavic. "He/she carries glory and fame"

Berkeley - English. "Lives at the birch tree meadow"

Berma - Spanish. "Verge"; "shoulder"

Bern - Old German. "Bear"

Bernadette - German. "Hardy"; "brave"; "strong as a bear"; Notable Bearer: Saint Bernadette was a French peasant girl whose 19th century visions of Virgin Mary prompted the establishment of the Roman Catholic shrine at Lourdes

Bernadine - French. "Strong as a bear"; "bear hard"

Bernice - Biblical. "Bringer of victory"

Beroud - Louis Béroud was a French painter of the late 19th & early 20th centuries

Berserker - Ancient Norse warrior who fought in a wild frenzy

Berta - Old English. "Bright"; popular during the Norman Conquest (11th century)

Bertha - Old German. "Bright"; "famous"; it died out as an English name after the Middle Ages, but was revived in the 19th century

Berthelot - French, German. "Son of a farmer"

Bertin/Burton - Old English. "Fortified town"; Notable Bearers: Sir Richard Burton (1821-1890) was an explorer of Africa and Asia; Burton Lorne Cummings is a Canadian musician, singer and songwriter

Bertram - Old German. "Famous raven"; the raven was the bird of Odin, the king of the gods in Norse mythology

Beryl - A transparent pale green, blue, or yellow mineral sometimes used as a gemstone

Besseta - Scottish. "My god is bountiful"; "god of plenty"

Beta - β The second letter of the Greek alphabet; the second star in a constellation

Betelgeuse/Betelgeux - Arabic. "The hand of Jawza"; Jawza was the old Arabic name for the constellation Orion; the star that marks the right shoulder in the constellation Orion

Bethany - A village near Jerusalem in the *New Testament* of *The Bible*

Bethel - Hebrew. "House of God"

Bethelina - English. "Little Beth"; the Phoenician symbol for B was originally named Beth, meaning "house"

Bethesda - Late Greek. "House of mercy"; in *The Bible*, a pool at Jerusalem alleged to have healing powers; a chapel or holy place

Bethia - Gaelic. "Life"; Scottish. "Daughter or worshipper of God"; Hebrew. "Maid-servant of Jehovah"

Bethzy - Hebrew. "My god is a vow"

Betlinde - Italian. "Beautiful"; Old High German. "Bright serpent"

Betsey/Betsy/Betzy - Greek. "Oath of God"; "God is satisfaction"

Beulah/Beaula - Hebrew. "To marry"

Beverly - English. "Beaver stream"; "from the beaver meadow"; first used as a boy's name in the late 19th century, it gradually came to be used as a girl's name; a fictional character in Stephen King's horror novel *It* (1986)

Bevis/Beauvis - French. "Handsome face"

Bharani - The second nakshatra (lunar mansion) in Hindu astronomy, ruled by the planet Venus

Bianca/Bianka - Italian. "White"

Bezimienny - Polish. "Anonymous; nameless"

Bifrost - Old Norse. "The tremulous way"; in Norse mythology, the rainbow bridge from Midgard (the earth) to Asgard (the home of the gods) that only the gods could travel upon

Bilancia - Italian. "Libra"

Billington - English habitational name for someone from Lancashire, Staffordshire, or Bedfordshire

Bion - Ancient Greek. "Life"

Birch - Topographic name for someone who lived by a birch tree or in a birch wood

Birdette/Burdett - An English surname popularly used as a given name

Bishoff/Bischoff - German. "Bishop"

Bishop - Old English. "Overseer from above"; a senior member of the Christian clergy, typically in charge of a diocese and empowered to confer holy orders

Bison - Greek. "Ox-like animal"

Bjorn - Icelandic. "Bear"

Blacwin/Blackwyn - A common surname in medieval times

Blade - Old English. "Wealthy glory"

Blair/Blaire - Gaelic. "Plain; field"

Blaise - French. "Lisp; stutter"

Blanchette - A given name or surname of French origin meaning "white or pale"; Notable Bearers: Andrulla Blanchette is a female bodybuilder; Cate Blanchett is an Australian actress

Bliss - Germanic, Old English. "Perfect happiness"; "great joy"

Blizenci - Afrikaans. "Gemini"

Bloodstone - In the ancient world, bloodstone (heliotrope) was considered to be the most beautiful of the jaspers; a deep, earthy green gem emboldened with spots of bright red

Blossom - Old English. "A cluster of flowers"; "to thrive, flourish"; popular alongside other floral names in the Victorian era

Blubelle/Bluebell - A blue, bell-shaped flower that has long been symbolic of humility and gratitude

Blu/Blue - A color intermediate between green and violet, as of the sky or sea on a sunny day

Bluford - A habitational name from a lost or unidentified place; the name occurs in English records of the 19th century but is now very rare

Blythe - Old English. "Joyous"; "kind"; "cheerful"; "pleasant"

Boa - A constrictor snake that bears live young and may reach great size

Boabdil - Moorish king of Grenada in the 16th century

Boadicea - A British queen who led an attempted revolt against the Romans in the 1st century

Boanerges - Hebrew. "Sons of wrath"; Greek. "Sons of thunder"; an epithet used by Jesus Christ

Boaz - Hebrew. "Swiftness"; In *The Bible*, the husband of Ruth

Bodebi - A small lost village in England

Bodhi - Sanskrit. बोधि "Awakening"; "enlightenment"; in Buddhism, the understanding possessed by a Buddha regarding the true nature of things

Boethius - Roman philosopher and statesman in the 5th century

Bogart - French. "Bow strength"

Bogdan/Bohdan - Slavic. "God's gift"

Bogomil/Bogumil - Slavic. "Dear to God"

Bohemia - Of a person with informal and unconventional social habits

Boise - French. "Wooded"

Bolverk - In Norse mythology, an alias used by Odin to win a poetry contest

Bolivar - A Basque habitational name

Bolivia - The country gets its name from Simon Bolivar, the military and political leader that changed the course of Colonial South America

Bolshoi - Russian. "Big"; "grand"

Bolvar/Bolva - Icelandic. "Curse"; Bolvar is a fictional character in the *World Of Warcraft* franchise

Bomber - Originally a nickname for combat aircraft or the pilots of such machines, but gained popularity after WWI as a given name

Bonnie - Old French. "Plump and healthy-looking baby"; used as a form of address for one's beloved or baby

Booker - Occupational name for someone concerned with books, generally a scribe or a binder

Boone - English. "Good"; "a blessing"

Boothby - Old Danish. "By a settlement"

Boratus - A fictional character in the *Star Trek* universe

Borawli - A stratovolcano with lava domes in Ethiopia

Borden - Old English. "Boar valley; swine pasture"

Borealis - Latin. "Pertaining to the north or north wind"

Boreas - Latin, Greek. "North wind"; "wind from the mountains"; Indo-European, Old Slavic. "Mountain"; in Greek mythology, the god of the north wind

Boris - Russian. "To fight"

Borivali - Marathi. "Town of berries"

Borivoi - The Duke of Bohemia in the 12th century

Bormo - The Celtic god of minerals and a healing deity associated with bubbling spring water

Borough - Old English. "Fortified castle; fortress"

Borrom - The god of the winds in Celtic mythology

Bosch - Middle Dutch. "Wood"; Notable Bearer: Hieronymus Bosch (1450-1516) was a Dutch draughtsman and painter and is widely considered one of the most notable representatives of Early Netherlandish painting

Boston - Named after a 7th century saint, originally called "Boltulf's Stone"

Botolph - Old German. "Wolf"

Boven - Dutch. "Boy"

Bovo - Latin, Greek. "A head of cattle"

Bowie - Gaelic. "Yellow; fair-haired"; Notable Bearer: David Bowie (1947-2016) was an innovative English singer, songwriter, and actor

Boyce - Middle English. "Lad"; "servant"

Bozhidar/Bozidar - Slavic. "Divine gift"

Bracken - Gaelic. "Speckled"; "spotted"; "descendant of Breacán"; Notable Bearer: 6th century Irish Saint Bracken was a famous healer

Bractor - A fictional character in the *Star Trek* franchise

Bradbury - Old English. "Broad town"

Braddock - Old English. "Broad oak"

Bradshaw - Old English. "Broad thicket"

Bradstreet - Old English. "Broad Roman road"

Bragi - The Norse God of poetry and eloquence; he was the son of Odin and husband of Idun

Brago - *Magic: The Gathering* legendary spirit creature

Brahma - Hindu, Sanskrit. "Worship; prayer"; in Hindu theology, the supreme and eternal essence or spirit of the universe; the chief member of the trinity (Brahma, Vishna, Siva); he is regarded as the creator of the universe

Bram - Hebrew. "Father of a multitude"; Notable Bearer: Abraham "Bram" Stoker (1847-1912) was an Irish author, best known today for his 1897 gothic novel *Dracula*

Bran - Irish. "Raven"; a mythical king of Britain; in Celtic mythology, the king of the underworld

Brando - Italian. "Brilliant raven"; "fiery torch"; "beacon"; Notable Bearer: Marlon Brando (1924-2004) was an American actor

Brannigan - Irish. A personal name from a double diminutive of Bran (raven)

Branwen - Welsh. "Fair raven"; a goddess in Celtic mythology

Braun - German and Jewish nickname referring to the color of hair, complexion or clothing

Brave - French. "Ready to face and endure danger or pain"; "showing courage"; Italian. "Bold"; Spanish. "Courageous"; "untamed"; "savage"

Bravo - Spanish, Portuguese. "Fierce, violent, and courageous"

Braxton - English. "Brock's town"; "Brock's settlement"

Brazen - English. "Bold"; "without shame"

Breeze - Old Spanish. "A gentle wind"

Brewster - English, Scottish. An occupational name for a brewer of beer or ale

Briar - English. "A thorned shrub"; Briar is thought of in reference to *The Briar Rose* (1890), a Brothers Grimm fairy tale that we know today by the name *Sleeping Beauty*

Briareus - Latin, Greek. "Strong"; in Greek mythology, a giant who fought with the Olympians against the Titans

Brice/Bryce - Celtic. "Swift"; Notable Bearer: Saint Brice, sometimes called Saint Britius, was a 5th century bishop of tours

Brick/Bric/Brik - Gaelic, German. "Swamp or wood"; Yiddish. "Bridge"; Slavic. "Dweller from a hilly place"; a fictional character in Tennessee Williams' play *Cat on a Hot Tin Roof* (1955)

Brigantia - In Celtic religion, the ancient goddess of the poetic arts, crafts, prophecy, and divination; she was the equivalent of the Roman Minerva and Greek Athena

Brigida - Italian. "High goddess"

Brimstone - Late Old English. "Burning stone"

Briony - Greek. The name of a flowering vine used in folk medicine

Briseis - In Greek legend, a pretty woman whose seizure by Agamemnon from Achilles, her captor, led to a quarrel between the two men

Bristo - Common name in farming families during the Revolutionary era

Bristol/Bristow - Old English. "Bridge"; "assembly place"

Brite/Bright - German, Old English. "Giving out or reflecting a lot of light"; "shining"

Brix - Danish form of Brixtus or Brice

Bronson - English. "Son of a dark man"

Bronte - English from Irish. "Descendant of Proinnteach"; the name Proinnteach means "bestower" in Gaelic; Notable Bearers: the Brontë sisters, Charlotte, Emily, and Anne, were 19th century English novelists

Bronx - In NYC, named for early Dutch settler Jonas Bronck; Notable Bearer: rockers Pete Wentz and Ashlee Simpson's child is named Bronx Mowgli Wentz

Brossmer - A fictional character in the *Star Trek* franchise

Brown - Found in Old Norse and Old English as a personal name referring to the color of the hair or complexion

Bruchner/Bruckner - German, Jewish from Yiddish. "Pavement; paver"; topographic name for someone living by a bridge or an occupational name for a bridge toll collector

Brumaire - French. "Fog; mist"; the second month of the French Revolutionary Calendar, adopted by the First Republic in 1793

Bruna - German, Italian. "Dark-haired"

Brunhild/Brunhilde/Brynhild - Old High German. "Fight"; "fighter in armor"; a queen of Iceland in the epic 5th century poem *The Song of the Nibelungs*

Bruno - Old German. "Brown"; three 10th and 11th century German saints, one of whom founded the Carthusian order of monks, bore this name

Brutus - Latin. "Heavy"; Notable Bearer: Marcus Junius Brutus (85-42 BCE), the statesman who conspired to assassinate Julius Caesar

Buccaneer - Derived from the Arawak word "buccan", a wooden frame on which Tainos and Caribs slowly roasted or smoked meat (mainly manatee); from it derived the French word "boucane" and hence the name "boucanier" for French hunters who used such frames to smoke meat from feral cattle and pigs on; English colonists Anglicized the word "boucanier" to "buccaneer"

Buckner - German and English surname referring to a male goat or deer

Buddha - Sanskrit. "Enlightened one"; this is a title applied to Siddhartha Gautama, the founder of Buddhism, as well as to a handful of other enlightened individuals

Buffalo - American bison; the name of several places in Canada and the USA

Buford - Old French. "Puffing and blowing"

Buller - Norman English. "Letter; document"; occupational name for a scribe or copyist

Bundy - A small, often crooked Australian tree with pendulous branches

Bunt - Middle High German. "Black and white coloration (specifically of a fur)"

Burgundy - French. A deep red color like that of burgundy wine

Burns/Byrne - Old English. "Be on fire"; German. "Consume by fire"

Burwell - Old English. "Town well"; "fort by a spring"

Buttercup - A cheery yellow wildflower; a fictional character in William Goldman's 1973 novel *The Princess Bride*

Buxenus - Celtic. "God of box trees"; in Gallo-Roman religion, Buxenus was an epithet of the Gaulish Mars, known from a single inscription found in Velleron

Buzz - American astronaut Edwin Eugene Aldrin, Jr. legally changed his given name to Buzz in 1988

Byblos - The ancient Phoenician port city of Gebal (called Byblos by the Greeks) on the coast of the Mediterranean sea in what is now Lebanon

Byron - Old English. "Cow shed"; Notable Bearer: English nobleman and poet Lord Byron (1788-1824)

C

Cadence/Kaydance - A sequence of notes or chords comprising the close of a musical phrase; the flow or rhythm of events

Cadet - Old Occitan. "Small dog"; a term designating the youngest member of a family; a young trainee in the armed services or police force

Cadmus - Greek. "He who excels"; "from the east"; in Greek legend, a Phoenician prince who founded Thebes and killed a dragon sacred to Mars

Cadog - Welsh. "Battle glory"

Caelian - One of the seven hills on which Rome was founded

Caerleon - Old Welsh. "Camp of the legions"; the original version of Chester; in Arthurian legend, a city where King Arthur held court

Caesar/Caesarea - Latin. "Leader"

Caiaphas - [KY-a-fuss] In *The Bible*, the high priest who presided at the trial that led to the condemnation of Jesus

Caillou - French. "Pebble"; "bald head"

Cain - Hebrew. "Spear"; "possessed"; in *The Bible,* Cain became the first murderer after killing his brother Abel in a fit of jealousy

Calbert - English. "Cowherd; cowboy"

Calchas - In Greek legend, a priest of Apollo who accompanied the Greeks during the Trojan War

Caldwell - English, Scottish, Irish. "Cold well; cold spring"; habitational name from any of several places in England and Scotland, variously spelled

Caledonia - Latin. "From Scotland"

Calhoun - Irish. "From the narrow forest"

Caliban - The second largest retrograde irregular satellite (moon) of Uranus; a cannibal in Richard Hakluyt's 1599 publication *Voyages*; a savage creature in William Shakespeare's 1611 play *The Tempest*

California - The name of a mythical island populated only by Amazon warriors who used gold tools and weapons in the popular early 16th century romance novel *The Adventures of Esplandian* by Spanish author Garci Rodriguez de Montalvo

Caligula - Gaius Caesar, Roman emperor from 37-41

Caline - French. "To cuddle; to make a fuss of"

Calixta/Callixta/Callista - Greek. "She who is most beautiful"; a mythological Roman nymph, daughter of the arcadian King Lycaon and mother of Arcas

Calliope - Latin, Greek. "The beautiful voiced"; in Greek mythology, the muse of eloquence and epic poetry

Calix - Latin. "Wine cup"

Calixtus - The name of three popes (also known as Callistus)

Callisto - In Greco-Roman mythology, a nymph who, because she was loved by Zeus (Jupiter), was changed into a bear by Hera (Juno); Zeus placed her among the stars as the constellation of the Bear

Calloway - Norman French. "Place of stones or pebbles"

Calpernia/Calpurnia/Culpernia - The third and last wife of Julius Caesar in the 1st century BCE

Calvert - Old English. "Herdsman"

Calvery - Latin. "Skull"; a hill outside of Jerusalem where the crucifixion of Jesus Christ took place

Calypso - In Homer's *The Odyssey* (8th century BCE), a sea nymph who did not let Odysseus (Ulysses) leave her island for seven years

Cambyses - Son of Cyrus the Great, the last median king of Prussia

Camelia/Camellia - English name for a flower; a popular name in the Victorian era

Camelot - A castle and court associated with the legendary King Arthur

Camenae - In Roman mythology, a nymph having prophetic powers who inhabited springs and fountains

Camile/Camille - French version of Camilla

Camilla - Latin. "Servant for the temple"; "Free born"; "noble"

Campbell - Gaelic. "Crooked mouth"; "wry-mouthed"; originally a nickname which over time became used as a surname, then a given name

Camulus - The name for a Celtic deity that the Romans equated to Mars

Canadice - Iroquois. "Long lake"; one of the minor Finger Lakes of New York; a seedless red grape

Canary - A small songbird in the finch family originating from the Macaronesian Islands that were first bred in captivity in the 17th century

Canaseraga - Iroquois. "Several strings of beads with a string lying across"; a village in upstate NY

Candace - The hereditary name of a line of Ethiopian queens

Candelaria - Spanish. "Candlemas"; given in honor of the church festival which commemorates the presentation of Christ in the temple and the purification of Mary

Candor - English. "The quality of being open and honest in expression"; "frankness"

Canicula - Latin. Diminutive of Canis (a dog)

Canis - Latin. "Dog"; a genus of the Canidae containing multiple species, such as wolves, coyotes, jackals, and dogs

Canopus - The brightest star in the southern constellation Carina

Canossa - An ancient town in northern Italy, the site of the penance of Henry IV of Germany, Holy Roman Emperor

Cantrelle - French. "Song"; "she is like a song"

Capella - Latin. "She goat"; a bright star in the constellation of Auriga; the third brightest star in the northern celestial hemisphere

Caper - English. "Skip or dance about in a lively or playful way"

Cappadocia - Biblical. "Sphere"; "buckle"; "hand"

Captain - Old French from Late Latin. "Head"; "the person in command of a ship"

Capulet/Capulette - The House of Capulet is one of fair Verona's two feuding families in William Shakespeare's *Romeo and Juliet* (1597)

Caravaggio - Michelangelo Merisi da Caravaggio was an Italian painter active in Rome, Naples, Malta, and Sicily from the early 1590's to 1610

Carina - A subdivision of the southern constellation Argo containing the bright star Canopus

Carlotta - Italian. "Strong"

Carlson - A patronymic surname meaning "Son of Carl"; it is rarely used as a given name

Carme - Hebrew. "Garden"; Greek. "She who cuts grain"

Carmella - Hebrew. "Vineyard"; "orchard"

Carmine - English. "Garden"

Carnation - French. "Flesh-colored"; popular in the Victorian era along with other flower names; a flower generally given on Saint Valentine's Day

Carnival/Carnivale - A season or festival of merry-making before Lent

Carolina - Latin. "Strong"

Carrick - Gaelic. "Rocky headland"

Carter - Irish, Scottish and English occupational name given to one who transports goods by cart or wagon

Carthage - An ancient city which was founded by Phoenicians in 814 BCE and destroyed by Romans in 146 BCE; Saint Carthage the Elder was an Irish bishop and abbot in the 6th century

Casanova - Catalan, Italian. "New house"; Notable Bearer: Giacomo Girolamo Casanova was an 18th century Italian adventurer and author

Cascade - French. "Waterfall"; "to fall"

Casimir/Casimira/Casimiro - Latin. "Peacemaker"

Casper/Caspar - Chaldean. "Treasurer"; considered one of the traditional names of the Biblical magi

Cassini - A satellite mission to explore Saturn and its moons

Cassiopeia - In Greek legend, the wife of Cepheus and mother of Andromeda; a northern constellation between Andromeda and Cepheus

Cassius - Latin. "Empty"; "vain"; this name was borne by several early saints; Notable Bearers: the birth name of American boxer Muhammad Ali (1942-2016), who was named after his father Cassius Clay (1912-1990), himself named after the American abolitionist Cassius Clay (1810-1903)

Castalia - A spring on Mount Parnassus that was sacred to Apollo and the Muses; its waters were considered a source of poetic inspiration

Castellan - Old French. "The governor of a castle"

Castor/Kastor - A star in the Gemini constellation; in Greco-Roman mythology, Castor and Pollux (Kastor and Polydeuces) were twin brothers, together known as the Dioskouroi

Caswell - Medieval English. "Watercress"

Catalina/Cataline - Portuguese. "Pure"

Cato - Latin. "Intelligent"; "shrewd"; Cato is the son of the great Marcus Cato, the brother of Portia and the the brother-in-law of Brutus in William Shakespeare's tragedy *Julius Caesar* (1599)

Catulus/Catullus - Roman lyric poet from 84-54 BCE

Cavalier - Southern French. "Knight"; "rider"

Cayenne - French. "Hot spice"

Cayson - Irish. "Courageous and tough"

Cecelia/Cecile - Latin. "Blind"; the blind Saint Cecile is the patron saint of music

Cecil - English. "Blind"; from the Roman clan name Caecilius

Cecrops - In Greek legend, the first king of Attica and founder of Athens; he is represented as half man, half dragon

Cedar - From the English word for the coniferous tree

Cedric - Celtic. "War chief"

Celestia - French. "Beauty"

Celestine - French from Latin. "Heavenly"; two of the five popes named Celestine have been canonized

Celza/Celsa - Latin variant of Celcus, a 2nd century Greek philosopher and opponent of early Christianity

Cena - Italian. "Mud"; Polish. "Price"; a nickname for a trader or dealer; Notable Bearer: John Felix Anthony Cena is an American professional wrestler

Centaur - Greek mythological creature with the upper body of a human and the lower body and legs of a horse

Centaurus - In Greek mythology, Centaurus is the father of the race of mythological beasts known as the centaurs or ixionidae; Centaurus is a bright constellation in the southern sky

Centurian/Centurion - The commander of a century in the ancient Roman army

Cepheus - A northern constellation near Cassiopeia; in Greek legend, the husband of Cassiopeia and father of Andromeda who was placed among the stars after his death

Cerberus - In Greco-Roman mythology, the three-headed dog guarding the gates of Hades

Ceres - A small planet with its orbit between Mars and Saturn; in Roman mythology, the goddess of agriculture, grain, and the love a mother bears for her child; she was the daughter of Saturn and Ops, the sister of Jupiter, and the mother of Proserpine

Cesarine - Of or about Caesar

Cestus/Caestus - An ancient battle glove, sometimes used in pankration; they were worn like today's boxing gloves, but were made with leather strips and sometimes filled with iron plates or fitted with blades or spikes, and used as weapons

Cevedic - Fictional character in the *Blake's 7* universe

Chacotay/Chakotay - A fictional character in the *Star Trek* franchise

Chah - Hindi. "Love"; "longing"; "desire"

Chai - Hebrew. "Life"; an Indian beverage made with aromatic spices and black tea

Chainer/Chayner - *Magic: The Gathering* legendary minion

Chakra - Sanskrit. "Wheel"; the centers of spiritual power in the human body

Chalcedony - A cryptocrystalline form of silicas composed of fine intergrowths of quartz and morganite

Chaldene - A moon of Jupiter

Chamaeleon - A small constellation in the southern sky named after the chameleon

Chamberlain - The name of an official in charge of the private chambers of his master in Norman France

Champion - Norman status name for a professional winner, especially an agent employed to represent one of the parties in a trial by combat, a method of settling disputes in the Middle Ages

Chancellor - A senior state or legal official

Chanda - Sanskrit, Pali, Tibetan. "Fierce"; "hot"; "passionate"

Chandler - Old English occupational name for a maker and seller of candles

Chandra - Sanskrit. "Shining"; a lunar god, identified with the Vedic lunar deity Soma; a NASA x-ray telescope observatory; *Magic: The Gathering* Planeswalker

Chandrama - Hindi. "Moon"

Chane/Cheyne/Shayne/Shane - French. "Oak hearted"; an Anglicized form of the Irish Seaghán, a variant form of Eóin which is a Gaelic cognate of John (God is gracious)

Chapman - Old English. "Market man; monger; merchant"

Chara - Greek. "Happiness; joy"

Charentais - A small muskmelon with a distinct fragrance and sweet orange flesh that is grown chiefly in France in a town of the same name

Charge/Charger - A horse trained for battle; a cavalry horse

Charis - Greek. "Grace, kindness and life"; in Greek mythology, a Charis is one of the goddesses of charm, beauty, nature, creativity and fertility

Charlet - Old German. "Free man (person)"

Charlton/Charleton - English. "Peasants' settlement"; Notable Bearer: American actor Charlton Heston (1923-2008)

Charm - Middle English, Old French, Latin. An object, action, gesture or chanted word that is believed to have magic power

Charmain/Charmaine - English. "Song"; an attendant to Cleopatra in William Shakespeare's *Antony and Cleopatra* (1607)

Charmer - English. "A delightful or fascinating person"; "an enchanter"

Charoite - A two-wheeled vehicle used in ancient Greece and Egypt

Charon - In Greek mythology, the boatman who ferries dead souls across the river Styx to Hades

Chauncey - English. "Chancellor"; "secretary"; "fortune"; "a gamble"

Chekhov/Chekov/Chekhova - Russian surname; Pavel Andreievich Chekov is a fictional character in the *Star Trek* universe

Cherika - Hindu. "The moon"

Cherub - A beautiful or innocent-looking child; a winged angelic being described in biblical tradition

Cherubina - Akkadian. "Blessing; blessed"; "like a cherub"; "little cherub"

Chesapeake - Algonquin. "At a big river"; "great shellfish bay"

Chess - English. "Camp of the soldiers"; a board game of strategic skill

Chessine/Chessie - Slavic. "At peace"

Chester - Latin. "Camp"; Notable Bearer: American president Chester A. Arthur (1829-1886)

Chevy - French. "Horseman"; "knight"; Notable Bearer: Cornelius Crane "Chevy" Chase is an American actor, comedian and writer

Cheyanne - An Algonquin tribe of the great plains and capital city of Wyoming, USA

Chicago - Derived from a French rendering of the Miami-Illinois word "shikaakwa" (a wild relative of the onion)

Chimera - The Greek monster killed by Bellerophon; a thing that is hoped or wished for but in fact is illusory or impossible to achieve; a mirage

Chiquita - Spanish. "Small"; a popular name in Central America in the 19th century

Chiron - In Greek mythology, the wisest of all the centaurs, famous for his knowledge of medicine

Chirp - Late Middle English. "To say something in a lively and cheerful way"

Chloris/Khloris - The goddess of flowers and a nymph of the Islands of the Blessed; she was the wife of Zephyros the Westwind and the mother of Karpos, god of fruit; her Roman name is Flora

Chondea - Sanskrit. "Illustrious"; "eminent"

Chopin - Old French. "To tipple"; "to drink to excess"; Notable Bearer: Fryderyk Franciszek Chopin (1810-1849) was a Polish composer and virtuoso pianist of the Romantic era

Christophorus - Greek, Latin. "Bearer of Christ"

Chrysanthemum - Greek. "Gold flower"

Chryseis - In Greek mythology, the beautiful daughter of Chryses, a priest of Apollo; seized by the Greeks in the Trojan War and given to Agamemnon, she was returned to her father only after Apollo caused a plague to fall on the Greek camp

Chrysostom - Greek. "Golden-mouthed"; Notable Bearer: John Chrysostom was archbishop of Constantinople in the 5th century

Chrystema - Latin. "Follower of Christ"

Cigno - Italian. "Swan"

Cincinnati - A city on the Ohio river named in honor of Quintius Cincinnatus, a Roman leader who became a legendary figure of Roman virtues

Cincinnatus - Dictator of Rome (458-439 BCE) who became synonymous with the Roman virtues of manliness and civic duty

Cinderella - French, German. "Ashes"; the name is identified with "rags to riches" thanks to a fictional character dating back to antiquity; the most famous tales include: the story of *Rhodopis*, first recorded by the Greek philosopher Strabo in the 1st century BCE; Charles Perrault's 1697 publication *The Little Glass Slipper*; the Brothers Grimm 1812 collection *Children's and Household Tales*; Disney's 1950 animated musical *Cinderella*

Cinnamon - Greek. An aromatic spice derived from the inner bark of any of several tree species falling within the genus Cinnamomum

Cintha - Greek. "From Mount Kynthos"; "hyacinth"; originally a masculine name

Citrine - French. "Lemon"; a transparent variety of quartz ranging in color from pale to golden yellow, honey or almost brown, and may contain rainbow or sparkle inclusions

Civility - English. "Formal politeness and courtesy in behavior or speech"; a popular virtue name among the Puritans

Claire/Clare/Clara - Latin. "Bright or clear"; "distinguished"; Notable Bearer: Twelfth century Saint Clare of Assisi (1194-1253) founded the Poor Clares order of nuns

Clancy - Irish. "The red-haired soldier's son"; "ruddy warrior"

Clarence - English. "Bright and clear"

Clariandra - Mash-up of Clare and Leandra

Claribel - Latin. "Clear"; "bright"; "pretty"; "fair"

Clarice - Variant of Clare

Clarimond -Medieval French. "Shining defender"

Clarity - English. "Lucidity"

Clarkson - English. "Son of the clerk"; refers to a scribe or secretary

Claudius - Latin. "Crippled"; Notable Bearer: Claudius was the fourth Roman Emperor reigning from 41 to his death in 54

Clay - Old English. "Settlement near the clay pit"

Cleanthes - Greek stoic philosopher of the 3rd century BCE

Clearchus - Spartan general in the 5th century BCE

Clement - Latin. "Mild"; "merciful"; the British nursery rhyme *Oranges and Lemons* refers to a church dedicated to Saint Clement, a disciple of Saint Paul; 14 popes have been named Clement

Clementine - Latin. "Little Clement"

Clemson - English patronymic short form of the personal name Clement

Cleonice - A genus of flies in the family tachinidae

Cleopatra - Queen of Egypt and mistress of Julius Caesar and Mark Antony from 69-30 BCE

Clever - Middle English. "Quick to catch hold"; Dutch, Low German. "Manually skillful"; "possessing mental agility"

Clifford - English. "Ford near a slope"; Notable Bearer: pianist Sir Clifford Curzon (1907-1982)

Clinton - English. "Settlement on a hill"; "from the headland estate"; Notable Bearer: William Jefferson Clinton served as the 42nd President of the USA

Clio/Cleo - Latin. "To celebrate"; Greek. "Fame, glory"; in Greek mythology, the muse of history

Clive/Clyve - English. "Lives at the cliffs"; Notable Bearers: 18th century British soldier and statesman Robert Clive; Clive Owen is an English actor; Clive Jay Davis is an American record producer

Cloanna/Khloanna - A combination of Chloris and Anna; a popular name in the 1920's

Cloelia - In Roman legend, Cloelia was a maiden who was given to an Etruscan invader as a hostage

Clorinda - Latin. "Renowned"; a fictional character in the epic poem *Jerusalem Delivered* by Torquato Tasso (1581)

Clothilda/Clotilda - French, German, Old High German. "Famous"; "to be esteemed"

Clotho - Latin, Greek. "To spin"; in Greek mythology, Clotho was one of the three fates, the spinner of the thread of human life

Clover - Herb of the pea family with small flowers of yellow, white or red; a person who believes laws are for the common good; a shamrock, an illustration of the Holy Trinity by Saint Patrick

Clyde - Scottish name for someone who lived by the banks of the River Clyde

Clyremnestra/Clytaemnestra - In Greek legend, the wife of Agamemnon

Clyrene - Popular in the early 1800's

Cobain - Old Norse. "Large"; "fair person"; Notable Bearer: Kurt Donald Cobain (1967-1994) was an American musician

Cobalt - A lustrous silvery metal which is the source of cobalt blue pigment

Cohen - Hebrew. כהן "Priest"; a common Jewish surname which represents an ancient biblical priestly heritage

Colbert - French, English. "Cool-bright"; Old Norse. "Bright helmet"; Notable Bearer: Stephen Tyrone Colbert is an American comedian, television host, actor, and writer

Colburn - English. "Cool stream"

Colette - French. "Necklace"; "victorious"; popular in the 15th century

Colonel - Italian. "Column of soldiers"; an army officer of high rank

Colony - Late Middle English. "Group of people"; the name originally referred to a settlement formed mainly of retired soldiers

Colorado - Spanish. "Colored red"; the name was applied to the Colorado River because of the red sandstone soil of the region, and came into use for the entire territory after the discovery of gold in the Pike's Peak region

Columbine - Latin. "Dove"; Notable Bearer: 6th century Irish abbott and missionary Saint Columba (521-597) converted the inhabitants of Scotland and Northern England to Christianity

Columbus - Latin. "Dove"; Notable Bearer: Christopher Columbus (1450-1506) was an Italian explorer who "discovered" the Americas

Comet - A cosmic snowball of frozen gases, rock and dust that orbits the Sun

Commander - A person in authority, especially over a body of troops or a military operation

Commodore - French. "Commander"; a naval officer of high rank; an 8-bit home computer introduced in January 1982

Comoros - Swahili. "The place of fire"; the name can be found on Arabic maps dating back to ancient times

Compton - Old English. "Short, straight valley settlement"

Comrade - Latin, Russian. "A companion who shares one's activities or is a fellow member of an organization"

Conchobar - In Irish legend, a king of Ulster; he was the guardian and intended husband of Deirdre

Concordia - Latin. "With one heart"; in Roman mythology, the goddess of harmony

Condor - A large New World vulture with a bare head and mainly black plumage, living in mountainous country and spending much of its time soaring

Congo - African. "Great river"

Connecticut - Native American. "Beside the long tidal river"

Connelly/Connolly - Gaelic. "As fierce as a hound/wolf"

Conquistador - A conqueror, especially one of Mexico and Peru in the 16th century

Conrad/Konrad - Old English. "Bold counsel"; the name of a 10th century bishop of Constance; it became popular in post-medieval England and France

Conradin - German. "Honest advisor"

Constance - Latin. "Firm of purpose"

Constantina - Italian. "Steadfastness"; Notable Bearer: Saint Constance (died 354) was the eldest daughter of Roman emperor Constantine the Great and his second wife Fausta

Constantine - Latin. "Constant"; "steadfast"; this name was borne by several Roman and Byzantine emperors including Constantine the Great (272-337), the emperor who made Christianity the official religion of the Roman Empire

Copper - A reddish brown metal that is a great conductor of energy and is useful for all types of spiritual purposes

Cora - A variant of the Greek Kore or Corina (maiden); Kore is an alternative name for the Greek goddess Persephone

Coral - A popular 19th century jewel name, from the pink semi-precious sea growth used to make jewelry and ornaments

Corallie - French variant of Coral

Corbeau - French. "Crow; raven"

Cordelia - Latin. "Heart"; Welsh. "Jewel of the sea"; French. "Heart of a lion"

Coreline/Coraline - Gothic variant of Coral

Corentina/Corentine/Coretin - Breton. "Hurricane"; Notable Bearer: 1st century bishop of Quimper in Brittany

Coristine - Italian. "To go in search or quest of"; "to seek the truth"

Cormic/Cormick - Gaelic. "Chariot driver"

Cornelia - 2nd century BCE mother of the two Roman tribunes known as the Gracchi

Cornelius - Latin. "Horn"; in the *New Testament* of *The Bible*, Cornelius is a centurion who is directed by an angel to seek Peter; after speaking with Peter he converts to Christianity, and he is traditionally deemed the first gentile convert

Cornett - The cornett, cornetto, or zink is an early wind instrument that dates from the Medieval, Renaissance and Baroque periods; it was used in what are now called alta capellas or wind ensembles

Cornix - A fictional princess character in Ovid's poem *Metamorphoses* (8 CE)

Cornucopia - Greek, Latin. "Horn of plenty"

Corretta - English. "From the round hill"; "seething pool"; "ravine"

Cortana/Curtana/Courtain - A ceremonial sword

Cortez - Spanish. "Courteous"; Notable Bearer: the Spanish explorer and adventurer Hernan Cortes (1485-1547) conquered the Aztec civilization of Mexico with only a small expeditionary force

Corvus - Latin. "Raven"; a small constellation in the southern celestial hemisphere

Cosgrove - Gaelic. "Victorious"; "triumphant"

Cosimina/Cosima/Cosimo - Greek. "Order"; "decency"; Notable Bearer: 4th century saint who was martyred with his brother Damian; they are the Patron Saints of medical doctors

Cosmina/Cosmin - Romanian saint

Cosmo - Greek. "Order"; "world"; of or relating to the world or the universe

Coso/Cosus - A Celtic god of war often associated with the Roman Mars

Costa - Greek. "Steady"; "stable"

Costellazione - Italian. "Constellation"

Costello - Irish. "Resembling a deer or fawn"; it is a common misconception that the name is Italian thanks to a mafia gangster and a 1940's comedy duo; Notable Bearers: Frank "the Prime Minister" Costello (1891-1973) was an Italian American mobster and head of the Luciano crime family; Louis Francis Cristillo (1906-1959), known by the stage name Lou Costello, was an Italian American actor and half of the comedy duo *Abbott and Costello*

Costner - A local name for a person who lived in Franconia; the name rose to prominence through the family's involvement in the social and cultural affairs of the area; Notable Bearer: Kevin Michael Costner is an American actor

Cotopaxi - Quechuan. "Shining peak"; the highest active volcano in the world, located in the Andes of central Ecuador

Courtois - Old French. "Refined"; "accomplished"

Cove - Old English. "Tent"; "hut"

Coyote - Mexican from Nahuatl. A wolf-like dog native to North America

Craven - Middle English. "Defeated"; Old French. "Crush; overwhelm"; Latin. "Burst"

Crawford - Old English. "Crow foot"

Creed/Credo - Latin. "A set of beliefs or aims that guide someone's actions"

Creek - Celtic. "Cliff"; "rock"; Old French occupational name for a basket maker

Creon - Greek. "Prince"; a figure in Greek mythology best known as the ruler of Thebes in the legend of *Oedipus Rex* (429 BCE), an Athenian tragedy by Sophocles

Cresent/Crescent - French. "To create"; the curved sickle shape of the waxing or waning moon

Cresentia - Latin. "Growing"

Cressida - Greek. "Origin"; titular character in William Shakespeare's *Troilus and Cressida* (1602)

Cricket - Old French. "To creak; to rattle" an insect that makes a chirping sound; originally a nickname for Christine and other "Chris" names; a bat and ball sport

Crimson - Of a rich deep red color inclining to purple

Crispin - Latin. "Curled or curly-haired"; Notable Bearers: Saint Crispin is the patron saint of shoemakers and is believed to have been martyred in the 3rd century

Cristoferi/Cristofori - Early Medieval English. "Annointed"; "follower of Christ"

Croatia - Russian. "Mountain chain"

Crockett - Middle English. "large curl"; Old Norman French. "Curl; hook"; Gaelic. "Son of Richard"

Crono - A fictional character in the *Chrono Trigger* universe

Cronus/Cronos/Kronos - The supreme god in Greek mythology until he was dethroned by Zeus; the youngest son of Uranus (Heaven) and Gaia (Earth)

Crosis - *Magic: The Gathering* legendary dragon

Cross - A mark, object, or figure used since antiquity as a symbol for the crucifixion of Jesus Christ

Crovax - *Magic: The Gathering* legendary human warrior

Crowe/Crow - A large, highly intelligent black bird which is said to symbolize death as well as intelligence, flexibility and destiny

Cruise/Cruize/Cruz - In Ireland, Cruise is an old surname which has been present since the Anglo-Norman invasion in 1169

Crux - Latin. "Cross"; a constellation in the southern sky in a bright portion of the Milky Way

Crystal - Greek. "Ice"; a colorless glass sometimes cut into a gemstone; used as a given name since the 19th century

Cupid - Latin. "Desire"; "love"; in Roman mythology, Cupid is the god of desire, erotic love, attraction and affection; he is often portrayed as the son of the love goddess Venus and the war god Mars; his Greek counterpart is Eros

Cuthbert - Middle English. "Well-known"; "bright and famous"

Cygnus - Latin. "The swan"; a prominent constellation in the northern sky; Cygnus is associated with the myth of Zeus and Leda in Greek mythology

Cyllene - Latin. "Sky"; "heaven"

Cynbel - Welsh. "Warrior chief"

Cyprian - Latin. "Of Cyprus"; Notable Bearer: 3rd century martyr Saint Cyprian was bishop of Carthage

Cyprine - A silicate mineral that is colored blue by copper

Cyra - Persian. "Moon"

Cyrax - A fictional character in the *Mortal Kombat* franchise

Cyrus - Persian. "Throne"; Notable Bearer: King Cyrus the Great founded the Persian empire in the 6th century BCE

D

Dack/Dak - English reference to the French town Dax; Notable Bearer: Rayne Dakota "Dak" Prescott is an American football quarterback

Daffodil - Synonymous with spring; a bulbous plant that typically bears bright yellow flowers with a long, trumpet-shaped center

Dagan/Dagon - Mesopotamian fertility and fish god; *The Torah* mentions him as the national god of the Philistines

Dagger - A knife with a very sharp point and two or more sharp edges

Daghatar - *Magic: The Gathering* legendary human warrior

Dagmar - Scandinavian. "Famous day"

Dagobert - Old Frankish. "Bright day"; Notable Bearer: Dagobert II was the king of Austrasia (676–679) and is recognized as a saint by the Roman Catholic Church

Daikolia - Greek. "Decency"

Daisy - Old English. "Day's eye"; a popular name in Victorian times

Dakkon - *Magic: The Gathering* planeswalker

Dakota - Native American. "Friend"; "ally"; another name for the Sioux or Lakota tribe or their language

Daksha - Sanskrit. दक्ष "Able"; "dexterous"; "honest one"; according to Hindu legend, Dakṣa is one of the sons of Lord Brahma who created Daksha, Dharma, Kamadeva and Agni from his right thumb, chest, heart and eyebrows respectively

Dalafilla - A stratovolcano in Ethiopia

Dali - Portuguese. "From there; from away"; Notable Bearer: Spanish surrealist painter Salvador Dali (1904-1989)

Dalibor - Slavic. "Fighting far away"

Damaine/Damien/Damion - Old Greek. "To tame"; "one who tames or subdues"; a fictional character in the 1976 horror film *The Omen*

Damara - Welsh. "Gentle"; a goddess of fertility in Celtic mythology

Dame - Old French. "Lady"; Latin. "Mistress"; originally a title of respect for a widow

Dametta - A fictional character in the *Final Fantasy* franchise

Damia - French. "Untamed"; feminine of Damien

Damiana - Greek. "One who tames, subdues"

Damon - Greek. "Gentle"; "to tame"; in Greek legend Damon was a loyal friend of Pythias; Notable Bearer: Matthew Paige Damon is an American actor, film producer, philanthropist and screenwriter

Damona - In Gallo-Roman religion, Damona was a goddess worshipped in Gaul as the consort of Apollo Borvo and Apollo Moritasgus

Damsel/Damselle/Damsella - French. A shortened form of Mademoiselle (a young, unmarried woman)

Damu - The god of vegetation and rebirth in Sumerian mythology

Damuzi - Syrian solar god who presides over the creative powers of spring; he is called "the Wise One" or "the Lord of Knowledge"

Danae - In Greek mythology, the mother of Perseus by Zeus

Danaus - In Greek mythology, the twin brother of Aegyptus, a mythical king of Egypt

Dancer - Old English occupational name for a dancer or acrobat

Dandy - A pet form of the name Andrew (manly; masculine)

Dane/Dain/Dayne - English. "From Denmark"

Danerys/Daenerys - A mash-up of Hebrew Daen (God is my judge) and Greek Erys, the goddess of discourse and destruction; a fictional character in the novel *A Game of Thrones* by George R. R. Martin

Danforth - Old English. "Hidden river crossing"

Danger - Latin. "Lord; master"

Dani - Hebrew. "God will judge"

Danielle/Daniella - Hebrew. "God is my judge"

Dante - Italian. "Enduring"; the poet Dante Alighieri wrote *The Divine Comedy* (1321) with its graphic description of medieval Hell known as "Dante's Inferno"

Danu - Celtic. "The flowing one"; Hindi. "Rain"; "river"; the mother of the Gods in Irish mythology and a Hindu river goddess

Danya - Ukrainian. "God's gift"

Daphnaie - In Greek mythology the Daphnaie are the spirit nymphs of the laurel trees

Darby - Irish. "Free from envy"

Daria/Darya - Persian. "He who holds firm the good"

Darien - Persian. "Good and wealthy protector"

Darius - Persian. "He possesses"; "rich and kingly"; Notable Bearer: Darius I (550-486 BCE) was the third king of the Persian Achaemenid Empire

Darla - Old English. "Darling"

Darling - Middle English. "Beloved one"; a very popular unisex name until the 14th century

Darmok - The title of an episode of *Star Trek* wherein the crew encounters a civilization which communicates only in metaphor

Darque - French. "The dark one from France"; "a day's work"; Old English. "Conceal"

Darth - According to George Lucas, "Darth is a variation of dark"; Darth Vader is a fictional character in the *Star Wars* universe

Darthula - Gaelic. "Daughter of Heaven"; Gothic. "Woman with beautiful eyes"

Darunia - Persian. "To possess"; "he who owns/possesses the well"; "he who maintains the well"

Darwin - English. "Dear friend"; Notable Bearer: 19th century naturalist Charles Darwin was the first major exponent of human evolution

Daruma - 達磨 A traditional hollow Japanese doll modeled after Bodhidharma, the founder of the Zen tradition of Buddhism

Dash/Dasher - English. "To run fast"

Dassuk - A fictional character in the *Doctor Who* franchise

Daster - Indonesian. "House dress"

Daugherty - Gaelic. "Unlucky"; "hurtful"

Davina - Scottish. "Beloved"; "friend"

Davinci - Latin. "Conqueror"; Notable Bearer: Leonardo da Vinci (1452-1519) was an Italian Renaissance polymath; his name at the time was simply Leonardo and he was from the town Vinci

Davros - A fictional character in the *Doctor Who* universe

Davula - Turkish. "Folk drum"

Dax - A town in southwestern France dating back to before the Roman occupation; Notable Bearer: Dax Randall Shepard is an American actor

Daxos - *Magic: The Gathering* legendary human soldier

Daxter - Latin. "Dexterous"; "right side"

Day - The period on a planet when its primary star is above the horizon

Daydream - English. "A series of pleasant thoughts that distract one's attention from the present"

Daylight - English. "The first appearance of light in the morning"; "dawn"

Dayton - English. "Day town"; "light town"

Deacon - In Catholic, Anglican, and Orthodox churches, an ordained minister of an order ranking below that of priest

Dean - Old English. "Valley"

Debrauna - Irish. "Great queen"; the goddess of speed in Celtic mythology

Decatur - Greek. "Pure"; Notable Bearer: Stephen Decatur was an early 19th-century naval hero after whom several US towns are named

December - Latin. "Tenth month"; originally the tenth month of the Roman calendar

Decima - Latin. "Tenth"

Decimus - This name was often given to the 10th child in large families; Notable Bearer: Decimus Junius Brutus Albinus was a Roman politician and general of the 1st century BCE who was one of the leading instigators in Julius Caesar's assassination

Deckard/Decker/Dekker - German. "Roofer"

Declan/Deklan - Irish. "Man of prayer"; "full of goodness"; Notable Bearers: Saint Declan founded a monastery in Ireland which has purportedly been the site of many miracles; Declan Patrick MacManus (Elvis Costello) is an English musician

Dedrick/Dedrix - Dutch, German. "Gifted ruler"

Dedun - Egyptian god of incense, prosperity and wealth

Deforrest/DeForest - French, Dutch. "From the forest"; Notable Bearer: Jackson DeForest Kelley (1920-1999) was an American actor, dammit, not a doctor

Degas - Old French. "Untilled"; Notable Bearer: Edgar Degas (1834-1917) was a French artist famous for his paintings, sculptures, prints, and drawings

Degore - A fictional character in the *OverSoul* game; House Degore is a knightly family in the novel *A Game of Thrones* (1996) by George R. R. Martin

Degory - Old French. "Lost"; "astray"; "destitute"; Notable Bearer: Degory Priest (1579-1621) was a member of the Leiden contingent on the historic 1620 voyage of the Mayflower

Deimos - Greek. "Dread"; Deimos is the smaller and outer of the two natural satellites (moons) of the planet Mars, the other being Phobos; Deimos was a god in Greek mythology, personification of terror; he was the son of gods Ares and Aphrodite and had a twin brother named Phobos

Deixis - The function or use of deictic (relating to or denoting a word or expression whose meaning is dependent on the context in which it is used) words, forms, or expressions

Deja - French, Spanish. "Already"; "remembrance"; "already remembered"; "remembered again"

Delanie/Delaina/Delaney - Old French. "From the Alder grove"

Delbert - English. "Bright day"; "sunny day"; "proud"; "noble"

Delcinia/Dulcinia - Latin. "Sweet"; "sweetness"; a name created by Cervante's fictional character Don Quixote for his idealized lady in *The Ingenious Nobleman Sir Quixote* (1605)

Deleware/Delaware - Old French. "Of the war"; English and French nickname for a soldier

Delfica - Italian. "Obscurely prophetic"; of or relating to Delphi or its oracles

Delfin - Spanish, Italian. "Dolphin"

Delia - From the name of the Greek island Delos, the birthplace of Artemis and Apollo in Greek mythology

Deliana - From the name of the Greek island Delos

Delilah - Hebrew. "Amorous"; "delight"; "languishing"; "temptress"; in the *Old Testament* of *The Bible*, Samson's mistress who tricked him into revealing the secret of his strength, then betrayed him to the Philistines

Delinda - Arabic. "Flower"; "vineyard"

Deliverance - Biblical. "Being rescued or set free"

Della - English. "Noble"

Delma - German. "Noble protector"

Delman - English. "Man from the valley"

Delora - Latin. "From the seashore"; "sorrows"

Delos - The island of Delos is one of the most important mythological, historical and archaeological sites in Greece; it is the alleged birthplace of the twins Artemis and Apollo

Delphia - Latin. "Dolphin"

Delphinia - Old English From Latin. "Dolphin"; Notable Bearer: 13th century French Saint Delphine

Delphyne - In Greek mythology, Delphyne is the name given to the monstrous serpent killed by Apollo at Delphi

Delta - The fourth letter of the Greek alphabet; the fourth star in a constellation; a code word used in radio communication; a piece of land shaped like a triangle, formed when a river splits into smaller rivers before it flows into the ocean; Notable Bearer: Delta Ramona Leah Burke is an American actress

Demelza - Cornish. "Fort on the hill"; quite popular in the mid 20th century

Demetro - Spanish. "Measure"; "rule"

Deneb - One of the three stars of the Summer Triangle constellation which anchors the tail of Cygnus the Swan

Deneka/Danika - [da-NEE-kah] Slavic. "Morning star"

Deniro - Italian. "Black"; likely originally a nickname for someone with black or dark hair

Denmark - Old German. "Threshing floor"; Old English. "Low ground"; Sanskrit. धनुस "Desert"; refers to the Norse mythological King Dan

Dennison - English from Greek. "The divine one of Nysa, god of the grape harvest"

Denton - Old English. "Village in a valley"

Denver - Old French. "Green valley"

Denya - A Southern Bantoid language of Cameroon in the Mamfe family

Deputy - A person whose immediate superior is a senior figure within an organization and who is empowered to act as a substitute for this superior

Dermot/Dermott - Irish. "Free from envy"; Notable Bearer: 12th century Irish king Dermot MacMurrough

Derrial - Derrial Book is a fictional character in the science-fiction series *Firefly*

Derry - Old German. "Gifted ruler"; "people ruler"

Dervla - Gaelic. "Daughter of Fal", Fal being an ancient name for Ireland

Desdemona - Greek. "Ill-fated"; Desdemona was the heroine of William Shakespeare's play *Othello* (1603); the leader of the railroad faction in *Fallout 4*

Desert - A dry, barren area of land that is characteristically desolate; in warm regions it is sandy dunes, in cold regions it is tundra or glaciers

Desiderata - Latin. "Desired things"; something that is needed or wanted; a prose poem from the 1920's by poet Max Ehrmann

Desmond - Irish. "South Munster"

Despoena/Despoina/Despoine - In Greek mythology, the daughter of Demeter and Poseidon and sister of Arion; she was the goddess of mysteries of Arcadian cults

Despona/Despina - Greek. "Lady"; "the equivalent of a ruler" most of the time it refers to the Virgin Mary, or "our lady"

Despot - A ruler or other person who holds absolute power

Desteran - A surname that was common in early Colonial America

Detroit - French. "The strait of Lake Erie"

Deva - Sanskrit. देव "Heavenly"; "divine"; "anything of excellence"; one of the terms for a deity in Hinduism; Deva is masculine, and the related feminine equivalent is Devi

Devi - [dee-vee or dee-VY] Sanskrit. देवी "Goddess"; the masculine form is Deva; both versions mean the same and are gender specific terms for a deity in Hinduism

Deville - Norman English. "Under the protection of God"

Devina - Latin. "Devine one"

Dew - Tiny drops of water that form on cool surfaces at night when atmospheric vapor condenses

Dexamene/Dexamine - Greek. "Of the strength of the right hand"; one of the Nereides in Greek mythology

Dexis - Greek. "Point of reference"

Dexter - A poetic form of the ancient Greek word "dexios" (right-handed, fortunate, skilled)

Dezra - A playable hero in the *Labyrinth of Ruin* franchise

Dhanishta - The 23rd nakshatra (lunar mansion) in Hindu astrology, corresponding to Delphini

Dhara - Sanskrit: धरा "Support"; in Hinduism, Dharā is one of the Vasus, the gods of the physical cosmos; he represents the Earth

Dharma - Buddhism. "Cosmic law and order"; "phenomena"; also applied to the teachings of Buddha

Dhatri - Sanskrit. "Earth"; a solar deity in Hinduism, and a god of health and domestic tranquility; his spirit can be called by drawing tantras and chanting Vedic hymns

Diamond - Greek. "Invincible"; "untamed"; a precious gemstone; a popular name in the Victorian era

Dianola/Dianoia - A term used by Plato for a type of thinking, specifically about mathematical and technical subjects

Diantha - Greek. "Flower"

Dias - Portuguese patronymic form of the medieval personal name Didacus

Dibella - Medieval English. "Of the beautiful"

Dickinson - Anglo-Saxon. "Son of Richard"

Dickon - The first recorded literary reference to the name is of a painting of King Richard III entitled *Dickon of York*; a character in *A Game of Thrones* (1996) by George R. R. Martin

Didacus - A Spanish Franciscan lay brother who served as among the first group of missionaries to the newly conquered Canary Island in the 15th century

Dido - Phoenician. "Virgin"

Dietrick/Dietrich - German. "Rich and powerful"

Dilaney/Delaney - Old French. "From the alder grove"; Irish. "Offspring of the challenger"; Gaelic. "Angel from heaven"

Dilys - Welsh. "Genuine"; "perfect"; "true"

Dinah - Hebrew. "Avenged, judged and vindicated"; in *The Bible*, Dinah was Jacob's only daughter

Diomedes - Greek. "Of Zeus"; "to think, to plan"; in Greek legend, Diomedes was one of the greatest heroes who fought against the Trojans

Dionisia - Medieval English reference to Saint Dionysius

Dionysius/Dionysios - The god of the grape harvest, winemaking and wine, of ritual madness, fertility, theatre and religious ecstasy in ancient Greek religion

Dior - French. "Golden"

Dioskouroi - The Dioskouroi (Dioscuri) were the star-crowned, twin gods of Saint Elmo's fire, an electrical discharge which appears on the rigging of ships portending deliverance from a storm

Ditty - A short, simple song

Dixon/Dickson - Scottish. "Dick's son"; allegedly originated upon the birth of the son of Richard Keith (12th century)

Django - African. "I awake"; it is best known as the nickname of Belgian jazz guitarist Jean Baptiste "Django" Reinhardt (1910-1953) whose fame has led to its use

Dobara - Urdu. "Again"

Docia - Greek. "Good reputation"; "comfort"; "God's gift"

Dogg - Medieval Scottish. "Son of the devotee of Dog"

Dolly - English. "Gift of God"; "of or like a baby doll"; Notable Bearer: Dolly Rebecca Parton Dean is an American country singer

Doloire - A tool and weapon used during the Middle Ages and Renaissance

Dolores - Spanish. "Sorrows"; a common nickname is Dottie/Dotty

Dominica - Latin. "Of the Lord"; Notable Bearer: Saint Dominic (1170-1221) founded the Dominican Order of Preaching Friars

Domitia - Of or about Saint Domitus

Domnola - A confirmation name of the early Byzantine Christian saints

Domri - *Magic: The Gathering* planeswalker

Donaghy - Old Irish. "Dark battle"

Donatello - Italian. "Gift"; "given by God"; Notable Bearer: Donato di Niccolò di Betto Bardi (Donatello) was an early Renaissance sculptor from Florence, known for his work in bas-relief, a form of shallow relief sculpture

Donnell - Scottish. "Great chief"

Donnovan/Donovan - Irish. "Brown-haired chieftain"

Dorado - Spanish. "The dolphin fish"; the Dorado constellation lies in the southern hemisphere

Doran - Irish. "Pilgrim"; "stranger"; "man from exile"

Doreen - Greek. "Beautiful"

Doretta - Greek. "Gift"

Dorilee - A popular girls name in the late 1800's

Doris - Greek. "Gift"; in Greek mythology, the daughter of Oceanus and mother of the sea nymph Nereids

Doritha - Greek. "Gift of God"

Dorothy/Dorothea - English. "Gift of God"; a fictional character in *The Wizard of Oz* (1900) by L. Frank Baum

Dorsett - Norman French. "Sweet to the eye"; "nice to look upon"

Dory - Old French. "Gilded"

Dosan - Korean. "Island mountain"; *Magic: The Gathering* legendary human monk

Doshie - Latin. "One who is a gift from God"

Dowsabel/Dowsabelle - An obsolete word for "sweetheart" that was popular in ancient times

Draco - Latin. "Dragon"; a constellation in the northern sky; Notable Bearer: Draco (650-600 BCE) was the first recorded legislator of Athens in Ancient Greece

Draconia/Draconius - Greek statesman who laid down a code of laws for Athens in 621 BCE that mandated death as punishment for minor crimes

Dragan - Serbian. "Dear"; "beloved"

Dragen - Slavic. "Dearly beloved"

Dragomir/Drahomira - Slavic. "Precious and peaceful"

Dragon - A legendary creature, typically scaled or fire-spewing and with serpentine, reptilian or avian traits that features in the myths of many cultures around world

Dragoslava - Slavic. "Dear; precious" + "fame; glory"

Drak - Slavic. "Dragon"

Drake - Old English. "Snake"; "dragon"

Draki - Old Norse. "Dragon"

Dralnu - *Magic: The Gathering* legendary zombie lord

Drana - *Magic: The Gathering* legendary vampire ally

Draper - English and Irish occupational name for a maker and seller of woolen cloth; the surname was introduced to Ulster in the 17th century

Drathro - A fictional robot character in the *Doctor Who* franchise

Draven - Due to the popularity of the 1990 film *The Crow*, the name may mean "Of the raven"; "child of sorrows"; "the raven"; "avenger"

Dravnik - Russian. "Dragon"

Drax - Drax the Destroyer is a fictional character appearing in the *Marvel Comics* universe

Drazhan/Drazan - Croatian. "Treasured"; "precious"

Drea - Greek. "Courageous"

Dream - A series of thoughts, images and sensations occuring in a person's mind during sleep; a cherished aspiration; ambition of ideal; a person or thing perceived as wonderful or perfect

Dreu - Greek. "Courageous"; "strong"

Drex/Drexel - German. "To turn"; Drex is a fictional character in the *Star Trek* universe

Drogo - Gothic. "To carry"; Saxon. "Ghost"; Slavic. "Precious; dear"; a fictional character in *A Game of Thrones* (1996) by George R. R. Martin

Druantia - Eternal mother goddess and mythological queen of the Celtic druids

Druid - A priest, magician, or soothsayer in the ancient Celtic religion

Druidia - Kingdom of Princess Vespa; a planet known for its large air supply which was nearly destroyed in the 1980's

Drummer - A percussionist who creates and accompanies music using drums

Drusilla - English from Latin. "Fruitful"; "dewy-eyed"; a popular name in the 1000's; a fictional vampire created by Joss Whedon

Drusus - A cognomen of ancient Rome

Druzy - A configuration of many tiny sparkling crystals on the surface of a bulky crystalline body

Duana - Irish. "Song"

Dudley - English. "From the people's meadow"

Dulcibella - Medieval Latin. "Sweet and beautiful"

Dulcie - Latin. "Sweet"

Dulcinia - Latin. "An overly elegant sweetness"

Dulzania/Dulzaina - A Spanish double reed instrument related to the oboe

Duma - Russian. "To think"; "to consider"

Dume - African. "The bull"

Dumuzi/Dumuzid - In Sumerian mythology Dumuzi is a shepherd god who represents the harvest season but also became a god of the underworld thanks to his wife, the goddess Ishtar

Duncan - Scottish. "Brown warrior"; Notable Bearer: Scottish king Duncan I was murdered by Macbeth in 1040

Dune - A mound or ridge of sand or other loose sediment formed by the wind, especially on the sea coast or in a desert

Dunia - Arabic. Used to describe the Earth in general

Dunovaria - A river off of Dorchester, made up of the Dunium and Varus, called "Durnium" by Ptolemy

Durand/Duran - French. "Firm"; "enduring"

Durbin - A French habitational surname

Durga - The warrior goddess in Hinduism whose mythology centers around combating evils and demonic forces that threaten peace, prosperity and dharma of the good

Durius/Durio - A personification in Celtic mythology of what is today known as the river Douro

Durst - Middle High German. "Boldness"; "thirst"

Dushara - Arabic. ذو الشرى "Lord of the Mountain"; a deity in the ancient Middle East

Duvall - French from Old English. "Dove"

Dwight - English surname referring to the Roman god of wine; Notable Bearer: American president Dwight David "Ike" Eisenhower (1890-1969)

Dwyfan - Celtic. "The father"; a primordial god of creation in Celtic mythology

Dymphna - A Christian saint in the 7th century, daughter of a pagan Irish king, she was patron saint of mental illness and spiritual disorders

Dystopia - An imagined place or state in which everything is unpleasant; a community that is undesirable or frightening

E

Eadwine - Old English. "Rich"; "happy" + "friend"

Eagle - Middle English nickname for a lordly, impressive, or sharp-eyed man

Ealgyth/Ealdgyth - Anglo-Saxon. "Old battle maid"

Earmengold - German. "Universal protection"

Earth - English, German. "Ground"; Earth is the only planet that wasn't named after a Greek or Roman god or goddess

Eartha - English. "Worldly"; Notable Bearer: Eartha Mae Kitt (1927-2008) was an American singer

Easter/Eastre - From the name of a pre-Christian goddess in England, Eostre, who was celebrated at beginning of spring

Ebeko - A highly active somma volcano on Northern end of Paramushir Island, Russia

Ebenezer - Hebrew. "Rock or stone of help"; in the *Old Testament* of *The Bible*, Samuel gave the name Ebenezer to a stone set up in recognition of God's assistance in defeating the Philistines; Ebenezer Scrooge is a fictional character in Charles Dickens' 1843 novel *A Christmas Carol*

Ebisu - The Japanese god of fishermen and luck; one of the Seven Gods of Fortune

Ebony - Greek. "Ebony tree"; "very dark brown or black color"; the name came as a companion/contrast to the word "ivory"

Echo/Ecko - A sound or series of sounds caused by the reflection of sound waves from a surface back to the listener; to be reminiscent of or have shared characteristics with

Eckhart - German. "Brave"; "strong"

Eclipse - When a celestial body obscures the light to or from another celestial body

Edelweiss - A European mountain plant signifying deep love and devotion

Eden - The biblical earthly paradise created by God to be inhabited by his first human creation

Edenia - Spanish. "Pleasure"; from the Hebrew Eden which was the garden-like home of Adam and Eve, the biblical parents of mankind

Edgar - English. "Fortunate and powerful"; Notable Bearers: King Edgar "The Peaceful" of England (943-975); American author Edgar Allen Poe (1809-1849)

Edie/Eadie - Old English. "Prosperity"; "wealth"

Edison - Old English. "Edie's son"; Notable Bearer: Thomas Alva Edison (1847-1931) was an American inventor and businessman

Edith - Old English. "Rich or blessed" + "war"

Edmonia - English, French. "Prosperous"; "protection"

Edon - Hebrew, Slavic. "Place of pleasure"

Edric - Anglo-Saxon. "Wealthy ruler"

Edwidge/Edwige - Teutonic. "Refuge from war"

Edwin - Old English. "Rich friend"

Edwina - English. "Rich in friendship"; "wealthy friend"

Eesha/Esha - Sanskrit. "Desire, pleasure or purity"; another name for the Goddess Parvati in Hinduism

Egbert/Ekbert - Old German. "Bright edge", such as that of a blade

Egeline - Popular name in Australia in the 1800's

Egeria - Latin. "Cumean"

Egon - German. "Strong with a sword"; Egon Spengler is a fictional character in *Ghostbusters* franchise

Egypt - Biblical. "That troubles or oppresses"; "anguish"

Eilaikai - Hawaiian. "Guide"; "leader"

Eileithyia - [EE-lee-thya] A goddess in Greek mythology who represented childbirth; the daughter of Zeus and Hera was born in a cave near Knossos, Crete, which became the main place of worship for the goddess

Eilika - Nordic, German. "Sword tip; sword edge"; Notable Bearers: Duchess Eilika of Oldenburg (Eilika Helene Jutta Clementine) is the wife of Georg von Habsburg; Eilika of Schweinfurt (1005–1059) was Duchess consort of Saxony

Einarr/Einar - Scandinavian. "Warrior chief"

Einstein - German, Jewish. "To enclose or surround with stone"; Notable Bearer: Albert Einstein (1879–1955) was a German theoretical physicist

Eir - In Norse mythology, the goddess of healing

Eira - Welsh. "Snow"

Eire - Irish. "Ireland"; from the name of a Gaelic goddess; Eriu is generally believed to be the matron goddess of Ireland, a goddess of sovereignty, or simply a goddess of the land

Ekhinda - A winery in Australia; a decoction in *Witcher*

Eladamri - *Magic: The Gathering* legendary elf warrior

Elaine/Laney - English. "Path; roadway"; in Arthurian legend, Elaine was mother to Sir Lancelot's son Galahad

Elan/Elon - Hebrew. "Tree"; "energy, style, and enthusiasm"; Notable Bearer: Elon Reeve Musk is the founder of SpaceX and co-founder of Tesla Inc.

Elba - From the name of the island off the west coast of Italy where Napoleon was exiled

Elbitha - Hebrew. "Beauty; grace"

Elbridge - Old English. "Old plank bridge"

Elbrus - Turkish. "Resembling a thousand mountains"

Elburn - A name that was brought to England when the Elburn family migrated to the region after the Norman Conquest in 1066

Eldon - English. "From the elves' valley"; "from the old town"

Eldorado - Spanish. "The golden one"

Electa - Latin. "Selected"

Electra - Greek. "Sparkling"; "the fiery sun"; the mythological daughter of Agamemnon; she was a central character in three Greek tragedies

Elegena - Old French. "Graceful and attractive in appearance or behaviour"

Elenor/Eleanor - Greek. "Light"; "torch"; "bright"

Elesh - Indian. "King"; *Magic: The Gathering* legendary praetor

Elesium/Elysium/Elysian - An ancient Greek conception of the afterlife where admission was reserved for mortals related to the gods and other heroes

Eleta - French. "Chosen"

Elfrida - English. "Good counselor"

Eliazar - Spanish. "God has helped"

Elika - Hebrew. "God will develop"

Eliphalet - Biblical. "The god of deliverance"

Elisheba/Elisheva - Hebrew. "Oath of my God"; "God is my oath"; in *The Torah*, the wife of Aaron, sister of Nahshon and daughter of Amminadab, from the tribe of Judah

Elisot - Old English from Hebrew. "Jehovah is God"; a fictional character in the *World Of Warcraft* franchise

Ellander/Ellender/Elender - Middle High German. "Strange"; "foreign"; a nickname for a stranger or newcomer

Ellery - English. "Joyful; happy"; Ellery Queen is the hero of a series of detective stories written by Frederic Dannay and Manfred B. Lee

Ellington - Old English. "Elf town"; "elf settlement"

Elliott - Greek. "Jehovah is God"

Elmer/Aylmer - Medieval English. "Noble"; "famous"

Elodie - French. "Foreign riches"

Eloisa - French from Old German. "Hale and wide"

Eloquence - Latin. "Speak out"; fluent or persuasive speaking or writing

Elora - Hebrew. "God is light"

Eloria - English. "God gives the laurel"; "the crown of victory"

Elpis - ἐλπίς In Greek mythology, Elpis is the personification and spirit of hope; she was depicted as a young woman, usually carrying flowers or cornucopia in her hands

Elspeth - Scottish. "Chosen by God"; "Consecrated by God"; a variant of Elizabeth; *Magic: The Gathering* planeswalker

Eluned - French. "Image"; "idol"; Notable Bearers: Saint Eluned, also known as Aled, was a 5th century virgin martyr; Welsh author Eluned Morgan (1870-1938)

Eluthia - The Greek goddess of childbirth and midwifery; she was connected with the annual birth of the divine child

Elvie/Elvy - Old English. "Elfin"; "good elf"; "noble friend"

Elvira - Spanish. "Truth"; "white"; "beautiful"; the heroine of Noel Coward's play *Blithe Spirit* (1941); a fictional character in Moliere's 1665 play *The Stone Feast*, the first legend of Don Juan; 1980's cult-movie TV hostess Elvira, Mistress of the Dark

Elvis/Alvis - Scandinavian. "All-wise"; Alviss was a dwarf in Norse mythology who was promised the hand of Thor's daughter, Thrud; Notable Bearer: Elvis Aaron Presley (1935-1977) was an American singer and actor

Elway - Gaining traction as a given name; Notable Bearer: John Albert Elway Jr. is a former American football quarterback

Elwood - English. "From the old forest"

Elysande/Elisande - Old French. "Temple path"

Elzar - Chef Elzar is a fictional character on the animated series *Futurama*

Elzbieta - Polish. "My God is bountiful"; "God is plenty"; a variant of Elizabeth

Ember - English. "Hot ashes"

Embeth - A blend of Emily and Elizabeth; Hebrew name roots from Aemilius and Elisheva

Emerald - Spanish. A precious green gemstone

Emeraude - French. "Emerald"

Emerick/Emmerich - Norman English. "Industrious leader"; German. "Power"; "work; labor"

Emeril - French. "A dark granular mineral"; Notable Bearer: Emeril John Lagasse III is an American celebrity chef

Emerson - Middle English. "Brave"; "powerful"; Notable Bearer: Ralph Waldo Emerson (1803-1882) was an American essayist, philosopher, poet and leader of the transcendentalist movement

Emesh - A Sumerian god of vegetation; Emesh was created alongside the god Enten to take responsibility on Earth for woods, fields, sheep folds, and stables; he is identified with the abundance of the Earth and with summer

Emmara/Ammara/Emmorah - The name of a 6th century woman who left her possessions to follow Mohammed, founder of Islam; a city in Iraq, the site of a major WWI battle; *Magic: The Gathering* legendary elf shaman

Emmeline/Ameline - French. "Industrious"; "hard worker"; Notable Bearer: British suffragette Emmeline Pankhurst (1858-1928)

Emmet - A pre-medieval girl's given name originating as a pet form of Emma

Emmony - Latin. "Flowed out"

Emory/Emery - Old German. "Industrious leader"; "home strength"; "brave"; "powerful"

Empath/Empathy - Greek. "Physical affection"; "passion"; a person with the ability to experience the mental or emotional state of another individual

Emperor - Latin. "Military commander"; "to command"; a sovereign ruler of great power and rank, especially one ruling an empire

Empire - Latin. "Settlement"; "farm"

Empousa/Empusa - A shape-shifting demigoddess in Greek mythology, said to have a leg made of copper

Emuze - Old French. "Entertain"; deceive"; Victorian twist on the word "amuse"

Ender - Turkish. "Very rare"; Andrew "Ender" Wiggin is a fictional character in a series of novels by Orson Scott Card

Endor - Also known as the "Forest Moon of Endor" and the "Sanctuary Moon", Endor is a fictional moon in the *Star Wars* franchise

Endora - Greek. "Light"

Endrek/Endrick - Old English. "Royal power"; "bold power"; *Magic: The Gathering* legendary human wizard

England - Old English. "Land of the Angles"; the Angles were one of the germanic tribes that settled in Great Britain during the early middle ages

Enid - Welsh. "Soul"; "life"; *Geraint and Enid* is one of the three Welsh Romances in Arthurian legend

Enki - The ancient Sumerian god of creation, intelligence, crafts, water, seawater, lakewater, fertility, semen, magic and mischief

Enkidu - Gilgamesh's companion in the ancient Mesopotamian poem *Epic of Gilgamesh* (2100 BCE); Enkidu embodies the wild or natural world

Enlil - Sumerian. "Lord storm"; Enlil, also known as Ashur, is the Mesopotamian god of wind, air, earth and storms

Enoch - Hebrew. "Dedicated"; in *The Torah*, this is the name of both the son of Cain and the father of Methuselah

Enten - A Sumerian fertility deity; he was said to have been created by Enlil as a guardian of farmers, along with the vegetation god Emesh; Enten is identified with the abundance of the earth and with the winter period

Enyo - A goddess of war and destruction in Greek mythology; Enyo was the sister and companion of Ares, and daughter of Zeus and Hera

Eocene - The Eocene Epoch, lasting from 56 to 33.9 million years ago, is a major division of the geologic time scale and the second epoch of the Paleogene Period in the Cenozoic Era

Eon - A major division of geological time, subdivided into eras; in Neoplatonism, Platonism and Gnosticism, Eon is a power existing from eternity, an emanation or phase of the supreme deity

Eonie - Used to describe someone who has an old soul; ageless

Eostre - The Germanic goddess of spring; also called Ostara or Eastre, she gave her name to the Christian festival of Easter (which is an older Pagan festival appropriated by the church), whose timing is still dictated by the moon

Ephara - *Magic: The Gathering* legendary enchantment god

Ephesus/Ephesos - Amazonian. "City of the Mother Goddess"; an ancient Greek city which, according legend, was founded by the tribe of the Amazons, great female warriors

Ephialtes - An ancient Athenian politician and an early leader of the democratic movement there

Ephraim/Efrayim - Hebrew. "Fruitful"; in the *Old Testament* of *The Bible*, Ephraim is a son of Joseph and Asenath and the founder of one of the 12 tribes of Israel

Ephrata/Ephrath - A biblical town in what is now Israel

Epicurus - Greek. "Wonderer"; Notable Bearer: Epicurus (341-270 BCE) was a Greek philosopher of the Hellenistic period

Epidarus/Epidaurus - A small city in ancient Greece

Epiona - Greek. "Soothing"; in Greek mythology, Epione was the goddess of the soothing of pain

Epiphany - Biblical. "A revelatory thought or manifestation of a divine being"; the Feast of the Epiphany, which commemorates the visit of the magi to the infant Jesus, takes place on January 6

Epoch - A period of time in history or a person's life, typically one marked by notable events or particular characteristics

Epona - Gaelic. "On horse"; in Celtic mythology, Epona is the patron goddess of mares and foals

Epsilon - The fifth letter of the Greek alphabet; the fifth star in a constellation

Equinox - Latin. "Equal night"; an astronomical event in which nighttime and daytime are of equal lengths

Erastus - Greek "Loved"; Erastus of Paneas is a steward in the *New Testament* of *The Bible*

Erato - Greek. "Desired"; "lovely"; in Greek mythology, Erato is the Muse of lyric poetry

Erebos/Erebus - Greek. "Deep darkness"; "shadow"; in Greek mythology, Erebus was often conceived as a primordial deity, representing the personification of darkness; *Magic: The Gathering* legendary enchantment god

Erecura - A Celtic earth goddess, often likened to Proserpina

Ereleuva - The mother of the Ostrogothic king Theoderic The Great

Ereshkigal - Sumerian. "Queen of the great Earth"; in Sumerian mythology, she was the goddess of Kur, the land of the dead or underworld

Eris - In Greek mythology, the goddess of discord

Eritrea - An ancient name, associated in the past with Greek Erythraia and Latin Erythræ

Erkanbald - Old High German. "Genuine"; "precious"; "bold"

Ermalinda/Ermelinda - Teutonic. "Serpent"

Ermina - Latin. "Noble"

Ermine - Old French. "Weasel"; Medieval Latin. "Armenian mouse"

Ernest/Ernust - Old German. "Serious"; "determined"; "vigor"

Ernesta - Spanish. "Serious; determined"

Ernis - Lithuanian. "Wolverine"

Eros - Greek. "Desire"; in Greek mythology, Eros was the Greek god of sexual attraction; his Roman counterpart was Cupid

Erra/Irra - An Akkadian plague god known from a poem of the 8th century BCE; Erra is the god of mayhem and pestilence who is responsible for periods of political confusion

Ershiba - French. "Your worship"; a lunar mansion (constellation) in Chinese astronomy

Ertai - *Magic: The Gathering* legendary human wizard

Erytheia - In Greek mythology, the spirit of immortality

Erzebet - [AIR-sa-bet] Hungarian. "Consecrated to God"; a variant of Elizabeth; Notable Bearer: Erzebet Báthory (1560-1614) was a Hungarian noblewoman accused of being the most prolific female murderer of all time

Erzulie - The Haitian voodoo goddess of love and the elemental forces; she is personified as a water snake, also called Ezili

Esau - In the *Tanakh*, the older son of Isaac and twin of Jacob; he is mentioned in the *New Testament* of *The Bible* as well

Escorial - A monastery and palace in central Spain built in the late 16th century by Philip II

Eshan - A planet in the *Star Wars* universe; Notable Bearer: Eshan Shanker is an Indian film actor

Esmeree - Old French from Latin. "Esteemed"; "loved"

Esmerelda - Spanish. "Emerald"

Essex - Old English. "East Saxons"

Estaline - Portuguese. Of or relating to Josef Vissarionovich Stalin (1878-1953), former General Secretary of the Central Committee of the Communist Party of the Soviet Union

Estella/Estelle - Old French from Latin. "Star"; a fictional character in the Charles Dickens novel *Great Expectations* (1861)

Esther/Ester - Persian. "Star"; the *Old Testament* of *The Bible* tells the story of Queen Esther, the Jewish wife of the king of Persia

Estienne - Medieval French. "An old or introverted soul"

Estoc/Estok - A type of sword in use from the 14th to 17th centuries in France and England

Estonia - A country in Northern Europe dotted with castles, churches and hilltop fortresses

Estrilda - Any of several small Old World finches, especially of the genus Estrilda, that have white, pink, or red bills of waxy appearance and are often kept as cage birds

Esus - Celtic. "Lord"; "master"; a powerful Celtic deity of vegetation; one of three gods mentioned by Roman poet Lucan in the 1st century, the other two were Taranis and Teutates

Eta/Etta - A pet form of Henrietta or Harriet

Eternity - English. "Time everlasting"

Ethel/Æthyl - Old English. "Noble"; in the middle ages, it was frequently used as the first element in Anglo-Saxon names, both masculine and feminine

Etheldreda - From the Old English Aethelthryth (noble, strength); Notable Bearer: Saint Etheldreda (636-679), later known as Saint Audrey, founded a monastery at Ely

Etheldria - A version of Etheldreda that gained popularity in Great Britain in the 1800's

Ethellyn - Old English. "Noble"

Ethereal - Greek. "Heavenly or spiritual"; "extremely delicate and light in a way that seems too perfect for this world"

Ethiopia - Greek. "The land of scorched faces"; the former name of the country was Abyssinia

Etienette - Ancient Greek. "Crown; garland; wreath" + "honor; reward; prize"

Etra/Ettra - French. "To be"

Etre - Breton. "Between"

Etro/Ettro - Italian. "Sky"; "air"

Eudialyte - Greek. "Well decomposable"; a somewhat rare, nine member ring cyclosilicate mineral; its name alludes to its ready solubility in acid

Eudocia/Evdokia - Greek. "Good deeds"; "she whose deeds are good"

Eudora - Greek. "God's gift"; in Greek mythology, Eudora was one of the nymphs of Hyades

Eudoxie/Eudoxia/Eudocia - Greek. "Comfort"; "good reputation"

Eugene - Greek. "Noble"; "well-born"; a common feminine and masculine given name since early times

Eugenia - Greek. "Well-born"; Notable Bearer: Saint Eugenia escaped persecution in the 3rd century by disguising herself as a man

Eulalia - Greek. "Sweet-speaking"; a teenage martyr and patron saint of Barcelona, Eulalia is associated with doves and peace

Eumalina - Hawaiian. "Calming"; "soothing"

Eumelia - Ancient Greek. "Melody"

Eunice - Greek. "Good victory"; "joyous victory"; "she conquers"; in *The Bible*, Eunice was a woman noted for being without hypocrisy

Euphemia - Scottish from Greek. "Auspicious speech or good repute"

Euphoria/Euphoric - Greek. "Born well"; "healthy"; a feeling or state of intense excitement and happiness

Euphrates - Biblical. "That which makes fruitful"; the Euphrates is the longest and one of the most historically important rivers of Western Asia

Euphraxia - Greek. "Of good cheer"; Notable Bearer: Euphraxia (380-410) was the daughter of a senator who distributed her fortune in charity, giving herself up to the practice of Christian perfection in an Egyptian convent

Euphrosene/Euphrosyne - One of the Three Graces in Greek mythology, the goddess of joy and mirth; one of the largest main belt asteroids; a common nickname is Phroso/Froso

Euporie/Euporia - In Greek mythology, Euporie is the goddess of abundance; one of the Pasiphae moons of Jupiter

Eura - Greek. "Justice"

Europa - The smallest of the four Galilean moons orbiting Jupiter; in Greek mythology, a Phoenician princess who was abducted and taken to Crete by Zeus in the guise of a bull

Eurus/Euros - Euros was the god of the east wind, one of the four directional Anemoi (Wind-Gods) in Greek mythology; he was associated with the season of autumn and dwelt near the palace of the sun god Helios

Euryale - Greek. "Far-roaming"; in Greek mythology, Euryale was the second eldest of the Gorgons, the three sisters that have hair of snakes

Eurydome - Greek. "Structure outside the areas"; in Greek mythology, she was the mother of the Three Graces by Zeus; one of the Pasiphae moons of Jupiter

Eustace - Greek. "Fruitful"; "productive"; Notable Bearer: Saint Eustace was a martyred 2nd century Roman soldier

Eustolia - Greek. "Fruitful"

Euterpe - Greek. "Rejoicing well"; "delight"; in Greek mythology, Euterpe was one of the Muses, the daughters of Mnemosyne fathered by Zeus

Eutopia/Utopia - Greek. "Good place"

Eutropia - Ancient Greek. "Well-mannered"; Notable Bearer: Eutropia was the 4th century daughter of Emperor Constantius Chlorus and Flavia Maximiana Theodora, and therefore half-sister of Emperor Constantine I

Evadene - In Greek mythology, the wife of Capaneus

Evalina - A form of Evalyn

Evalyn/Evelyn - English. "Life"

Evander - The name is borne in Roman mythology by the son of Hermes; Evander was father of Roma and he founded a town called Pallenteum which eventually became the city of Rome

Evandros - Greek. "Manly"

Evangela - Greek. "Brings good news"

Evangeline - French. "Bringer of good news"

Eve - Hebrew. "life"; "living"; "lively"; the biblical mother of the human race in who tasted the forbidden fruit, precipitating the fall of man

Evening - Old English. "Dusk falling"; "the time around sunset"

Ever - Old English. "At all times"; "at any time"

Everest - Greek. "Well-pleasing"; Mount Everest is the highest mountain in the world

Everett/Evered - Old English. "Strong, brave or hardy as a wild boar"

Evergreen - English. "Having an enduring freshness, success, or popularity"; a plant that has leaves throughout the year

Everild - Old English. "Boar battle"; "strong as a boar"

Everly/Everley - English. "From the boar meadow"; "from Ever's meadow"; Notable Bearers: the Everly Brothers were a 1950's/1960's singing duo; a fictional character in the *Sookie Stackhouse Series* of novels by Charlaine Harris

Evgeniya - Greek. "Well born"; Russian. "Noble"; a variant of Yevgeniya

Evola - Italian topographic name; Notable Bearer: Baron Giulio Cesare Andrea Evola was an Italian philosopher, painter, and esotericist (1878-1894)

Evolve - Latin. "Make more complex"

Exa/Exie - Hebrew. "Adorned"; American. "Habit"; "permanent feature of someone's character"

Exava - *Magic: The Gathering* rare legendary human cleric

Exerpa - Latin. "Plucked out"

Explorer - A person who examines or evaluates an unfamiliar area; an adventurer

Exura - Latin. "I burn"; "I consume"; "I kindle"

Ezekiel - Hebrew. "God strengthens"; in *The Bible* Ezekiel was a prophet among the captives taken to Babylon at the first fall of Jerusalem

Ezili - The Haitian voodoo goddess of love and the elemental forces; she is personified as a water snake, also called Erzuli

Ezio - Greek. "Eagle"; *Ezio* (1728) is an opera libretto by Metastasio

Ezra - Hebrew. "Help, helper"; Notable Bearers: Ezra was a religious reformer in the 5th century BCE; American poet Ezra Pound (1885-1972)

Ezuri - *Magic: The Gathering* legendary elf warrior

F

Fabia - A diminutive of Fabiola

Fabiana - From the Roman clan name Fabius (bean grower)

Fabienne - French form of Fabiana

Fabiola - Saint Fabiola was a 4th century nurse and Roman matron of rank who gave up all earthly pleasures and devoted herself to the practice of Christian asceticism and charitable work

Fable - A short story conveying a moral, often associated with Aesop

Fafner/Fafnir - Norse. "A mythical dragon"; *Fafner in the Azure* is a Japanese mecha drama anime series

Fairy/Faerie - Latin. "The fates"; a small imaginary being of human form that has magical powers

Falco - Latin surname or German given name related to falconry; Notable Bearer: Edith Falco is an American actress

Falcon - Birds of prey that are widely distributed on all continents of the world except Antarctica; they are closely related to raptors of the Eocene Epoch

Falcor/Falkor - A fictional dragon character in Michael Ende's 1979 novel *The Neverending Story*

Fallon - Irish. "Supremacy"

Fancy - Middle English. "Elaborate in structure or decoration"; "of high quality"

Fanny - French. "Free one"

Faramond/Faramund - Old German, Old Norse, Old English. "To journey; to travel"

Fargo - Spanish. "From the fenced pasture"

Farmer - Gaelic. "Son of the husbandman"; Old English occupational name; trending as a given name for both boys and girls

Farrah - Arabic. "Happy"; Notable Bearer: Farrah Leni Fawcett (1947-2009) was an American actress, model, and artist

Fausta - Italian. "Lucky"

Faustina - Latin. "Fortunate"

Fawkes - Norman French. "Falcon"

Fawn - Old English. "Make or be glad"; English. "Young deer"

Fay/Faye - Old English. "Loyalty"; "belief"; Middle English. "Fairy"

Fayte/Fate - Greek. "Destiny"

Februa - An ancient annual festival in Rome to avert evil spirits and purify the city; originally called Lupercalia; a spring cleansing ritual which gives the month of February (Februarius) its name

February - From the Latin Februa, the name of a purification festival held in this month

Federic - Scandinavian. "Peaceful ruler"; "peace" + "power"

Feldon - English topographic name for someone who lives in or by a field

Feldspar - An abundant rock-forming mineral typically occurring as colorless or pale-colored crystals

Felice/Felicia - Latin. "Happy"

Felipa - Spanish feminine form of Phillip (lover of horses)

Felis - Latin. "Fortunate, lucky or happy"

Felix - Latin. "Lucky"; "successful"; it was acquired as a nickname by the 1st century BCE Roman general Sulla; a biblical governor of Judea who imprisoned Saint Paul; *Felix the Cat* is a cartoon character from the silent film era

Fenella - Gaelic. "White shoulder"

Fenn/Fenne/Fehn - Middle English. "Marsh; bog"; a topographic name for someone who lived in a low-lying marshy area

Feodora - Russian. "God's gift"; Notable Bearers: Princess Feodora of Leiningen (1807-1872) and Princess Feodora Victoria Auguste Marie Marianne (1879-1945) were the half-sister and first great-grandchild of Queen Victoria, respectively

Ferdinand - Old German. "Safe, peaceful travels"; Notable Bearer: Ferdinand Magellan (1480-1521) was a Portuguese explorer who set out to discover a western sea route to the spice islands

Fergus/Feargus - Celtic. "Vigorous or forceful man"

Ferguson - Celtic. "Son of Fergus"

Ferne/fern - A feathery green plant that loves shade

Ferris - Celtic. "Rock"; a fictional character in the 1986 film *Ferris Bueller's Day Off*

Fewell - Scottish. "People"; a family name since the late 5th century, though the Saxon invasions mixed the native Scottish bloodline with conquering noblemen in 1200

Fezzik - A fictional character in the novel *The Princess Bride* (1973) by William Goldman

Fidelia - Latin. "Faithful"

Fielding - English. "Lives in the field"

Figaro - A fictional cat who first appeared in the children's novel *The Adventures of Pinocchio* (1883)

Fiji - An independent archipelago of over 800 islands in the south Pacific Ocean

Fillmore - Norman English. "Very famous"; Notable Bearer: Millard Fillmore (1800-1874) served as the 13th president of the USA

Finbar/Finbarr/Finbarre - Irish. "Fair-headed one"; Notable Bearer: Saint Finbarr (550-620) was the patron saint of and diocese of Cork city; in Irish folklore, Finbarr was the king of the fairies

Finch - Middle English occupational name for someone who caught and sold finches

Finetta - A variant of Hebrew Josephine (Jehovah increases)

Finlan/Fenlon - Irish. "Fair; white"

Finley - Anglicized Gaelic. "Fair-haired warrior"

Finn/Fynn - Old Norse. "White or fair"

Finnian/Finian - Anglicized Gaelic. "Little fair one"

Fintan - Irish. "White fire"; "white bull"; in Irish mythology Fintan mac Bóchra, known as "the Wise" was a seer who accompanied Noah's granddaughter Cessair to Ireland before the deluge; there have been 74 saints with this name

Fionn - Fionn mac Cumhail was a legendary Irish hero who became all-wise by eating an enchanted salmon

Fionnla - Scottish. "Fair-haired soldier"; Notable Bearer: Fionnla Dubh Mac Gillechriosd (Black Finlay, the son of Christopher) was a 15th century Scottish ancestor of the leading lines of the Macraes from Kintail

Firefly - A soft-bodied beetle with luminescent organs representing light and illumination in spirituality

Fisher/Fischer - English occupational name for one who obtained his living by fishing or living by a fishing weir

Flannery - Irish. "Red valor"; Notable Bearer: American author Flannery O'Conner (1925-1964)

Flavius - Latin. "Golden"; "yellow-haired"; Notable Bearer: Flavius Aetius (391-454) was a Roman general

Fleet - Old English. "Stream"; "estuary"; a country's navy

Fleetwood - Old English. "Wooded stream"

Fletcher - Anglo-French. "Arrow"; "to fletch"; "to furnish an arrow with a feather"; an English occupational name for someone who made arrows

Flora - The indigenous plant life occurring in a particular region or time; the corresponding term for animal life is fauna; Flora and Fauna were used as twin names in medieval times and again in the Victorian era

Florabelle - Latin, Italian. "Beautiful flower"

Florence - Latin. "Blossoming"; English version of Florentia

Florentia - Latin. "Flowering"; "in bloom"; Notable Bearer: Saint Florentia was a 6th century Spanish martyr

Florentine - French form of Florentia (blooming)

Floriana - French. "Flower"

Florida - Spanish. "Flowering"

Flossie - In Roman mythology, the goddess of flowers

Flower - Middle English."Blooms"; "to bloom"

Flute - A family of musical instruments in the woodwind group; a fictional character in William Shakespeare's comedy *A Midsummer Night's Dream* (1595)

Flyssa - A Berber traditional sword of the Kabyles tribe during the 19th century

Folcard/Foulcard - A monk of Saint Bertin's in Flanders

Folk - Old English. "People in general"; of or relating to the traditional art or culture of a community or nation

Ford/Fordy/Fordley - Middle English. "River crossing"; topographic name for someone who lived near a ford

Fordham/Fordwin - Anglo-Saxon. "Ford by a settlement"; "wading place"

Fordson - A brand name of tractors and trucks manufactured by Henry Ford & Son, Inc. in the early 1900's; a nickname is Fordy

Foreman/Forman/Formon - Old English. "Leader"; "spokesperson"

Forester - Old English. "Dweller or worker in the forest"

Fornax - The Fornax Dwarf Spheroidal is an elliptical dwarf galaxy in the constellation Fornax; Fornax is a constellation in the southern sky, partly ringed by the celestial river Eridanus

Forseti - Norse god of justice

Forsythe - Scottish. "Man of peace"

Fortuna - The goddess of fortune and the personification of luck in Roman religion; equivalent to the Greek goddess Tyche

Fortune - Chance or luck, especially good luck

Fossil - Latin. "Dug up"; "dig"; the remains or impression of a prehistoric organism preserved in petrified form or as a mold or cast in rock

Foster - Middle English. "One who keeps the forest"

Fox - An omnivorous mammal related to the dog; Fox William Mulder is a fictional character in *The X-Files* franchise

Foxglove - Old English. "Faerie folk"; a plant with vivid flowers which range in color from various purple tints through pink, light gray, and white

Francine - Latin. "From France"; "free one"

Francis - Latin. "Frenchman"; Notable Bearers: Saint Francis de Sales (1567-1622) is the patron saint of writers; Saint Francis of Assisi founded the Franciscan order of friars in the 16th century; navigator Sir Francis Drake was an English sea captain of the Elizabethan era ; philosopher Francis Bacon (1561-1626) served both as Attorney General and as Lord Chancellor of England

Franco - Italian, Portuguese and Spanish reference to the Germanic tribe of the Franks who invaded Gaul during the Migration Period

Franziska - German. "Free"; a Victorian-era royal name

Fredonia - English. "Freedom"; Latin. "Place of freedom"

Frey - Norse god of weather

Freya - Old Norse. "Lady"; a goddess in Norse mythology famous for her fondness of love, fertility, beauty and fine material possessions

Friar - Middle English. Old French. "Brother"; "monk"; a nickname for a pious person or an occupational name for someone employed in a monastery

Friday - Old English. "Day of Frige", a result of an old convention associating the Norse goddess Frigg with the Roman goddess Venus, with whom the day is associated in many different cultures

Frigg - Old Norse. "Beloved"; in Germanic mythology, Frigga (Old Norse), Frija (Old High German), Frea (Langobardic), and Frige (Old English) is a goddess; in nearly all sources, she is described as the wife of the god Odin; in Old High German and Old Norse sources, she is also connected with the goddess Fulla

Fronzie/Fronzy - Hindi. "Frontier"

Fuchsia - A vivid, purplish-red color like that of the sepals of a typical fuchsia flower

Fulbert - Fulbert of Chartres was the Bishop of Chartres from 1006 to 1028 and a teacher at the Cathedral school there

Fulke - Old German. "People"; "chieftain"; it is cognate with the French Foulques, the Italian Fulco and the Swedish Folke

Fulla - The goddess servant of Frigga in Norse mythology

Fuller/Fulleretta - British occupational name for a person who fulls cloth; a popular name in the late 1800's

Fulton - Scottish. "Bird enclosure; bird settlement"; popular in the 13th century

Futen/Fujin - 風神 The Japanese god of wind and one of the eldest Shinto gods

G

Ga/Ge - Gaelic, referring to Gaea, Greek Earth goddess

Gabriella - Italian. "Woman of god"

Gacrux - A bright red giant star in the Crux constellation (Southern Cross)

Gaddock - *Magic: The Gathering* legendary kithkin advisor

Gadley - Celtic. "Heath near the wasteland"

Gadriana - Feminine of Hadrian, Roman emperor in the 2nd century

Gaea/Gaia/Gaiea - Greek earth goddess and mother of the Titans

Gaetana/Gaetano - Italian. "From Gaete"

Gaete - According to tradition, the town was named after the elderly nurse of Aeneas, who died after fleeing with him from the ruins of Troy

Galactica - Of or relating to a galaxy, especially the Milky Way; *Battlestar Galactica* is an science fiction media franchise

Galapagos - Spanish. "Turtle"; the Galápagos Islands is a volcanic archipelago in the Pacific Ocean; Charles Darwin visited in 1835, and his observation of Galápagos' species later inspired his theory of evolution

Galatea/Galatia - Greek . "White as milk"; in Greek mythology, Pygmalion fell in love with the statue of Galatia, so Aphrodite brought it to life for him

Galaxia - Latin. "Milky way"; in new age mythology, the mother goddess corresponding to Gaia, but on a galactic level

Galaxy - Greek. "Milky"; a gravitationally bound system of stars, stellar remnants, interstellar gas, dust, and dark matter

Galen/Galena/Galina - Greek. "Calm"; from Galenus, a Greek physician whose research provided a basis for accepted medical practices for 1500 years

Galene - Greek. "Calm sea"; one of the famous nereids (mermaids/sea nymphs) in Greek mythology, she was the goddess of calm seas

Galileo - Italian. "From Galilee"; the name allegedly honors Jesus Christ, who was also called "the Galilean" in the *New Testament* of *The Bible*; Notable Bearer: Galileo Galilei (1564-1642) was an Italian polymath and a central figure in the transition from natural philosophy to modern science

Gallagher - Irish Gaelic clan based most prominently in what is today County Donegal

Gallant - Middle English. "Brave, heroic and chivalrous"; Old French. "Have fun"; "make a show"; "pleasure; rejoicing"

Galloway - Scottish. "Foreigner"; "from the place of the foreign Gaels"

Galveston - Arabic. "Triumphant"; a name borne by various Moorish chieftains in Spanish history and legend, notably the father-in-law of Al-Mansur, 10th century vizier of Córdoba

Galvez - The mountainous borders of Spain whose name is derived from the the Visigothic Gundesaelf (battle elf)

Galya/Galia - Hebrew. "God shall redeem"; Russian. "Calm"

Gamel - Old Southern French occupational name for a textile worker, miller, or baker

Gamma - The third letter of the Greek alphabet; the third star in a constellation

Gandalf/Gandolph - Old Norse. "Wand elf"; this name belongs to a dwarf in *Völuspá*, a 13th century Scandinavian manuscript; a fictional character in a series of novels by J. R. R. Tolkien

Ganesha - Sanskrit. गणेश One of the best-known and most worshiped deities in the Hindu pantheon; Hindu denominations worship him regardless of affiliation

Gangnrad/Gagnrad - In Norse mythology, a pseudonym used by the god Odin when he visited Vafthrudnir

Ganymede - The most massive moon of Jupiter and the ninth largest object in our Solar System; in Greek mythology, a divine hero whose homeland was Troy

Garcia/Garsea - Spanish from Basque. "Bear"

Gareth - Old French. "Gentle"; Sir Gareth was a Knight of the Round Table in Arthurian legend

Garrat/Garrett - One of the many baptismal surnames to have been derived from the popular names of Gerard and Gerald in 12th Century England

Garrison/Garriston - Middle English. "Protection"; "spear-fortified stronghold"; "son of Garret"

Garruk - *Magic: The Gathering* planeswalker

Garrus - French. "War"; Garrus Vakarian is a fictional character in BioWare's *Mass Effect* franchise

Garuda - A legendary bird or bird-like creature found in Hindu, Buddhist and Jain mythology; he is the vahana of the Hindu god Vishnu

Garza - A Galician and Basque noble surname and the Spanish equivalent of Heron

Gaspar - Spanish. "Treasure"; the original spelling of Caspar

Gatsby - Old English. "The Great"; "left-handed cat, god, or person from Gat"; *The Great Gatsby* is a 1925 novel written by F. Scott Fitzgerald

Gauntlet - An armored glove, as worn by a medieval knight

Gavril - Russian. "Worships god"

Geb - The Egyptian god of the Earth and later a member of the Ennead of Heliopolis; he had a viper around his head and was thus also considered the father of snakes

Gefion - The Norse fertility goddess often associated with a plow

Gelder - Middle English. "Sterile animal herdsman"; occupational name for a person responsible for looking after oxen and castrated horses

Gemma - Italian. "Gem"; "gemstone"; Notable Bearer: Gemma di Manetto Donati (1266-1329) was the wife of medieval Italian poet Dante Alighieri; Gemma Madoc Teller Morrow is a fictional character in the *Sons of Anarchy* TV series

Gemmeke/Gemeke - German female personal name that was popular in the 1600s

Gemmes/Gemme/Gem/Jem - Old French. "Precious stone"; occupational name for a jeweler; Jem is a fictional character in Harper Lee's controversial 1960 novel *To Kill a Mockingbird*

General - A commander of an army or an army officer of very high rank

Genesis - The origin or mode of formation of something; a famous book in *The Torah* and *The Bible*

Geneva - Native American. "Juniper tree"; the city of Geneva, NY was named so after a misunderstanding of the printed word Seneca, the name of the lake on which Geneva sits

Genevive/Genevieve - German. "Of the race of women"; "white wave"; Notable Bearer"; Saint Genevieve, the patron saint of Paris, believed to have protected the city from Attila the Hun

Georgette - A French diminutive of the Greek George (tiller of the soil)

Georgia - The US State of Georgia is named after British King George II

Georgiana - Catalan, English, Greek, Romanian. "Farmer"

Georgina - French version of Georgia

Geraldine - German. "Mighty with a spear"; "rules by the spear"

Geralf - *Magic: The Gathering* legendary human wizard

Gerbert - Old German. "Leather preparer"

Gerlinda/Gerlinde - Old German. "Soft or tender with a spear"

Germany - Old High German. "People"; "nation"

Geronimo - Greek. "Sacred name"; Notable Bearer: Geronimo (1829-1909) was a prominent leader and medicine man from the Bedonkohe band of the Chiricahua Apache tribe

Gerra/Girra - The Babylonian and Akkadian god of fire, derived from the earlier Sumerian deity Gibil

Gersham/Gershom - Hebrew. "A sojourner there"; according to *The Bible*, Gershom was the firstborn son of Moses and Zipporah; the text claims that the name is a reference to Moses' flight from Egypt

Gerta - Teutonic. "Warrior"

Gertrude - Old German. "Strong spear"; the name of Hamlet's mother in the Shakespearean tragedy *Hamlet* (1609)

Gerutha - In Norse mythology, the goddess of charity

Gervase - Celtic. "Servant spear"; Notable Bearer: Saint Gervase was a martyr who died in Milan in the 2nd century

Geryon - In Greek mythology, a fearsome giant who dwelt on the island Erytheia; the son of Chrysaor and Callirrhoe, the grandson of Medusa and the nephew of Pegasus

Geshtu/Gestu - A minor god of intelligence in Sumerian and Akkadian mythology; legend says that he was sacrificed by the great gods and his blood was used in the creation of mankind

Geth/Gethin - Old Welsh. "Strong lord or ruler"

Getty/Geddy - Gaelic. "Winged"; Notable Bearer: Geddy Lee Weinrib is a Canadian musician, singer, and songwriter

Ghana - African. "Warrior king"

Giacomo - Italian. "Supplanter"

Giana - Italian. "God is gracious"

Gibbiana/Gibiona - From the common medieval personal name Gib, a short form of Gilbert

Gibbon - Medieval English. "Bright, famous youth"

Gideon - Hebrew. "Destroyer"; "one who has a stump in place of a hand"; "a hewer"; the Gideons are a Christian organization distributing Bibles to schools, hospitals, and hotels; *Magic: The Gathering* planeswalker

Gilbert - German. "Bright pledge"; the Normans introduced this name to England, where it was common during the Middle Ages

Gilda - English. "Golden"

Gilgamesh - The main character of *Epic of Gilgamesh* (2100 BCE), an Akkadian poem that is widely considered the first great work of literature

Gillian - Latin. "The first down on the chin"; "downy-bearded"; the name was traditionally unisex and was popular in the 16th century

Gilligan - Gaelic. "Lad"; Gilligan is a fictional character in the 1960s TV show *Gilligan's Island*

Giordiana - Italian feminine of Jordan, for the Jordan River

Gipson/Gypson - Medieval short form of the name Gilbert (bright pledge)

Gisa - Hebrew. "Cut stone"

Gisella - German. "Pledge"

Giza - Hebrew. "Cut stone"; a city in Egypt where the ancient Egyptian pyramids and the Sphinx are located

Glacier - Latin. "Ice"; a slowly moving mass or river of ice formed by the accumulation and compaction of snow on mountains or near the poles

Gladys - Welsh. "Royalty"; "princess"

Glenanna/Glenette - French. "Anne's glen"; "glen of the stepping stones"

Glenna - Gaelic. "Valley"; "from the den"

Glinda - Welsh. "Fair; good"; Glinda "the Good Witch" is a fictional character in *The Wizard of Oz*, a children's novel written by L. Frank Baum in 1900

Glissa - *Magic: The Gathering* legendary elf

Glisten/Glistine - Old English. "Shine"; "glitter"

Gloriana - Latin. "Glory"; in Edmund Spencer's poem *The Faerie Queene* (1950) this was the name of the title character, a representation of Queen Elizabeth I

Godberta/Godbertha - Old High German. "God"; "deity"; "divine being" + "light"; "bright"; "clear"; "shining one"; this was a common name of royalty and saints

Godeliva/Godelieve - Old German. "God love"; Notable Bearer: Saint Godelieve (1049-1070) is the only married female martyr recognized as a saint by a medieval pope

Godiva - Old English. "Gift of God"; Notable Bearer: Lady Godiva (990-1067) was an English noblewoman who rode naked through the streets of Coventry to protest the high taxes imposed by her husband on the townspeople

Godric - Old English. "Power of God"; "god ruler"; this name was popular during the Norman conquest

Godwin/Godwine - Old English. "Friend of God"

Goethe/Gothe - Middle High German. "Godfather"

Gogh - Cornish. "Smith"; Notable Bearer: Vincent Willem Van Gogh (1853-1890) was a Dutch Post-Impressionist painter

Gold - A rare noble metal considered to be precious since antiquity

Golda - Israeli. "The precious metal"; Notable Bearer: Golda Meir (1898-1978) was an Israeli teacher, stateswoman, and fourth Prime Minister of Israel

Goldberg - Jewish. "Gold hill"; Notable Bearer: William Scott Goldberg is an American professional wrestler

Goliath/Golyat - Hebrew. "Uncover; reveal"; a giant Philistine who is slain by David in the *Old Testament* of *The Bible*

Gomatha - A heavenly cow-like goddess portrayed in Hinduism as the mother of all dairy animals

Goodman - Old English. "Good man"; in Scotland, the term denoted a landowner who held his land not directly from the crown but from a feudal vassal of the king

Gordiana - Italian feminine of Jordan, for the Jordan river

Gordon - Scottish. "From the marshes"; a surname and given name adopted from a Scottish place name; one of Scotland's great clans

Gore - Middle English. "Triangular"; a habitational name for someone who lived on a triangular piece of land; Notable Bearers: Albert Arnold Gore Jr. is an American politician and environmentalist; Eugene Luther Gore Vidal (1925-2012) was an American writer and public intellectual

Gormadoc - A character in *Middle-earth*, the fictional setting of much of British writer J. R. R. Tolkien's legendarium

Gortyna - A sacred place; once a major Roman city that later became the seat of the first Christian Bishop of Crete

Gorya - Russian. "Earth-worker"; "farmer"

Goteleib - Nordic. "Good legacy"; "heir of God"

Gotham - English. "Homestead where goats are kept"; Gotham is a fictional American city in the *DC Comics* universe

Gothique/Gothic - Belonging to or redolent of the dark ages; used in the 17th and 18th centuries to mean "not classical" (not Greek or Roman)

Gottfried - Jewish. "God" + "peace"

Gozer - Fictional Sumerian god in the *Ghostbusters* franchise

Graciela - Latin. "Favor"; "blessing"

Grady - Gaelic. "Noble, illustrious one"

Grafton - Middle English. "Grove town"

Graham - Scottish. "Grant's homestead"

Graii/Graeae/Graiae - In Greek mythology, three aged sea deities with only one eye and one tooth among them; they were the guardians of their sisters, the Gorgons

Grannus - In the Celtic mythology, Grannus was a deity associated with spas, healing thermal and mineral springs, and the sun; he was regularly identified with Apollo

Grant - Scottish. "Grand"; Notable Bearer: Ulysses Simpson Grant (1822-1885) served as the 18th president of the USA

Grantham - Old English. "Village built on gravel"; "snarler"

Gratiana/Gratiano - Italian. "Grace"

Graven/Greven - Old English. "Engrave an inscription or image on a surface"; *Magic: The Gathering* legendary human warrior

Gray/Grey - English. "Gray-haired"

Grayling - English. "Gray-haired"; "pleasant"

Grayson - English - "Son of the reeve"; "gray-haired"; "son of Gray"

Grecia - Spanish. "Who has God's friendship"

Green/Grene - One of the most widespread English and Irish surnames, dating back to before the 7th century; the color of nature

Gregor/Grigor - Scottish. "On the watch"

Gregoria - Spanish. "Vigilant"

Gregorius/Gregorios - Latin. "Watchful; alert"

Gretel - An Old German short form of Margarete (pearl)

Gretta - Dutch diminutive of Gretel (pearl)

Griffin/Griffon/Gryphon - A legendary Welsh creature with the body, tail, and back legs of a lion, the head, wings and talons of an eagle

Grimnir - In Norse mythology, a name Odin uses when he visits his foster son Geirrod, King of the Goths

Griselda - Old German. "Dark battle"

Grisha - Russian. "Watchful"

Groening - Middle Low German. "Yellowhammer"; an occupational name for a bird catcher; Matthew Abraham Groening is an American cartoonist

Grohl - David Eric Grohl is an American musician who rocks too hard because he's not a mortal man

Grover - English. "Grove dweller"; Stephen Grover Cleveland (1837-1908) was the 22nd and 24th president of the USA

Gru/Grue - English. "To be frightened; to shudder with fear"; a predator invented by Jack Vance and featured in the *Zork* series

Grus - Latin. "Crane"; a bird constellation in the southern sky

Guatemala - Spanish. "Land of trees"; a heavily forested and mountainous nation

Guilford - Old English. "Golden river crossing"

Guinevere - Welsh. "Fair; white"; Sebara. "Phantom"; "magical being"; in Arthurian legend, Queen Guinevere was the beautiful wife of King Arthur

Guinness - Celtic. "Chosen son of Gus"; a very popular name in Ireland

Gulde/Gulden - Middle High German. "Gold"; "golden"

Gulliver - Old French nickname which was given to a particularly covetous or acquisitive person; *Gulliver's Travels* is a 1726 novel by Jonathan Swift

Gullveig - Norse. "Gold branch"; in Norse mythology, the sorceress and seer who had a great love and lust for gold

Gunnar/Gunnarr - Old Norse. "Fighter; soldier; attacker"; the Vikings used the name to describe a brave and bold warrior

Gunnora - Old German form of Gunnvor

Gunnvor - Old Norse. "Wary in battle"

Gunter/Gunther - Old German. "Battler; warrior"

Guru - In Hinduism and Buddhism, a spiritual teacher, especially one who imparts initiation

Gussie - Latin. "Great; magnificent"

Gustave/Gustav/Gustaf - Old Swedish. "Staff of the Geats, Goths, or Gods"

Gustavine - Medieval Slavic. "Glorious guest"; Swedish feminine of Gustav

Guthrie - Gaelic. "Windy place"; "son of Uchtre"

Guyana - Native American. "Land of many waters"

Gwendlyn/Gwendolyn - Welsh. "Fair"; "blessed"; "white-browed"

Gwenllian - Welsh. "Flaxen-haired"; popular among medieval Welsh royalty; Notable Bearer: Gwenllian Ferch Llywelyn (1282-1337) was the only child of Llywelyn Ap Gruffudd, the last native Prince of Wales

Gwenna - Short form of Gwendlyn

Gwenore - A mash-up of Gwen and Lenore that was used in the early 1800's

Gwinnette - A regional name from the ancient principality known as Gwynedd, which was named for its overlord, Owain Gwynedd

Gwydion - Old Welsh. "Born of trees"; Gwydion was a hero, magician and trickster in Celtic mythology

Gyllenhal/Gyllenhaal - A Swedish family name that originated from a crown homestead in South Härene Parish

Gypsy - Egyptian. "Bohemian traveler"

H

Habondia - Latin. "To flow in waves"; the queen of abundance in Celtic mythology

Hachiman - Japanese. 八幡神 The Shinto and Buddhist god of archery and war and the divine protector of Japan and its people; his symbolic animal messenger is the dove

Hadad/Adad - Mesopotamian god of weather, hurricanes, storms, thunder and rain

Hadar - Beta Centauri, also known as Agena or Hadar, is a triple star system in the southern constellation of Centaurus

Hades - In Greek mythology, Hades was the god of the underworld; he was a son of the Titans Cronus and Rhea and the brother of Demeter, Hestia, Hera, Zeus, and Poseidon

Hadwisa - Isabella, Countess of Gloucester (1173-1217), was the wife of John of England; a depiction of her as a witch appears in *The Devil and King John*, a 1943 novel by Philip Lindsay, where she is called Hadwisa

Hagar - Hebrew. "Flight"; in the *Old Testament* of *The Bible*, Hagar is the concubine of Abraham and mother of Ishmael, the founder of the Arab people

Hagen - Middle Low German. "Protected place"

Haiku - Japanese poem traditionally evoking images of the natural world

Haimo - Old Norse. "Home"

Hale/Hayle/Hail - Old German. "Strong and healthy"; pellets of frozen rain that fall in showers from cumulonimbus clouds

Haline - Greek. "Salty"; "saline"; "of or relating to the degree of saltiness"

Hall - English, Scandinavian. "A spacious residence"; a topographic name for someone who lived in or near a hall or an occupational name for a servant employed at a hall

Halluce - "Big toe/great toe"; form of hallucinate

Halo/Haylo/Haloh - A circle of light around the sun, moon or other luminous body caused by refraction through ice crystals in the atmosphere; used in religious art as a symbol of holiness

Hamal - The brightest ancient equinox star in the northern constellation of Aries

Hamilton - Scottish. "Crooked hill"; habitational name from what is now a deserted village in the parish of Barkby; Notable Bearer: Alexander Hamilton (1757-1804) was one of the founding fathers of the USA as well as the founder of The Federalist Party, the US Coast Guard and *The New York Post* newspaper

Hamlet - Old German. "House; home"; most often associated with William Shakespeare's 1609 play *The Tragedy of Hamlet, Prince of Denmark*

Hamlin - German. "Loves the little home"

Hamon/Hammond - Norman English. "High protection"

Hampton - English and Scottish habitational name for someone from any of the numerous places called Hampton

Hamza/Hamzah - A letter in the Arabic alphabet; Notable Bearer: Ḥamzah ibn 'Abdul-Muṭṭalib (570-625) was a companion and paternal uncle of the Islamic Prophet Muhammad

Hani - The god of toxicity and poisons in Akkadian mythology, and one of the attendants of the storm god Adad

Hannibal - Phoenician, Carthaginian. "Mercy of Baal"; Notable Bearer: Hannibal Barca was a 3rd century BCE general, considered one of the greatest military commanders in history

Hans - German. "Gift from God; God has been gracious"; Hans Gruber is a fictional character in the Christmas film *Die Hard* (1988)

Hapi - An ancient Egyptian deity, the personification of the Nile flood

Happiness - English. "The state of being joyous, cheerful, or content"

Harbard - An alias used by Odin while disguised as a ferryman during a fight with Thor

Harbor - Old English. "Give a home or shelter to"; a place on the coast where vessels may find shelter

Harding - Dutch. "Hardy; brave; strong"

Hardy - Old French "Bold; courageous"; Irish. "Son of the hard lad"

Harka - Arabian. "The burner"; a god in pre-Islamic mythology who was the personification of the scorching heat of the desert

Harlan/Harlon - English. "From the hare's land"

Harlequin/Herlequin - Old French. "A mute character in a traditional pantomime"; "a joker or jester"; King Herla Cyning is a legendary leader of the mythical Germanic Wild Hunt and is credited as inspiring the word Herlequin

Harmon/Harman - Old High German. "Army"; "protector: a surname dating back before Christ; Notable Bearers: Daniel Harmon is an American writer and actor; Thomas Mark Harmon is an American actor

Harmony - The playing of musical tones together as chords; a pleasing arrangement of parts

Harpalyke/Harpalyce - Greek. "Song contest"; a very tiny gray moon of Jupiter; in Greek mythology, this name is attributed to two female characters

Harper - A musician who plays the harp; Notable Bearer: Harper Lee, author of the controversial 1960 novel *To Kill a Mockingbird*

Harrah/Hara - Biblical. "A hill"; "showing forth"

Harriet/Hariette - English. "Rules the home"; Notable Bearer: Harriet Tubman (1820-1913) was a Civil War nurse, suffragist and abolitionist who led slaves to freedom along the Underground Railroad; she was born Araminta "Minty" Ross, but changed her name in 1849 when she escaped slavery

Harrison - Old English. "Son of Harry"; Notable Bearer: Harrison Ford is an American actor

Hart - English, North German. "Stag"; Yiddish. "Hard"; Irish. "Descendant of Art"

Hartford - Old English. "Hardy ford"

Hartley - Old English. "Tongue of land in the fork of a river"

Hartwell - Old English. "Horse stream"

Harvard - Old English. "Army guard"; Notable Bearer: Harvard was an 11th century thane of Lincolnshire

Harvey - Old Breton. "Iron"; "blazing"

Hasta - Spanish. "Until"; a lunar mansion in Hindu astrology

Hatcher - Southern English topographic name for someone who lived by a gate marking the entrance to a forest or other enclosed piece of land

Hathor - An ancient Egyptian goddess who personified the principles of joy, feminine love, and motherhood

Hattie - A pet form of Harriet

Hattusha/Hattusa - The name of an archaeological site that is the former capital of the Hittite empire

Haukim - A pre-Islamic deity who was concerned with arbitration and the law; he is often mentioned together with Anbay, another god of justice

Haven - English. "Place of safety; shelter"

Havoise - Old German. "Sanctuary in battle"

Havran - One of the nakshatras (constellations) in Hindu astronomy

Hawaii - Hawaiian. "Place of the Gods"

Hawk/Hawke - A diurnal bird of prey; a person who advocates an aggressive or warlike policy, especially in foreign affairs

Hawkin/Hawking - Middle English. "Falconry"; Stephen William Hawking (1942-2018) was an English theoretical physicist, cosmologist, and author

Hawsey - Old German. "Hare"; the animal with many supernatural and unlucky aspects plays an important part in medieval folklore

Hawyse/Hawise - Old French. "Big battle"; the Normans introduced this name to England; Notable Bearer: Hawise of Rennes (1037-1072) was sovereign Duchess of Brittany from 1066 until her death

Haywood - English. "From the hedged forest"; Notable Bearer: Haywood Nelson is an American actor

Haze/Hays/Hayes - Gaelic. "Descendant of Aodh (fire)"; "descendant of Aed (an Irish mythological god)"

Hazel/Haezel - A popular medieval name representing the tree or the color

Hector/Hektor - Greek. "To check"; "restrain"; in Greco-Roman mythology, Hektor was a legendary Trojan champion who was killed by the Greek Achilles

Hedetet - A scorpion goddess of the ancient Egyptian religion; Hedetet resembles Serket in many ways, but was in later periods merged into Isis; she was depicted with the head of a scorpion, nursing a baby

Hedonia - English. "Pleasure; enjoyment; satisfaction"

Hefner - German and Jewish occupational name for a potter; Notable Bearer: Hugh Marston Hefner (1926-2017) was the founder and editor-in-chief of *Playboy* magazine

Hegelina - Medieval English. "Angel"

Heidar/Hayder - Arabic. حيدر "Lion"

Heimdall - In Norse legend, the watchman of the Norse gods and owner of the horn Gjall; Heimdall is the son of nine mothers; often identified with Rig, the creator of three races of men

Heka - Egyptian. "Magic"; Heka was the god of magic and medicine and was the personification of magic itself in ancient Egyptian lore

Heket - A frog goddess in Egyptian religion who was said to protect women in childbirth

Heleanor - Greek. "Other; foreign"; "sunray"

Helena/Helene - Greek. "Light"; "torch"; "bright"; in Greek legend, the beautiful wife of the king of Sparta whose abduction by the Trojan Prince initiated the Trojan War

Helewise/Heloise - Old German. "Hale and wide"

Helga/Helge/Helka - Old Norse. "Holy"; "blessed"

Helgi - Scandinavian. "Being dedicated to the gods"

Helia - Greek. "Of the sun"

Heliod - *Magic: The Gathering* legendary enchantment god

Helios - The personification of the sun in Greek mythology; he is the son of the Titans Hyperion and Theia

Hemingway - English habitational name from a lost or unidentified place; Notable Bearer: Ernest Miller Hemingway (1899-1961) was an American novelist

Hemlock - Poisonous herbs of the carrot family having finely cut leaves and small white flowers; a drug or lethal drink prepared from the poison hemlock

Hemma - Indian. "Premier"; "beast"; traditionally given to boys of the Hindu religion

Henderson - Scottish. "Son of Hendry"

Hendrix/Hendrik - Scandinavian. "Rules this household"; Notable Bearer: James Marshall Hendrix (1942-1970) was an American rock guitarist, singer, and songwriter

Hendry - Scottish variant of Henry

Henley - English. "High clearing"

Henna/Hennah - Finnish. "Home ruler"; in Arabia, it is a form of temporary body art using a dye prepared from the hina plant

Henon/Hinon - Native American. "Thunder leader"; Hinon was the Iroquois god of thunder

Henrietta/Henriette - French. "Keeper of the hearth"; "rules her household"

Henrika - Swedish. "Rules the home"

Hepburn - A family name of the Anglo-Scottish Border; Notable Bearers: Audrey Hepburn (1929-1993) was a British actress; Katharine Houghton Hepburn (1907-2003) was an American actress

Hepzebah/Hepzibah - Hebrew. "She is my delight"

Hera - In Greek mythology, the wife of Zeus who was the queen of heaven and the goddess of marriages; she is equated to the Roman Juno

Heracles - Latin. "Glory of Hera"; "glorious gift"; in Greek mythology, Heracles was the son of Zeus and Hera; he is cognate with the Roman Hercules

Hercules - A Roman hero and god famous for his strength and for his numerous far-ranging adventures; he was the son of Jupiter and Alcmene and was the equivalent of the Greek divine hero Heracles

Herkimer - Quartz crystals (Herkimer diamonds) that were discovered in and around the Mohawk River Valley

Herla - Herla King was a legendary leader of the mythical Germanic Wild Hunt and the name from which the Old French term "herlequin" may have been derived

Herleve/Herleva - Old Norse. "Army"; "honor"; "noble"; Notable Bearer: Herleva of Falaise (1003-1050) was a commoner and the mother of King William the Conqueror

Herlewin - Old German. "Free man"; "noble man"; Notable Bearer: Ethelmaer, also called Herlewin, was a 12th century English ascetic writer

Herman - Old German. "Army man"

Hermes - Greek. "Messenger of the gods"; in Greek mythology, Hermes is the god of trade, wealth, luck, fertility, animal husbandry, sleep, language, thieves, and travel; he is equivalent to the Roman Mercury

Hermina/Hermione - Spanish, Greek. "Messenger"

Hermod - The son of the god Odin in Norse mythology

Hermogene - Biblical. "Begotten of Mercury"

Hero - A person who is admired or idealized for courage, outstanding achievements, or noble qualities

Herodias - Feminine form of Herod; In *The Bible*, she is a sister of Herod Agrippa and the wife of Herod Antipas

Hershel - Yiddish. "Deer"

Hersilia - Spanish, Greek. "Delicate"; in Roman mythology, Hersilia was the wife of Romulus, Rome's founder

Hertha - German. "Of the Earth"

Hervor - Old Norse. "Lady of spring"

Hesiod/Hesiodos - Greek. "To throw song"; Notable Bearer: Hesiodos was Greek poet who was active around the same time as Homer (750-650 BCE)

Hesper - Greek. "Evening star"

Hester - Persian. "Star"; "myrtle leaf"

Hestia - Greek. "Hearth; fireside"; in ancient Greek religion, Hestia is a virgin goddess of the hearth, domesticity, and the family

Heston - Old English. "Brush wood"; Notable Bearer: Charlton Heston (1923-2008) was an American actor and political activist

Hetfield - Anglo-Saxon family name; Notable Bearer: James Alan Hetfield is an American musician

Hetty - French. "Ruler of her household"

Hex - Pennsylvania Dutch. "Cast a spell; bewitch"; hex signs are a form of Pennsylvania Dutch folk art; barn paintings, usually in the form of stars in circles, began to appear on the landscape in the early 19th century

Hezekiah - Hebrew. "God is my strength"; "God has strengthened"; according to *The Torah*, Hezekiah was the son of Ahaz and the 13th king of Judah

Hibernia - The classical name for the island of Ireland, taken from Greek geographical accounts; during his exploration of northwest Europe in 320 BCE, Pytheas of Massilla called the island Ierne

Hibiscus - A common name in ancient Rome, referring to the flower

Hieronymus/Hieronymos - Latin, Greek. "With a sacred name"; it corresponds to the English name Jerome; Notable Bearer: Hieronymus Bosch (1450-1516) was a Dutch draughtsman and painter

Hieropolis - An ancient city located on hot springs in classical Phrygia in southwestern Anatolia

Hikaru - Japanese. "Light"; Hikaru Kato Sulu is a fictional character in the *Star Trek* franchise

Hiker - A person who walks for long distances, especially across country.

Hild/Hilda - Old Norse. "Battle"; Hild was a Valkyrie who conveyed fallen warriors to Valhalla in Norse mythology

Hildebrand/Hildebrant - Old Norse. "Battle sword"; companion of Theodoric the Great in Norse mythology

Hildegard - Old High German. "Battleguard"

Hiltrude/Hiltrud - Old German. "Strength in battle"

Himalaya - Sanskrit. "Abode of snow"

Himalya/Himalia - The largest irregular satellite (moon) of Jupiter; in Greek mythology, Himalia was a nymph who produced three sons with Zeus

Hindley - English. "Doe clearing"

Hippolyte - Greek queen of the Amazons, a female warrior tribe

Hiraeth - Welsh. "A homesickness tinged with grief or sadness over the lost or departed"; "feeling of longing, yearning, nostalgia, wistfulness, or an earnest desire for the ways of the past"

Hiram - Hebrew. "Exalted brother"; a king of Tyre in the *Old Testament* of *The Bible*; as an English given name, Hiram came into use after the Protestant Reformation

Hirudo - Greek. "Leech"; an obsolete old western constellation

Hixus - *Magic: The Gathering* rare legendary human soldier

Hobbes - Old English. "Bright fame"; an Old German variant of Robert; Notable Bearer: Thomas Hobbes was a 17th century English philosopher after whom Bill Watterson named his popular cartoon stuffed tiger

Hodge - Medieval short form of Roger

Hodiny - A Czech constellation that is cognate with Horologium

Hogan/Hogyn - Irish. "Young"; Cornish. "Mortal"; Welsh. "Stripling"; Terry Gene Bollea (Hulk Hogan) is an American professional wrestler regarded by many as the greatest of all time

Holden - Old English. "From the hollow in the valley"; Holden Caulfield is a fictional character in J. D. Salinger's novel *The Catcher in the Rye* (1951)

Holland - Old English. "Ridge land"; Dutch. "Wood land"

Hollandine - Louise Hollandine (1622-1709) was the daughter of Elizabeth, nominal Queen of Bohemia

Hollianra/Holliandra - Old English habitational name for a brave man who lived by the clearing by the hollow

Holliday/Holiday - Habitational name for someone who lived near the mountain called "Holy Day" (Croagh Patrick) in the country of Annandale

Hollis - English. "Dweller at the holly trees"

Holmar - Old Norse. "Small island"; Notable Bearer: Hólmar Örn Eyjólfsson is an Icelandic footballer

Holon/Hollon/Hollan - Hebrew. "Little sand"; Anglo-Saxon. "A small, protected place"

Homer - Greek. "Security"; "helmet maker"; "pool in a hollow"; Notable Bearers: Homer was a Greek poet in the 8th century BCE who authored *The Iliad* and *The Odyssey*; Homer Simpson is a fictional character in the longest running animated series, *The Simpsons*

Homura - Chinese. 炎 "Blaze or flame"; a genus of moths

Honden - Japanese. "Main hall"; the most sacred building at a Shinto shrine

Honduras - Italian. "Depths"; the country was named in 1502 by Christopher Columbus for the deep waters off the coast

Honey - Old English, Dutch, German. "Sweet, sticky liquid made from nectar by honeybees"

Honeycutt - Old English. "Honey cottage"

Honolulu - Hawaiian. "Sheltered harbor"; "calm port"

Honora/Honoria - Irish. "Honor"

Honorine/Honorina - Latin. "Honor"; Notable Bearer: Saint Honorina (died 303) is the oldest, most revered virgin martyr in the Normandy area of France

Hopper - English and Scottish occupational name for a professional tumbler or acrobat

Horace - Latin. "Hour in time"; "timekeeper"; Notable Bearer: Quintus Horatius Flaccus (65-8 BCE) was a Roman poet known as Horace in the English-speaking world

Horatio - Italian. "Timekeeper"; derived from the Roman clan name Horatius; the close friend of Hamlet in William Shakespeare's *The Tragedy of Hamlet, Prince of Denmark* (1599)

Horatius - Latin. "Hour"; "time"; "season"; Notable Bearer: Quintus Horatius Flaccus (Horace) was a Roman lyric poet, satirist, and critic in the 1st century BCE

Horik - Old Norse. "Kingly"; "kingpin"; the assumed name of two viking kings in Denmark in the 8th and 9th centuries

Horologium - Refers to Horology (the science of timekeeping); a faint constellation in the southern sky

Hortence/Hortense - French from Latin. "Gardener"; Notable

Bearers: Hortense Allart (1801-1879) was an Italian French feminist writer and essayist; Hortense de Beauharnais (1783-1837) was the step daughter of Napoleon and Queen consort of Holland

Horton - Old English. "Farm on muddy soil"; Horton the Elephant is a fictional character in children's books written by Dr. Seuss

Horus - Egyptian. "Falcon"; "high"; in Egyptian mythology, Horus was the god of light, often depicted as a man with the head of a falcon

Hosanna - Biblical. "Save I pray thee"; "keep; preserve"

Hoshi - Japanese. "Star"

Houston - Scottish. "From Hugh's town"; a city in Texas named for American general Sam Houston

Howland - English. "From the chief's land"

Hrodrich - Old German. "Famous ruler"; "famous king"

Hubert - German. "Bright heart": Saint Hubert was an 8th century bishop who is considered the patron saint of hunters

Huberta - German. "Intelligent"

Huckleberry - A regional American name for a berry similar to a small blueberry; it is thought of as a name chiefly because of Mark Twain's illustrated novel *Adventures of Huckleberry Finn* (1884)

Hudson/Hutson - Old English. "Son of Hudde"; a medieval given name and nickname for both Hugh and Richard; New York's Hudson River and Canada's Hudson Bay were both named after Henry Hudson, an English explorer

Hugard - Anglicized variant of the Old French Huguenot

Hugo - German. "Bright in mind and spirit"; "intelligence"

Huguenot - Old French. "House follows"; "oath follows"

Humility - English from Latin. "Humbleness"

Humphrey/Humfrey - German. "Bear cub"; "peace"; Notable

Bearer: 9th century Saint Humfrey, bishop of Therouanne, had a following in England among Norman settlers

Huna - Old English, Hebrew, Hindu, Indian. "Golden necklace"

Hurakan/Huracan - Taino. "God of the storm"; Mayan. "Heart of sky"; in native legend, Huracan was the Mayan god of wind, storm, fire and one of the creator deities who participated in all three attempts at creating humanity

Hurricane - A rapidly rotating storm system with a spiral arrangement of thunderstorms that produce heavy rain; depending on its location and strength, a tropical cyclone is referred to as a hurricane, typhoon, tropical storm, cyclonic storm, tropical depression, or cyclone

Hush - Scottish. "Unexplained"

Huxley - Old English. "Hugh's meadow"; Notable Bearer: Aldous Leonard Huxley (1894-1963) was an English writer

Hyacinth - In Greek legend, a flower that sprouted from the blood of the youth Hyacinthus, who was accidentally killed by Apollo

Hyaline - Greek. "Transparent; like glass"; a thing that is clear and translucent like glass, especially a smooth sea or a clear sky

Hydra - A dragon killed by Hercules

Hymn - Old French, Old English from Latin. "Song of praise"; Greek. "Song or ode in praise of gods or heroes"; Hebrew. "Song praising God"

Hyperion - Greek. "The high one"; in Greek mythology, Hyperion was one of the 12 Titan children of Gaia (Earth) and Uranus (sky or heaven)

Hypolite/Hippolyta - Greek. "Horse-freer"; Hippolyta was an Amazonian queen with a magic girdle in Greek mythology

Hythonia - *Magic: The Gathering* legendary gorgon

I

Iah - Egyptian. "Moon"; a lunar deity in ancient Egyptian religion

Iat - An Ancient Egyptian goddess of milk and, by association, of nurturing and childbirth

Iapapa - A berry in the *Pokemon* franchise which has healing powers

Iapetus - Greek. "A Titan"; the third largest moon of Saturn

Ice - Frozen water, a brittle, transparent crystalline solid; diamonds

Ichabod/Icabod/Ikabod - Hebrew. "No glory"; Notable Bearers: In the *Old Testament* of *The Bible*, Ichabod is the grandson of Eli and the son of Phinehas; Ichabod Crane is the main character in Washington Irving's novel *The Legend of Sleepy Hollow* (1820)

Icharus/Icarus/Ikaros - In Greek mythology, Icarus was the son of Daedalus, locked with his father inside the Labyrinth by Minos, they escaped from the maze using wings devised from wax, but Icarus flew too close to the sun and the wax melted, plunging him to his death

Icheb - A fictional character in the *Star Trek* franchise from the Brunali homeworld

Ida - German. "Labor; work"; a mountain in West Turkey, south east of ancient Troy; the name is associated with Old Norse goddess Iounn

Idabel/Idabelle - Swedish form of Ida

Idaho - Shoshone. "Gem of the mountains"

Idalia - Greek. "Behold the Sun"

Idalina/Idaline - English, German, Spanish, Teutonic. "Working noble"

Idella/Idelle - Celtic, Welsh. "Bountiful"

Ide/Ides - Latin. "13th or 15th day of the month"; Irish. "Thirst; thirst for goodness or knowledge"; Notable Bearer: Íte ingen Chinn Fhalad (475-570), also known as Ita, Ida or Ides, was an early Irish nun and patron saint of Killeedy

Idonea - Latin. "Suitable"

Idunn - Norse. "Active in love"

Ignatius - Latin, Etruscan. "Fiery one"; Notable Bearer: Ignatius of Antioch, also known as "The Fire-Bearer", was an early Christian writer and bishop of Antioch in the 1st century

Igner/Ignar - A fictional character in the animated series *Futurama*

Ignis - Latin mix. "Fiery"

Igor - Russian. "Warrior of peace; Ing's warrior"; Ing was the Norse god of peace and fertility; from the Scandinavian name Ingyar

Igwisi - The Igwisi Hills are a volcanic field in Tanzania

Ihy - A child deity in Egyptian legend, the god of music, joy and jubilation

Ilargia/Illargia - Basque. "The light of the moon"; "moonlight"

Ilbertus - Old English. "Noble; bright"

Iliad - *The Iliad* is an ancient Greek epic poem in dactylic hexameter, traditionally attributed to Homer; it is generally considered to have been written in the 8th century BCE

Ilian - Arabic. "Big"; "spiritual"; Hebrew. "The Lord is my God"; a popular name in Bulgaria

Ilimuda - Merapi. "The one who makes fire"; a volcano the island of Flores, Indonesia

Illinois - Illini. "The best people"; derived from the word "Illiniwek", the tribal name of the Illini, which is made up of 12 Native American tribes

Ilona - Hungarian. The traditional name of the faeries of the Magyar folklore; a common story is that Ilona is cognate with the Greek given name Helen

Iktomi - In Lakota mythology, Iktomi is a spider-trickster spirit and a culture hero for the Lakota people; alternate names for Iktomi include Ikto, Ictinike, Inktomi, Unktome, and Unktomi; these names are due to the differences in tribal languages, as this spider deity was known throughout many of North America's tribes

Imani - Kiswahili. "Faith"

Immerse - Latin. "To plunge in; dip into"

Imogene - Celtic. "Maiden"; "girl"

Imperial - Late Middle English via Old French from Latin. "Majestic; magnificent"

Impressa/Impresa - An emblem or device with a motto used in the 16th and 17th centuries

Inanna - The ancient Sumerian goddess of love, beauty, sex, desire, fertility, war, combat, justice, and political power; she was later worshipped by the Akkadians, Babylonians, and Assyrians under the name Ishtar

Inari - Japanese. "Carrying rice"; "rice load"; Inari (also known as Oinari) is the Japanese kami (spirit) of foxes, fertility, rice, tea and Sake, agriculture and industry, general prosperity and worldly success; she is one of the principal kami of Shinto

Incubus - Middle English from Latin. "Nightmare"; a Lilin-demon in male form who, according to mythological and legendary traditions, lies upon sleeping women; its female counterpart is "succubus"

Indiana - English. "Land of the Indians"; "Indian land"

Indica - Feminine derivative of Indigo, which is a deep blue dye from an Indigofera plant; a female strain of the marijuana plant

Indigo - A color of the rainbow.; a deep blue dye made from the Indigofera plant

Indonesia - Greek. "Indian islands"

Indra - Sanskrit. "Possessing drops of rain"; the name of an ancient Hindu warrior god of the sky and rain; he is the chief god in the Hindu text *Rigveda*

Inessa - Russian. "Chaste"

Inez - Greek. "Poor, pure or chaste"; a form of the given name Agnes

Infinity - Late Middle English, from Old French and Latin. "Endless"

Ingeborg - Scandinavian from Old Norse. "Stronghold; protection"

Ingen - Old Irish. "Maiden; girl"

Ingram - German. "Ing's raven"; Ing is the Norse god of peace and fertility

Ingrid - Scandinavian. "Ing's ride"; Ing is the Norse god of peace and fertility

Inigo/Eneko - Castilian from medieval Basque. "My little (love)"; Inigo Montoya is a fictional character in William Goldman's 1973 novel *The Princess Bride*

Innogen - Celtic. "Maiden or girl"

Inspire - Middle English from Old French from Latin. "Breathe or blow into"; the word was originally used of a divine or supernatural being and hence means "to impart a truth or idea to someone"

Io - The innermost of the four Galilean moons of the planet Jupiter; it was named after the mythological character Io, a priestess of Hera who became one of Zeus' lovers

Ioannina - A city in ancient Greece often called Yannena

Iola - Greek. "Violet-colored dawn"; sister of Iphitus in Greek lore

Ion - The illegitimate child of Creusa and the god Apollo in Greek mythology; an atom or molecule with a net electric charge due to the loss or gain of one or more electrons

Ionnia - The leader of Heldren's village council in *Pathfinder*

Iosif - Russian. "God adds"; Hebrew. "He will enlarge"

Ioskeha - [I-yus-kah] Iroquois. "Little sprout; maple sapling"; in Huron mythology, Ioskeha is one of the twin grandsons of Ataensic, the Sky Woman; Ioskeha and Tawiscara (Flint) exist in natural balance with each other, with Ioskeha representing creation, life, day, and summer, while his brother represents destruction, death, night, and winter

Iota - The ninth letter of the Greek alphabet; the ninth star in a constellation

Iounn - In Norse mythology, a goddess associated with apples and youth

Iovita - Latin. "Young; vigorous"

Iowa - From Ioway, the French transcription of Ayuway, which is what the Illini and Meskwaki called the tribe

Iphiginia/Iphigenia - Greek. "Strong born"; "born to strength"; "she who causes the birth of strong offspring"; the daughter of Agamemnon and Clytemnestra in Greek mythology

Iraya - A predominantly Pagan people inhabiting the mountainous interior of Northern Mindoro in the Philippines

Ireland - The modern Irish "Éire" evolved from the Old Irish word "Ériu", which was the name of a Gaelic goddess; Ériu is generally believed to have been the matron goddess of Ireland, a goddess of sovereignty, or simply a goddess of the land

Irene/Eirene - Greek. "Peace"; this was the name of the Greek goddess who personified peace, of the Horai; the name was also borne by several early Christian saints

Iridescence - Greek, Latin. "A lustrous rainbow-like play of color"

Iriria - [ee-ree-ree-AH] The Bribri earth goddess; Iriria was the daughter of the Tapir, who was the sister of the culture hero Sibú; Sibú sacrificed his niece to transform her into the Earth; because of this, both Iriria and tapirs were venerated by the Bribris

Iris - Greek. "Rainbow"; in Greek mythology, Iris is the goddess of the rainbow; the colored part of the eye; a flower featured dominantly in art

Irkalla - In Mesopotamian mythology, Irkalla is the underworld from which there is no return

Irma/Irmin - Old German. "War goddess"

Irmgard - Old High German. "Strong; protection"; the name of an 11th century German saint

Irminia - Greek. "Universal"; "whole"

Iroas - *Magic: The Gathering* god of honor and victory

Iron - Anglo-Saxon. "Holy metal"; the *Periodic Table of Elements* symbol Fe comes from the Latin word "ferrum"; iron was known in prehistoric times and was used to make the swords during the Crusades

Iroquois - French from Algonquin-Basque. "Killer people"

Irtishe - A river in Siberia, China and Kazakhstan; chief tributary of the Ob river

Irving - Scottish. "Green river"; "sea friend"

Isa/Esa/Ysa - Esa, the Wolf, is the creator god and culture hero of the Shoshone, Bannock, and Northern Paiute tribes

Isabeau - French. "My god is bountiful; god of plenty"; Notable Bearer: Isabeau of Bavaria became queen of France when she married King Charles VI in 1385

Isabel/Isabella - Medieval Occitan form of Elizabeth; it spread throughout Spain, Portugal and France, becoming common among royalty by the 12th century

Isabelline - An amorphous pale yellow-gray-cream color most often seen in horse's coats or bird's plumage

Isabetta - Italian. "Pledged to god"

Isadora - Greek. "Gift of Isis"; this name is Greek even though Isis in an Egyptian deity

Isao - Japanese. 功 "Achievement"; 勲 "meritorious"; 績 "exploits" 公 "public"; 勇夫 "brave; man"; 勇雄 "brave; masculine"

Iscariot - Aramaic. "Man from Kerioth"; Notable Bearer: Judas Iscariot (died 30 CE) is most famous for revealing the identity of Jesus Christ to the masses

Isha/Esha - A wolf god in Shoshone mythology

Ishkhara/Ishara - The Mesopotamian goddess of love and mother of the seven Sebettu; she was often identified with Ishtar as a fertility goddess

Ishmael - Hebrew. "God listens"; Abraham's first son in *The Tanakh*, *The Quran* and *The Bible*; Ishmael was born to Abraham and Sarah's handmaid Hagar (Hājar); according to the *Genesis* account, he died at the age of 137

Ishtar - Persian. "Easter"; Babylonian goddess of love, war and fertility.

Isidore/Isadore - Greek. "Strong gift"; Saint Isadore of Seville tried to convert Spanish Jews to Christianity during the 7th century

Isis - Egyptian mythical goddess of magic and sister to Osiris; Isis was the most powerful of the female gods

Island - Old English. "Watery; watered"; any piece of sub-continental land that is surrounded by water

Isle/Isla - Scottish, derived from Islay, an island and two rivers in Scotland

Isobel - Scottish. "God is my oath"; Notable Bearer: Isobel of Huntingdon (1199-1251) was a Scottish princess and ancestor of Robert the Bruce, King of Scotland

Isocrates - An ancient Greek rhetorician who was one of the ten Attic orators; Isocrates made many contributions to rhetoric and education through his teaching and written works

Isolde - Welsh. "Beautiful; fair"

Isonoe - In Greek mythology, Isonoe was one of the Danaides (daughters of Danaus) and was transformed into a spring after her death

Isperia - *Magic: The Gathering* legendary sphinx

Israel - Hebrew. "May god prevail"; "he struggles with god, god perseveres"; in *The Bible* when Jacob was in his 90's, as a token of blessing, God changed his name to Israel

Istvan - Hungarian. "Crowned with victory"

Italy/Italia - Latin. "Land of cattle; calf land"; the country's ancient name was originally spelled "Vitalia"

Itzelle/Itzel - Mayan. "Rainbow goddess"; it is most likely a variant of Ixchel; in Maya culture, Ixchel was the goddess of midwifery and medicine

Iulia - Latin. "Young"

Iuliana - Romanian version of Latin Julia

Ivah - Biblical. "Iniquity"

Ivory - English. "White"; "pure"

Ixidor - *Magic: The Gathering* planeswalker and wizard legend

Ixion - In Greek mythology, Ixion was king of the Lapiths, the most ancient tribe of Thessaly

Ixionidae - Any of a group of icy asteroids that orbit the sun primarily in the region between Jupiter and Neptune; a race of monsters in Greek mythology also known as centaurs

Iya - In Lakota mythology, Iya is a storm monster, brother of Iktomi the spider

Izanagi - Japanese. "He who invites"; Izanagi is a deity born of the seven divine generations in Japanese mythology and Shinto

Izanami - Japanese. "She who invites"; in Japanese lore, Izanami was a goddess of both creation and death, as well as the former wife of the god Izanagi

Izar - Spanish. "Star"

Izetta - *Izetta: The Last Witch* is a 2016 Japanese anime television series

J

Jabez/Jabes - Hebrew. "He makes sorrowful"; in the *Old Testament* of *The Bible*, this character's mother stated, "I gave birth to him in pain"

Jace/Jase - A masculine given name, often a shortened version of Jason; *Magic: The Gathering* planeswalker

Jacinta - Greek. "Beautiful"

Jackal - A wild dog that feeds on carrion, game, and fruit and often hunts cooperatively

Jacquie - Hebrew. "May god protect"; feminine of the English name Jacques, which originated from the Hebrew Jacob

Jacy - Native American. "Moon"; "creator of all plant life"

Jade - An ancient stone, used as the birthstone for May; it represents the fourth chakra (heart) and is the 12th anniversary stone

Jadwiga - Polish. "Battle"; "fight"

Jadzya/Jadzia - Polish. "War battle"

Jagger - English name for someone who owned and/or managed a team of pack horses; Notable Bearer: Sir Michael Philip "Mick" Jagger is an English singer

Jago - Spanish, Cornish. "Supplanter"

Jakko - Hebrew. "Jacob"; In the *Old Testament* of *The Bible* Jacob is the son of Isaac and Rebecca and the father of the 12 founders of the 12 tribes of Israel

Jamaica - Taino. "Land of wood and water"; "land of springs"; the name of an island in the Caribbean sea which Indigenous Taino inhabitants called "Xaymaca"

Jamarion - Arabic. "Good looks; beauty"

Jamettus - "Supplanter"; from James, a classic name derived from the Hebrew Jacob

January - Anglo-Saxon. "Month of the wolf"; the month is named after Janus, a Roman god

Janus - In ancient Roman religion and mythology, Janus is the god of beginnings, gates, transitions, time, duality, doorways, passages, and endings; he is usually depicted as having two faces because he looks to the future and to the past

Jareth - Jareth, the Goblin King is a main character in the 1986 movie *Labyrinth*

Jarret/Jarrett - Old German. "Brave"

Jarvis/Jarvi - Finnish. "Lake"

Jasper/Jazper - Persian. "Treasurer"; this name was traditionally assigned to one of the wise men who were said to have visited the newborn Jesus

Javis - Old German. "Spear"

Jawza - Arabic. "Central one"; the old Arabic name for the constellations Orion and Gemini

Jaxon/Jackson - Old English. "God has been gracious; God has shown favor"

Jaya - Sanskrit. "Victory"

Jayla - African. "One who is special"

Jazz/Jaz - English. "Energy; excitement; excitability; very lively"; nickname for Jasmine or Jasper; given name in reference to the genre of music

Jazmin/Jasmine - Persian. "Yas flower"

Jedi - Hebrew. "Beloved by God"; an order of individuals in the *Star Wars* franchise who are able to use the "Force"

Jefferson/Gefferson/Geofferson - English. "Son of Geoffrey"; Notable Bearer: Thomas Jefferson (1743-1846) was a Founding Father and the third President of the U.S.

Jeleva - *Magic: The Gathering* legendary vampire wizard

Jemima - Arabic. "Little dove"; in *The Bible*, she is one of Job's three daughters who were known as the most beautiful women of their time; the other two were Keziah and Keren

Jenga - Swahili. "To build"

Jennett/Jennet/Jenett - Old French. "God is gracious"

Jeptha - In *The Bible*, Jephthah is a judge over Israel for a period of six years

Jeremine - French from Hebrew. "The Lord raises up"

Jerusha - Biblical. "Banished"; "possession"; "inheritance"

Jeska - Polish pet form of the personal name Jan (God has been gracious)

Jessalyn - Hebrew. "He sees"

Jessamine - French variant of Jasmine

Jessamy - Persian. "Jasmine flower"; "gift from god"

Jessop - Hebrew. "Jehovah increases"

Jester - Old French. "Joke; exploits"; Middle English. "Buffoon, mimic or professional reciter of romances"

Jesterka - The Czech variation of the Lacerta (lizard) constellation

Jestina - Welsh. "Just"; "upright"

Jethro - Hebrew. "Abundance"; according to the *Old Testament* of *The Bible*, Jethro was a Midianite priest who sheltered Moses when he fled Egypt; he was the father of Zipporah, who became Moses's wife

Jett - American. "Free"; From the English word "jet", meaning either a airplane powered by a jet engine or a black glossy, semi-precious stone; Notable Bearers: Jett Travolta, son of John Travolta; Jett Lucas, son of George Lucas

Jetta - Latin. "Jet black"

Jewel - Middle English from Old French "Game; play"; Latin. "jest"; a precious stone

Ji - Korean. 智 "Wisdom"; 池 "pond"

Jiao - Chinese. "Beautiful"; "delicate; tender"

Jin - Chinese. 金 "Gold; metal; money"; 锦 "tapestry, brocade, embroidered"; 津 "ferry"

Jezebel - In the *Old Testament* of *the Bible*, the wife of Ahab, King of Israel

Jinsy - English. "God is gracious"; from Jane, feminine of John

Jiro - Japanese. "Second son"

Jitu - Swahili. "Accurate (exact or careful conformity to truth)"

Jizo - Japanese. "Earth treasury"; "Earth store"; "Earth matrix"; "Earth womb"; Notable Bearer: Jizo was a bodhisattva (a person who is able to reach nirvana but delays doing so out of compassion in order to save suffering beings) primarily revered in East Asian Buddhism and usually depicted as a Buddhist monk

Joann - Hebrew. "God is gracious"

Jobe/Job - Hebrew. "Persecuted"; Job is a central character in *The Bible*; in rabbinical literature Job (Iyov) is called one of the prophets of the Gentiles

Jocasta - Greek. "Shining moon"; the mother and wife of Oedipus in Greek mythology; once they learned their marriage was incestuous, Oedipus blinded himself and Jocasta committed suicide

Joette - American, Hebrew. "Jehovah increases"

Johanna/Johanah - Hebrew. "Gift from god"; Stricklandian. "The great one"

Jolanta - Greek. "Violet flower"

Jolene - Hebrew. "God shall add"; "she who shall increase"

Jolie - French. "Beautiful"

Jolon - Native American. "Valley of the dead oaks"

Jolrael - *Magic: The Gathering* legendary human spellshaper

Joplin - English. "The afflicted"; this name is related to Hebrew Job; Notable Bearer: Janis Lyn Joplin (1943-1970) was an American rock singer and songwriter

Jordan - Hebrew. "Descend"; "flow down"; from the name of the river that flows between the countries of Jordan and Israel

Josce - Nordic. "Raised"; "who pardons"

Josephine - French. "May Jehovah add (to the family)"; French empress Joséphine de Beauharnais (1763-1814) was the wife of Napoleon Bonaparte

Joses - Usually regarded as a form of Joseph, occurring many times in the *New Testament* of *The Bible*

Jourdain - French variant of Jordan; the name was originally used in the Middle Ages for a child baptized in holy water from the river Jordan

Journey - A trip or expedition

Joutsen - Finnish. "Swan"; a cognate of the constellation Cygnus

Jove - Greek. "Bright"; Jupiter, also called Jove, is the chief ancient Roman and Italian god; like Zeus, the Greek god with whom he is identical, Jupiter was a sky god

Joven - Spanish. "Young"

Joyous - English. "Full of happiness"; Latin. "Lord"

Juanita - Spanish. "God is gracious"

Juda - The fourth son of Jacob and Leah in the biblical book of *Genesis*

Judas - Hebrew. "Praise; the praised one"; in *The Bible*, the apostle Judas Iscariot betrayed Jesus Christ for thirty pieces of silver

Jude - Hebrew. "Praise; praised one"

Judge - Latin. "Law"; "to say"; an English occupational name for an officer of justice or a nickname for a solemn and authoritative person thought to behave like a judge

Judine - Swedish. "Woman of Judea"

Judith - Hebrew "Woman of Judea"; in the *Old Testament* of *the Bible*, the wife of Esau

Judson - English. "Son of Jordan"

Jue - A Chinese lunar mansion (constellation)

Julene - Latin. "Young"

Julia - An orange and black American butterfly with long narrow forewings, found chiefly in tropical regions

Juliana - Latin. "Youthful"; Juliana was queen of the Netherlands

Julienne - French. "Young; youthful"

Juliette/Juliet - Juliet Capulet was a main character in William Shakespeare's 1597 play *Romeo & Juliet*

Julius - Greek. "Downy-bearded"; Latin. "Devoted to Jove"; the name of a Roman family, most famously the dictator Gaius Julius Caesar

July - French, Latin. "Youthful"; "Jove's child"

Jun - Chinese. 君 "King; ruler"; 俊 "talented; handsome"; 军 "army"

June - Latin. "Young"; in Roman mythology, Juno was protectress of women and of marriage; June is therefore known as the bridal month

Juniper - Latin. "Youth producing"; "evergreen"; a shrub or bush that bears berry-like cones

Junius - Roman family name which was possibly derived from the name of the Roman goddess Juno; Notable Bearer: Lucius Junius Brutus was the founder of the Roman Republic in the 6th century BCE

Juno - An ancient Roman goddess, the protector and special counselor of the state; she is the daughter of Saturn, the sister of the chief god Jupiter and the mother of Mars and Vulcan

Jupp - A "crusader" name introduced to the British Isles in the 12th century by knights returning from the Holy Land

Justina - An Italian virgin martyr who converted Saint Cyprian

Justus - The fourth Archbishop of Canterbury; he was sent from

Italy to England by Pope Gregory the Great, on a mission to Christianize the Anglo-Saxons from their native paganism, probably arriving with the second group of missionaries despatched in 601

Jyeshtha - Hindu. "The eldest"; the Hindu goddess of inauspicious things and misfortune; the 18th nakshatra (lunar mansion) in Vedic astrology

K

Kaervek - *Magic: The Gathering* legendary human shaman

Kagemaro - *Magic: The Gathering* legendary demon spirit

Kahlo - Frida Kahlo (1907-1954) was a Mexican-American artist known for self-portraits and admired as a feminist icon

Kai - Estonian. "Pier"; Finnish. "Warrior"; Hawaiian. "Ocean"; "ocean water"

Kaiser/Keyser - Middle High German. "Emperor"; from the Latin imperial title Caesar

Kakoset - A Finnish constellation

Kaldra - *Magic: The Gathering* legendary demon

Kaleo - Hawaiian. "Sound"; "voice"

Kaleko - Greek. "Holdeth fast"

Kalitas - *Magic: The Gathering* legendary vampire warrior

Kallisto/Callisto - One of the 67 moons of Jupiter, discovered by Galileo Galilei

Kalyke/Calyce - A retrograde irregular satellite (moon) of Jupiter named after the Greek mythological figure Kalyke or Calyce

Kamahl - Arabic. "Perfection and excellence"; Persian. "Beauty, perfection, excellence, completion, utmost level"

Kamala - Hindi, from Sanskrit. "Lotus"; "pale red"

Kami/Kammy - Kami is one of the twin creator gods of the Bakairi tribe; together with his brother Keri, Kami adapted the world for humans to live on, and taught them to use fire and hunt; Kammy is a female magikoopa in the *Paper Mario* video games

Kana/Kayna - Japanese. "One who is powerful"

Kanae - [kah-NYE] Japanese. "Beautiful one"

Kanalon - A Greek Orthodox convent in the northeast of the Greek region of Thessaly

Kang - A Chinese name that dates back to the Han Dynasty; Kang the Conqueror is a fictional supervillain appearing in *Marvel Comics*; Kang and Kodos are a duo of fictional characters in the animated television series *The Simpsons*

Kannon - The god or goddess of mercy in Buddhist lore

Kansas - Known as "The heartland", Kansas is a midwestern U.S. state with great plains and rolling wheat fields; it was named after the Kansa Indian tribe which inhabited the area

Kantwell/Cantwell - Old English. "Spring; stream"; the name is common in Ireland and England

Kanyon/Canyon - A deep gorge, typically one with a river flowing through it

Kappa - The 10th letter of the Greek alphabet; the 10th star in a constellation

Karador - *Magic: The Gathering* legendary centaur spirit

Karametra - *Magic: The Gathering* legendary enchantment creature

Karazorel - Superman's cousin in the *Marvel* universe

Karlov - *Magic: The Gathering* legendary spirit advisor

Karma - Sanskrit. "Actions are fate"; Buddhist and Hindu concept of inevitable effect of one's life actions

Karn - *Magic: The Gathering* planeswalker

Karnak - The Karnak Temple Complex comprises a vast mix of decayed temples, chapels, pylons, and other buildings in Egypt

Karona - Indian. "Merciful"; "forgiving"

Karrthus - *Magic: The Gathering* legendary dragon

Karthica/Karthika - Tamil, Hindi. "Bestower of courage"; an Indian feminine given name derived from the god Kartikeya

Kartikeya - Sanskrit. "The son of the six Pleiads"; the Hindu god of war; he was the son of Parvati and Shiva and the brother of Ganesha

Kasimir - Slavic. "Enforces peace"; the Patron Saint of Poland and a favored name of Polish royalty

Kasserine - The Battle of Kasserine Pass was a series of battles in February 1943 when raw American troops had their first major battlefield encounters with the German army

Katana - Persian. "Honorable"; Japanese. "Sword"

Katar/Katara - A type of push dagger from South Asia

Katerina - Greek. "Pure"

Katniss - Edible aquatic plant of the genus Sagittaria; Katniss Everdeen is the fictional heroine of the *Hunger Games* trilogy by Suzanne Collins

Katya/Katja - Russian diminutive form of Yekaterina, which is a Russian form of Katherine

Kauai - Polynesian. "A favorite place around one's neck"

Kauket - Egyptian. "Bringer-in of the night"; in ancient Egyptian mythology, Kauket represented darkness in combination with her male aspect Kek; she was associated with the dusk

Kauri/Kauris - Polynesian. "A New Zealand tree"

Kaysa - Swedish. "Pure"

Keanu - Hawaiian. "The cool breeze"; Notable Bearer: Keanu Charles Reeves is a Canadian actor, director, producer, and musician

Keaton - English. "Place of hawks"

Keats - English. "Herdsman"; Notable Bearer: John Keats was an English Romantic poet

Keerthana - Indian. "Devotional song"; usually given to girls of the Hindu faith.

Kek - Egyptian. "Raiser up of the light"; in Egyptian mythology, Kek was the deification of the concept of primordial darkness; his female counterpart was Kauket

Kekoa - Hawaiian. "The warrior"

Keldon/Kelton - Old English. "Town of the heels"

Kendrick - Anglo-Saxon. "Family ruler"

Kennah - Welsh. "Greatest champion"

Kennedy - Gaelic. "Helmeted chief"; John Fitzgerald Kennedy (JFK) served as the 35th President of the United States from January 1961 until his assassination in November 1963

Kenobi - African. "Heart"; Swahili. "Soul"; a religious belief of African origin involving witchcraft; Obi-Wan Kenobi is a legendary Jedi master in the *Star Wars* franchise

Kentaro - Japanese. "Sharp"; "big boy"

Kentaur - Old German. "Centaur"

Kenton - English. "Royal chieftain"

Kentucky - Iroquois. "Land of tomorrow"

Kenya - Kikuyu, Embu, Kamba. "God's resting place"

Kenyatti/Kenyatta - African. "Musician"

Kenyon - Old English. "Ennion's mound"; Celtic. "Blonde"; Welsh. "Rabbit"; Notable Bearer: Kenyon Hopkins (1912-1983) was an American composer of jazz and film scores

Kepler - German. "Hatter; cap maker"

Keranos - *Magic: The Gathering* legendary enchantment god

Kerberos - Latin from Greek. "Spotted"; in Greek mythology, this was the name of the three-headed dog that guarded the entrance to Hades

Keren - Hebrew. "Horn of antimony"; antimony was used in ancient times as a cosmetic; in the *Old Testament* of *The Bible*, Keren was one of Job's three beautiful daughters, along with Jemima and Keziah

Kermit - Irish. "Son of Dermot"

Kerouac/Kirouac - Breton. "Wet soil hamlet"

Kerr - English and Scottish topographic name for someone who lived by a patch of wet ground overgrown with brushwood; a legend grew up that the Kerrs were left-handed, one theory is that the name is derived from a Gaelic word meaning "wrong-handed"; "left-handed"

Kestrel - Bird of prey. North American Kestrel, formerly called the NA Chickenhawk, ultimately derived from Old French "crecelle" (rattle), which refers to the sound of its cry

Ketu/Kettu - In Hindu astrology Ketu represents karmic collections both good and bad, spirituality and supernatural influences

Keziah - Hebrew. "Sweet-scented spice"; Keziah, Keren and Jemima were Job's three fair daughters in *The Bible*; this name was popular with Puritans in the 17th century

Khaleesi - Fijian. "Queen"; a royal title in the 1996 novel *A Game of Thrones* by George R. R. Martin

Khan - Turkish. "Ruler"; "nobleman"; this was originally a hereditary title among Tartar and Mongolian tribesmen, but is now very widely used throughout the Muslim world as a personal name; Khan Noonien Singh is a fictional character in the *Star Trek* franchise

Khepri - A god of creation, the movement of the sun, and rebirth in ancient Egyptian mythology

Kherty - Egyptian. "Lower one"; Kherty, also known as Cherti, was an ancient Egyptian Earth god and a god of the underworld who sailed the boat which carried the deceased on their last journey

Khonsu - Egyptian. "Traveller"; in ancient Egyptian mythology, Khonsu was the god of the moon, his name nodding to the nightly travel of the moon across the sky; he and Thoth marked the passage of time

Kiefer - Old German. "Pine tree"; Notable Bearer: Kiefer William Frederick Dempsey George Rufus Sutherland is a British-born Canadian actor

Kiku - Japanese. "Chrysanthemum"; the flower is the symbol of the Japanese emperor; the name fell out of fashion in Japan after the defeat of imperial Japan in WWII

Killeen - Irish from Gaelic. "Bright-headed"

Killian - Irish. "Strife or battle"; "small"; "fierce"; originally spelled Cillian

Kimber - Anglo-Saxon. "Royal fortress"

Kimberlee/Kimberly - English. "From the wood of the royal forest"

Kincaid - Scottish. "The steep place"; Gaelic. "The head of the rock"

King - Old English. "Ruler"; the male ruler of an independent state, especially one who inherits the position by right of birth

Kinsey/Kynsey - Old English. "Royal victory"

Kiora - Aboriginal, Celtic, Gaelic. "Little and dark"; "love"

Kipling - English. "Cybbel's cottage"; Notable Bearer: Rudyard Kipling (1865-1936) was a British novelist born in India who wrote *The Jungle Book* and other works

Kirahvi - Finnish. "Giraffe"; the name of a Finnish constellation

Kiran/Kieran/Keiran - Sanskrit. करिण "Dust"; "ray of light"

Kirk - Scottish, Danish, Middle English. "Church"; a topographic name for someone who lived near a church; James Tiberius Kirk is a fictional character in the *Star Trek* franchise

Kishar - In Mesopotamian mythology, Anshar and Kishar are the twin horizons of sky and earth

Kismet - Turkish. "Fate; destiny"

Knight - In the Middle Ages, a man who served his sovereign or lord as a mounted soldier in armor; in current times, a man awarded a nonhereditary title by the sovereign in recognition of merit or service and entitled to use the honorific "Sir" in front of his name

Knossos - In Greek mythology, King Minos dwelt in a palace at Knossos

Knox - English, Scottish. "From the small hill"; Notable Bearers: celebrity offspring Knox Leon Jolie-Pitt; Scottish reformer and leader during the Protestant Reformation, John Knox (1513-1572); Mickey and Mallory Knox are fictional characters in the 1994 film *Natural Born Killers*

Kodos - Kang and Kodos are a duo of fictional recurring characters in the animated television series *The Simpsons*

Kohen - Hebrew. "Priest"; in Jewish tradition Kohens are distinguished as hereditary priests directly descended from the biblical Aaron

Koi - Hawaiian. "Urge; implore"; the Hawaiian equivalent of Troy

Kolaghan - *Magic: The Gathering* legendary elder dragon

Koli - A Finnish constellation

Kolmio - Finnish. "Triangle"; a constellation in Finnish astrology

Kona - Hawaiian. "Lady"

Kolya - Russian. "Of the conquering people"

Konicek - Czech. "Small horse"; "hobby"

Koontz/Kuntz - German. "Bold adviser"; Notable Bearers: Alan Kuntz (1919–1987) was a Canadian ice hockey player; Dean Ray Koontz is an American author

Korben/Corben/Korbin/Corbyn - French. "Raven"; Korben Dallas is a fictional character in the film *The Fifth Element*

Kore - Greek. "Pure"

Kosovo - Greek. "Blackbird"

Koth/Kotz - Middle Low German. "Cottage; hovel"; a status name for a day laborer who lived in a cottage and owned no farmland; *Magic: The Gathering* planeswalker

Kotka - Polish. "Cat"; a Finnish constellation

Kourion - Archaeological site located on the west coast of Limassol in the small town of Episkopi

Kozilek - [koh-zah-LEEK]; *Magic: The Gathering* legendary eldrazi creature

Kozoroh - Czech. "Ram"; a variant of the constellation Capricorn

Krenko - *Magic: The Gathering* legendary goblin warrior

Kresh/Creche - A representation of the Nativity; a group of young animals (such as penguins or bats) gathered in one place for care and protection usually by one or more adults; *Magic: The Gathering* legendary human warrior

Krittika - Indian. The third nakshatra; the name of a star

Krond - *Magic: The Gathering* legendary archon

Kruphix - *Magic: The Gathering* legendary enchantment god

Kruzitko - A Czech lunar mansion (constellation)

Krypton - A distant planet which orbits a red sun, as well as the homeworld of Clark Kent in the *Superman* franchise

Kubrik/Kubrick - Stanley Kubrick (1928-1999) was an American film director, screenwriter, and producer

Kuiper - A circumstellar disc in the outer solar system extending from the orbit of Neptune

Kujo/Cujo - *Cujo* is a 1981 psychological horror novel by American writer Stephen King

Kultakala - Czech. "Goldfish"; the name of a constellation in Czech astrology

Kurki - Finnish. "Crane"; a royal family and a constellation in Finland

Kyanite - A blue or green crystalline mineral

Kynthia - Greek. "Moon"

Kytheon - *Magic: The Gathering* legendary human soldier

L

Labna - A mesoamerican archaeological site and ceremonial center of the pre-columbian Maya civilization, located in the Puuc Hills region of the Yucatan Peninsula

Labyrinth - A complicated irregular network of passages or paths in which it is difficult to find one's way; a maze

Lacerta - Latin. "Lizard"; a constellation that contains 12 stars with planets sometimes referred to as "Little Cassiopeia"

Lady - Old English. "Bread kneader"; usually refers to someone in charge of a household, and therefore of high rank

Lafayette - French nobleman Marquis de Lafayette (1757-1834) went to fight for four years in the American Revolution

Lake/Layke - An area filled with water, localized in a basin, that is surrounded by land

Lakelyn - American. "Beautiful lake"; the name was given to boys in the 1800s but is currently finding popularity as a girls name

Lakota - Referring to the Native American tribe or their language; has been used as a twin's name (the other being Dakota or Sioux)

Lambda - λ The 11th letter of the Greek alphabet; the 11th star in a constellation

Lambert - English, French, Dutch, German. "Land; territory"; "bright; famous"

Lamer - French. "From the sea"

Lanai - Hawaiian. "Terrace; veranda"

Lance - Old French. "Spear"

Lancelot - French. "Servant"; Sir Lancelot was a knight of King Arthur's *Round Table* and adulterous lover to Queen Guinevere

Lando - An Italian given name and a surname; Notable Bearers: Pope Lando was Roman Catholic Pope from 913 to 914; Lando was a 7th Century Bishop of Rheims; Lando was a 13th century archbishop of Messina; Lando Calrissian is a fictional character in the *Star Wars* franchise

Landrius - Landrius Ravenfall is a fictional character in the *World Of Warcraft* franchise

Landry - Anglo-Saxon. "Ruler"

Langdon - Old English. "Long hill"

Lanzo - Italian. "Spear; lance"; "land"

Lao - A Cantonese form of Liu

Laozi - Chinese. 老子 "Old Master"; an ancient Chinese philosopher and writer

Lapis - Egyptian baby name, from the precious blue stone Lapis Lazuli

Laquatus - *Magic: The Gathering* nightmare horror

Laquelle - French. "Which; that"

Lares - Latin. "God of the household"

Larimar - Also known as the Dolphin Stone, Blue Pectolite, Atlantis Stone, and Stefilia's Stone named by the Dominican who re-discovered it in 1974 by combining the first letters of his daughter's name (Larissa) and the Spanish word for the sea (mar)

Larissa - A nymph in Greek mythology who was the daughter of Pegasus; an ancient city in Greece which meant "citadel"

Lark/Larke - Middle English. "A songbird"

Larken/Larkin - Old English. "Silent"; "fierce"; was likely used as a nickname for a brave warrior

Lars/Larz - Latin. "Crowned with laurel"; Notable Bearers: Lars Ulrich is the Danish drummer of heavy metal band Metallica; Lars Barriga is a fictional character in the animated series *Steven Universe*

Lathan - Hebrew. "Gift from God"

Lato - Hungarian. "To see"; a nickname for a wise person or an occupational name for a clairvoyant; Polish. "Summer"; nickname for someone who was born or baptized in summer

Latona - In Greek mythology Latona (Leto) is a daughter of the Titans Coeus and Phoebe, the sister of Asteria, and the mother, by Zeus, of Apollo and Artemis

Latula - Derived from "Tula", the Hindu sign for Libra

Latulia/Tullia - Spanish, Latin. "Heavy rain; downpour"; From the ancient Roman family name Tullius

Laurentina - Latin. "The place of the laurel trees; place of honor and victory"; feminine of Lawrence, dating from time of the Romans

Laux - Old German. "Lynx"

Lavah - Greek, Hebrew. "To unite; to remain"; "to borrow or lend"; also spelt Lava when referring to molten liquid borne by volcanoes

Lavender - Old French. "To wash"; Latin. "bluish"; Lavender Brown is a fictional character in the *Harry Potter* series by J.K Rowling

Lavinda - A name used in Russia and the Ukraine, related to the Latin Lavinia

Lavinia - Latin. In classical mythology, the daughter of King Latinus and the wife of Trojan Hero Aeneas, who named the city Lavinium in her honor

Lavish - English. "Sumptuously rich, elaborate, or luxurious"

Lawler - Gaelic. "Half sick"

Lawson - English. "Son of Lawrence"; Latin. "Someone from Laurentum"

Layne/Lane - A French surname with occupational origins to signify a person who worked in wool; Notable Bearer: Layne Thomas Staley (1967-2002) was an American musician

Laysan - Hawaiian. "Egg"; the name refers to the the shape of the island and to how much life springs from it

Lazareth - Hebrew. "God has helped"

Lazaro - Spanish. "Help of God"

Lazarus - Greek. "God is my help"; In *The Bible*, Lazarus was brother to Mary and Martha and was raised from the dead after four days

Lazuli - [LAH-zoo-lee] Persian. "Heaven; sky"; used for the color blue because of the lapis lazuli gem

Leander - Hero and Leander were two lovers celebrated in Greek legend

Leandra - Greek. "Lioness"; feminine of Leander

Lear - German. "Clearing"; Old English. "Cheek; face"; *King Lear* is a tragedy written by William Shakespeare in 1606

Lebanon - Biblical. "White"; "essence"

Leda - Greek. Spartan queen in Greek mythology who gave birth to Helen after being visited by Zeus in the form of a swan

Ledger/Leger - Old French from German. "People; tribe"; "spear"; Notable Bearer: 7th-century bishop of Autun, whose fame contributed to the popularity of the name in France

Leela/Leilah - Sanskrit. "Play"; Turanga Leela is a fictional character in the animated series *Futurama*

Leeloo/Leelou/Lylou/Lilo - A French female given name; a character in the sci-fi film *The Fifth Element* (1997)

Legacy - Something, usually honor, handed down by a predecessor

Legend - An extremely famous or notorious person, especially in a particular field

Leia - Hawaiian. "Child of heaven; heavenly flowers"; Hebrew. "Languid; relaxed"; a name borne from *The Torah* by the elder sister of Rachel and the first wife of Jacob; Princess Leia Organa is a fictional character in the *Star Wars* franchise

Leif - Old Norse. "Heir"; "descendant"

Leila/Layla - Arabic. "Night; dark beauty"; Persian. "Dark-haired"; its usage in England began with George Byron's *The Glamour* (1813)

Leilani - Hawaiian. "Heavenly lei (flower necklace)"

Lennon - Irish. "Lover"; Gaelic. "Little blackbird"

Lennox - Scottish. "A nobleman"; "elm trees"; a fictional character in William Shakespeare's *Macbeth* (1606)

Lenore - Greek. "Light"; the departed love of the narrator in Edgar Allan Poe's legendary poem *The Raven* (1845)

Lentin/Lenten - Of, in, or appropriate to Lent

Lentokala - Finnish. "Flying fish"; the equivalent of the constellation Volans

Leofwin/Leofwine - Leofwin was a medieval Bishop of Lichfield in the 11th century

Leonard - English, German, Irish, Dutch. "Lion strength"; "lion-strong"; "lion-hearted"; Notable Bearer: Leonard was the name of a Saint in the Middle Ages period, known as the patron saint of prisoners

Leonardo - Portuguese. "Lion; bold"; Notable Bearers: Leonardo da Vinci (1452-1519) was an Italian Renaissance polymath; Leonardo Wilhelm DiCaprio is an American actor, film producer, and environmental activist

Leonice - Old Greek. "Strong; brave man"; Latin. "Lion"

Leonidas - A Greek masculine name, from Leon (lion); the name Leonidas is over 2,500 years old as evidenced by Leonidas I, a great hero-king of Sparta in the 5th century BCE

Leonie/Leoni - Latin. "Lioness"

Leonis - Old German. "Lion strength"

Leonona/Leonora - A version of the Greek "Helen"; in Greek mythology, the abduction of Zeus's mortal daughter Helen sparked the Trojan War

Leontine - Latin. "Lioness"

Leopold - German, Latin. "Brave lion"; "brave people"

Leota - German. "Of the people"

Lesnar/Lesner/Lessner - Slavic. "Forest"

Lesotho - A kingdom in southern Africa

Lesta - Russian. "From Town of Leicester"

Lestat - Lestat de Lioncourt is a fictional vampire character appearing in several novels by Anne Rice

Lester - Old English. "Roman town or walled city"

Letha - Greek. "Forgetful"

Leticia/Letizia - Latin. "Joy; gladness; delight"; one of the epithets of Ceres, Roman goddess of fertility and abundance

Lewella/Luella/Louella - English. "Famous elf"

Lexy - Greek. "Man's defender"

Liberace - Old German. "Noble, bright and famous"; Notable Bearer: Władziu Valentino Liberace (1919-1987) was an American pianist, singer and actor

Libya - Biblical. "The heart of the sea"

Liege - A feudal superior or sovereign in medieval times

Lilac - A flowering pale purple shrub

Liliana - Italian. "Regarding the lily"; a flower which is a symbol of innocence, purity, and beauty; *Magic: The Gathering* planeswalker

Lilikoi - A type of Hawaiian passion fruit; an exotic baby name not commonly used in the continental US

Lilith - Hebrew. "Night monster"; "storm goddess"; in Jewish folklore, a female demon and the first wife of Adam

Lilium - Greek. "True, white lilies"; as exemplified by the Madonna lily

Lillian - English, derived from the flower name Lily (a symbol of innocence, purity and beauty)

Limerence - English. "Involuntary, life-altering love"

Limerick - A humorous verse of 3 long and 2 short lines rhyming "aabba", popularized by an English artist in the 1800s

Lincoln - Old English. "Roman colony at the pool; lakeside colony"; the name of an early Roman settlement in England, used as both a surname and a first name; Notable Bearer: American president Abraham Lincoln (1809-1865) presided over the Union during the Civil War and brought about the emancipation of slaves

Linessa - Greek. "Flaxen haired"; feminine of Linus; one of Apollo's sons who was a music teacher of Hercules in Greco-Roman mythology

Linnie - German, Latin. "Soft; tender"; "beautiful"

Linus - Greek. "Flax"; in Greek legend he was the son of the god Apollo; Notable Bearer: Pope Linus was the second bishop and pope of Rome in the 1st century

Liora/Liara - Hebrew. "God's gift of light to me"

Lisbeth - Hebrew. "Oath of God"; "God is satisfaction"

Littleton - English. "Small settlement"

Liu - Chinese. "Flowing"

Liviana - Latin. "To envy; envious"; feminine of the Roman family name Livianus

Livingston - Habitational name in Scotland named after a man named Levin who appears in several 12th century charters

Livonya/Livonia - A historic region on the eastern shores of the Baltic Sea; popular given name in the mid-1900's

Lizabeta - The Nordic variant of Elizabeth (oath of god)

Lizeth - Pet form of Elizabeth, derived from Hebrew Elisheba; in *The Bible*, Lizeth a kinswoman of the virgin Mary and mother of John the Baptist

Lleuad - Welsh. "Moon"

Lo - Old English. "To call attention or to show wonder or surprise"

Loki - Old Norse. "To break"; a Norse god who was associated with magic and fire

Lola - Spanish. "Lady of sorrows"

Lolita - Spanish. "Little Lola"; "little sorrows"; a fictional character in the novel *Lolita* (1958) by Vladimir Nabokov

Lolite - Greek. "Violet (color)"; is sometimes used for the name of the iolite gem

Lombardi - Originally indicated someone who came from the Lombardy region in Italy; the region got its name from the Lombards, a Germanic tribe who invaded in the 6th century; Notable Bearer: Vincent Thomas Lombardi (1913–1970) was an Italian-American football player and coach

London - Latin. "Fierce"; the city is the capital of England and was founded in the 1st century

Lonestar - Texas is nicknamed "The Lone Star State" to signify its former status as an independent republic, and as a reminder of the state's struggle for independence from Mexico; Lone Starr is a fictional character in the Mel Brooks spoof *Spaceballs* (1987)

Lorcan - Irish. "Little fierce one"; a name rich in Irish history as belonging to several kings, including the grandfather of the most famous high king of Ireland, Brian Boru

Lord - Someone or something having power, authority, or influence; a master or ruler

Lorelai - In Germanic legend, Lorelei was a beautiful siren who sat upon a rock in the Rhine River and lured sailors to shipwreck and death

Lorenzo - Italian, Spanish from Latin. "From Laurentum"

Loretta - Latin. "Bay laurel"; "little Lora"

Lorne - Medieval Latin. "Province"; an early Scottish chieftain and place name; Notable Bearers: Lorne Michael Lipowitz is a producer and writer best known for *Saturday Night Live*; Lorne Hyman Greene (1915-1987) was a Canadian actor, radio personality and singer

Lorraine - French. "From Lothair's kingdom"; he was a ruler of the region during the 9th century

Lorthos - *Magic: The Gathering* legendary octopus

Lorton - Old English. "The roaring one"

Lothar - German. "Renowned warrior"; Sir Anduin Lothar is a fictional character in the *World Of Warcraft* franchise

Lottie - French. "Tiny and feminine"; a nickname for Charlotte; a feminine form of Charles

Lotton/Lawton - Old English. "Settlement on or near a hill"; "settlement by a burial mound"

Lotus - Egyptian flower that symbolizes purity of the body, speech and mind; this is because, though the flower is rooted deeply in mud, it blooms without any trace of impurities

Louilla - English. "Famous elf"

Louise - French. "Famous warrior"; "renowned fighter"; this name became popular in the middle of the 19th century

Louisiana - US State named after Louis XIV, King of France from 1643-1715; when Rene-Robert Cavelier claimed the territory drained by the Mississippi river for France, he named it "La Louisiane"

Louvenia - Alternate form of Lavinia; peaked as a given name in the 1880's

Lovell - Anglo Norman French. "Wolf"; was originally given as a nickname to a fierce or shrewd person

Lovisa - German. "Renowned warrior"

Lowry/Lowrie/Lowery - Gaelic. "Descendants of Labhradha"

Loyal - Giving or showing firm and constant support or allegiance to a person or institution

Luan - Albanian. "Lion"; Vietnamese. "Justice; fair; transparent"; Celtic. "Warrior"; Scottish. "Yew tree"

Lucia - Italian. "Graceful light"; Saint Lucia was a virgin martyr in the 4th century; her name is invoked against eye disease

Lucian/Lucien - Old French. "Light"; Notable Bearers: Lucian of Samosata (born 120 CE) was a satirist and rhetorician who wrote exclusively in the Greek language during the Second Sophistic; Lucien Bonaparte (1775-1840) was the younger brother of Napoleon Bonaparte

Lucida - Latin. "To shine"

Lucille - Latin. "Shining"; Notable Bearer: Lucille Désirée Ball Morton (1911–1989) was an American actress, comedian, model, film-studio executive, and producer

Lucinda - Latin. "Illumination"; mythical Roman goddess of childbirth and giver of first light to newborns; also refers to (the virgin) Mary as "lady of light"

Lucky - English. "Fortunate; blessed; favored; charmed"

Lucretia - Latin. "Profit"; derived from the Roman clan name Lucretius

Lucrezia- Latin. "Profit; wealth"; a form of the Roman name Lucretius

Ludmilla/Ludmila - Slavic. "People; dear love"

Ludovic - French from Old German. "Famous warrior"

Ludwig - German. "Famous"; "war, battle"; Notable Bearer: Ludwig van Beethoven (1770-1827) was a German composer and predominant musical figure in the transitional period between the Classical and Romantic eras

Luigi - Italian. "Renowned fighter"; Luigi is Mario's younger, taller twin brother and is a major protagonist of the *Mario Bros.* franchise

Lula - Choctaw. "Leaping waters"; Creek. "Town"; once a nickname for the Tallulah waterfalls

Lumen - Latin. "Light"; in a poetic manner lumen may refer to the eyes; Lumen Pierce is a fictional character in the TV series *Dexter*

Luna - Latin. "The moon"; in Greek mythology, Luna is one of the names of Artemis, the moon goddess

Lunam - Gaelic. "Descendant of Luan (the hound)"; originally a nickname for a fast runner

Lunette - French. "Moon"; denoting a semicircular horseshoe

Lunita - Italian, Latin. "Little moon"

Lupine - Latin. "Wolf"

Luru/Luruni/Lurunio - A god of death in Celtic mythology

Luther - Old German. "Lute player"

Lutie/Lute - German. "Army people"; Lutie Cameron Brewton, character in *The Sea of Grass* (1937) by Conrad Richter; Lootie, Princess Irene's fond nurse in *The Princess and the Goblin* (1872) by George MacDonald

Luxe - Latin. "Luxurious"

Luxemborg/Luxembourg - A castle built in the high middle Ages; modern historians link the etymology of the word with "letze" (fortification), which may have referred to either the remains of a Roman watch tower or to a primitive refuge of the early middle ages

Luxor - Arabic. "The palaces"; a city on the east bank of the Nile river in Egypt

Lydia - Greek. "Beautiful"; "noble one"

Lylas - Arabic. "Night"; "dark beauty"; popular acronym in the 1990's meaning "love you like a sister"

Lynx - Greek. "Light; brightness"; a medium-sized wild cat

Lyra/Lyre - Greek. "Lyrical"; a medieval instrument

Lyric/Lyrique - A form of the Greek "lyre"; (of poetry) expressing the writer's emotions, usually briefly and in stanzas or recognized forms

Lysander - Greek. "Liberator"; "one who is freed"; in Greek history, Lysander was a Spartan naval commander in the 4th century BCE; a fictional character in William Shakespeare's comedy *A Midsummer Night's Dream* (1595)

Lysias - Biblical. "Dissolving"

Lysithea - A moon of Jupiter named after the mythological Lysithea, daughter of Oceanus and one of Zeus' lovers

Lyton/Lython - Norse. "From the farm; from the meadow"

M

Mace/Mase - Hebrew. "Of the seed of Aharon the priest"; Japanese. "Space"; "strait"

Macedonia - A landlocked Balkan nation of mountains, lakes and ancient towns with Ottoman and European architecture

Madagascar - Island nation off the southeast coast of Africa; home to thousands of animal species, rainforests, beaches and reefs found nowhere else on Earth

Madden - Anglo-Saxon from Gaelic. "Dog"; *Madden NFL* is an American football video game series named after Pro Football Hall of Famer John Madden

Madeline - Aramaic. "Elevated; great; magnificent"; form of Magdalene, known for Saint Mary Magdalene

Mademoiselle - French. "Damsel"; a title or form of address used of or to an unmarried French-speaking woman

Madge - Persian. "Child of light"

Madonna - Italian. "My lady"; respectful form of address similar to the French "madame"; used to signify Virgin Mary or art depicting her as a mother

Mae - Originally used as a pet form of Mary or Margaret, more recently associated with the name of the month; from the Latin "maius"

Maestro - Italian. "Master"; a distinguished musician, especially a conductor of classical music

Maeve/Maev/Maiv - Irish. "Intoxicating"; "she who intoxicates"; Queen Maeve was ruler of Connacht in the Ulster Cycle of Irish mythology

Maeven - A variant of the Irish "Maeve" with strong ties to mead, an ancient honey wine that was consumed at weddings

Magdala - Aramaic. מגדלא "Elegant"; "great"; "tower"; the hometown of Mary, mother of Christ

Magdalena - Czechoslovakian. "Woman from Magdala"; the biblical Mary Magdalene came from Magdala, an area near the sea of Galilee

Magic - Greek. "Art of a magus"; something that has a delightfully unusual quality

Magnus - Late Latin. "Great"; this name has been used by many saints, dating back to the 2nd century; Notable Bearer: Magnus Olafsson (1024-1047), known as Magnus the Good, was king of Norway and Denmark

Maia - Greek mythological goddess of increase, the eldest and most beautiful of the pleiades; in Roman mythology, she was an earth goddess after whom the month of May is named

Maiden - Old English. "Young girl"

Maine/Mayne - Nautical term which refers to the region being a mainland separate from the many surrounding islands

Maisie - Scottish. "Child of light"

Majestic - Latin. "Greatness; dignity; honor; excellence"

Majesty - Latin. "Royal bearing; dignity"; from Magestus, Roman goddess of honor

Makani - Hawaiian. "Wind"

Maksim - Slavic from Latin. "The Greatest"

Malachite - A bright green mineral that typically occurs in masses and fibrous aggregates with azurite and is capable of taking a high polish; a fictional character in the animated series *Steven Universe*

Malady - Irish. "Melody"; Old English. "My lady"

Malawi - Bantu. "Lake"; an English-speaking South African country

Malaysia - English. "Gift of god"; a country in Southeast Asia, the word refers to the Malay ethnic group

Malcovich/Malkovich - Slavic family name; Notable Bearer: John Malkovich is an American actor, producer, and director

Maleficent - Latin. "Harmful; baleful"; "wicked, prone to evil"; a fictional character in Disney's animated film *Sleeping Beauty* (1959)

Mali - Welsh. "Bitter"

Malta - Greek. "Honey"; an island country located in the central Mediterranean Sea

Malvenia - Irish. "Sweet"

Manala - Finnish. "The space (or area) under the earth"; in Finnish mythology, Manala is the realm of the dead

Manali - Italian, Hindu. "Bird"

Manannan - Gaelic. "Son of the sea"; a sea deity in Irish and Scottish mythology

Mandoline - A musical instrument created in Italy near Naples; its ancestor, called the mandorre, was an instrument with stiff strings

Mandulis/Mandulus - A sun god of Lower Nubia; he is usually depicted wearing a crown of ram horns surmounted by high plumes, sun disks and cobras

Manes - In Roman mythology, the deified souls of dead ancestors

Manfred - Old High German. "Man of peace"; "peace to mankind"; Notable Bearer: Manfred von Richthofen (1892-1918) was the Red Baron of World War I

Mangala - Sanskrit. "Red"; the name for Mars, the red planet; lord of Mangal Dosha in Hindu texts

Manhattan - Lenape. "Island of many hills"

Manor - Israeli. "Loom"; Old English. "A unit of land (originally a feudal lordship)"

Manson - Anglo-Saxon from Scandinavian. "Son of Magnus"

Maple - A tree or shrub with lobed leaves, winged fruits, and colorful autumn foliage, grown as an ornamental or for its timber or syrupy sap

Mapp - Latin. "Loveable"

Maralen/Maraline/Marilyn - A blend of the English given names Mary and Lynn; is use began in the 1920s, and it peaked in popularity by the 1930s; *Magic: The Gathering* legendary elf wizard

Maraxus - *Magic: The Gathering* legendary human warrior

Marcella - Latin. "Warlike"; "martial and strong"; "young warrior"

March - Middle English from French. "To walk"; "to trample"; since March was the first month of the new year in ancient Rome, some historians believe the Romans named March after Mars, the Roman god of war

Marchesa - Italian feminine version of a marquis (a nobleman ranking above a count and below a duke); no Italian noblewomen are named Marchesa, it is simply a title attached to their given name

Marduk - Sumerian. "Calf of the sun; solar calf"; a late-generation god from ancient Mesopotamia and patron deity of the city of Babylon

Margarita/Margarite - Spanish, French. "Little pearl"

Margery/Marjorie - Persian. "Child of light"

Margot - French. "Pearl"

Mariann/Marianne - French compound of Marie (wished-for child; rebellion) and Anne (favor, grace)

Marieke - Dutch. "Wished-for child"

Marigold - English. Refers to both the flower and the mother of Jesus (Mary's gold)

Mariner - Sailor; a person who directs or assists in the navigation of a ship

Marino - Spanish, Galician. "Sailor"; from Latin "marinus" (of the sea)

Mario - Latin. "Hammer"; refers to Mars, the Roman god of war; the main character in the *Mario Bros.* franchise

Marion - French from Hebrew. "Sea of bitterness"; "sea of sorrow"

Marionette - French. "Little Mary"; in medieval France, string puppets were often used to depict biblical events, with the Virgin Mary being a popular character, hence the name

Marisha/Mariska - Russian., Hebrew. "Bitter"

Marmaduke - Gaelic. "Follower of Saint Maedoc"; "leader of the seas"

Marozia - Latin. "Mistress or lady of the sea"; Notable Bearer: Marozia (890–937) was a Roman noblewoman who was the alleged mistress of Pope Sergius III and was given the titles Senatrix and Patricia of Rome by Pope John X

Marrone - Southern Italian. "Chestnut"

Marshall - Frankish. "Horse servant"; Scottish. "Love of horses"

Martha - Aramaic. "Lady"; In *The Bible*, Martha was the sister of Lazarus and Mary (of Bethany) known for her obsession with housework

Martok - A fictional Klingon warrior in the *Star Trek* franchise

Marvelle - French. "Miracle"

Marybelle - English, derived from Mary (biblical mother of Christ) and Belle (beauty)

Masha - A Russian diminutive of Maria

Master - Old English, Old French, Latin. "More; more important"

Matar - Hebrew. "Rain"

Mather - English. "Powerful army"

Mathias/Matthias/Matthaios - The apostle chosen to replace the traitor Judas Iscariot in *The Bible*; Notable Bearer: Matthias I was king of Hungary in the 15th century

Matilda/Mathilda - Germanic Gothic. "Might; strength in battle"

Matlock - Old English. "Meeting-place oak"

Matrix - Middle English. "Womb"; Latin. "Breeding female"

Mattock - Old Welsh. "The goodly one"; a versatile hand tool similar to the pickaxe

Maude - Irish. "Strong battle maiden"; German. "Strength in battle"; used in Australian slang for a bushman's pack

Maui - In Hawaiian mythology Māui was a trickster who created the Hawaiian Islands by having his brothers fish them out of the sea; he was also responsible for binding the sun and slowing its movement

Maureen - Irish, Latin, Gaelic, Old French. "Great"; "little Mary"; "dark-haired"; Hebrew. "Wished-for child"; "rebellion"

Maurice - Latin. "Moorish"; "dark-skinned; "swarthy"

Mauve - A pale purple color named after the mallow flower

Maverick - English. "An independant human who avoids conformity"

Mavis - English. "Song thrush"

Maxima - Latin, Russian. "Miracle-worker"

Maxine - Roman. "Greatest"; "bright; noble"

Maxwell - Scottish. "Great spring"; "great stream"

May - English feminine given name; it is derived from the name of the month, which comes from Maia, the name of a Roman fertility goddess; also used as a pet form of Mary or Margaret.

Mayael - *Magic: The Gathering* legendary elf shaman

Maybelle - French. "The belle of May"

Mayble/Mable - Pet form of Amabel (beautiful; loving; lovable)

Maynard - Old German. "Hardy, brave or strong"; an ancient name whose history on English soil dates back to the wave of emigration that followed the Norman Conquest of England in 1066

Maze/Mayze - Scottish. "Pearl; child of light"

Mazelina - Medieval variant of Matilda

Mazirek - *Magic: The Gathering* legendary insect shaman

Mazzaroth - Hebrew. "A garland of crowns"; a term for the zodiac or the constellations thereof

McFadden - Scottish, Irish. "Son of little Patrick"

McKellan/McKellen - Celtic. "Harmony" or "little rock"

McKennah - Irish, Scottish. "Respect and love"; the Celtic god of fire

McMahon - Irish. "Good calf"; this was the name of two unrelated chieftain families in counties Clare and Monaghan

McQueen - Scottish. "Pleasant"; Notable Bearers: Terence Steven "The King of Cool" McQueen (1930–1980) was an American actor; Alexander McQueen is a British fashion house

Meadow - A field; earthy American name, used in families with Summer, Autumn and the like; Meadow Soprano is a fictional character on the TV series *The Sopranos*

Meagen - [MEE-gen] Welsh. "Pearl"; "strong"

Meander - English. "To follow a winding course"; in Greek mythology, the patron saint of the Maiandros River (after which he was named)

Medomai - [mih-DOH-me] Greek. "To think; to intend; to plan"; *Magic: The Gathering* creature

Medusa - Greek. "To protect; to rule over"; in Greek mythology, one of the gorgons (women with snakes for hair)

Mehen - Egyptian. "Coiled one"; a mythological snake god; *Mehen*, or *The Game of Snake*, was a board game played by ancient Egyptians until about 1000 BCE

Mehitable/Mehetabel - Biblical. "God rejoices"

Melancholia/Melankolia - Greek. "A beautiful view of sadness and understanding"

Melanthe - Greek. "Dark flower"

Melatiah - Biblical. "Deliverance of the lord"

Melba - Australian. "From Melbourne"; Notable Bearer: Dame Nellie Melba (1861–1931) was an Australian soprano opera singer after whom the dessert "Peach Melba" was named

Melchior - Hebrew. "King"; "splendor; light"; Saint Melchior was one of the Biblical Magi who visited the infant Jesus after he was born

Melek - Arabic. "Angel"; *Magic: The Gathering* legendary wizard

Melira - *Magic: The Gathering* legendary human scout

Mellifluous - Late Latin. "Honey flow"; (of a voice or words) "sweet or musical; pleasant to hear"

Melite - One of the Naiads, daughter of the river god Aegaeus, and one of the many loves of Zeus and his son Heracles

Melody - Greek. "Song"; "to sing"

Melona - Greek. "Song"; "canary yellow"

Melpomene - Greek. "To sing"; "the one that is melodious"; "to celebrate with dance and song"; initially the muse of chorus, Melpomene later became the muse of tragedy in Greek mythology

Melucine/Melusine - In European folklore, Melusine was a water fairy who turned into a serpent from the waist down every Saturday

Melvador - English family name in Colonial America

Melville - Scottish habitational name from any of the various places in Normandy called Malleville

Melvin - Scottish, Irish from Gaelic. "Gentle chieftain"

Memory/Memorie - Old English. "Something remembered from the past; a recollection"

Menelaus - Greek. "Vigor; rage; power"; "wrath of the people"; in Greek mythology, Menelaus was a king of Mycenaean Sparta, the husband of Helen of Troy, and the son of Atreus and Aerope

Menilly - Cahuilla "Moon maiden"; the Cahuilla goddess of the moon who taught the people the arts of civilization

Mensa/Mensah - A constellation in the Southern sky

Meraki - Greek. "Doing something with soul, creativity or love"; when you put something of yourself into what you are doing

Mercer - English, Scottish. "Merchant"; originally a surname for someone trading in textiles (mercery)

Mercia - Anglo-Saxon. "From Mercia"

Mercury - The smallest and innermost planet in our solar system; in Roman mythology, Mercury is the patron god of financial gain, commerce, eloquence, communication, travelers, boundaries, luck, trickery and thieves; he is also the guide of souls to the underworld

Meribor - A fictional character in the *Star Trek* universe

Meridith - Welsh. "Protector of the sea"

Merieke/Marieke - [muh-RYE-kuh] Dutch. "Wished-for child"

Merit/Merritt - English. "Wished-for child"

Meriwether - Middle English. "Happy weather"; Notable Bearer: Meriwether Lewis (1774–1809) was an American explorer, soldier, and public administrator

Merlin - Celtic. "Sea hill"; "sea fortress"; the name was most famously borne in Arthurian legend by the magician helper and guide of King Arthur

Merlot - French. "Blackbird"; a dark blue-colored wine grape

Merope - In Greek mythology, one of the seven pleiades, the daughters of Atlas and Pleione

Merrill - English. "Shining sea"

Meryl - Latin. "Blackbird"

Mesa - Spanish. "Table"; a flat-topped mountain commonly found in the southwest

Messiah - Hebrew. "Anointed One"

Methuselah - Hebrew. "Man of the dart/spear"; "his death shall bring judgement"; in *The Hebrew Bible*, the man reported to have lived to be 969 years old

Mezarim - Biblical. "The mourning of Egyptians"

Miami - Algonquin. "Downstream people"

Mica/Micah - Hebrew. "Who is like God"; "who is like Yahweh"; a shiny silicate mineral with a layered structure, found as minute scales in granite and other rocks, or as crystals; the name of several people in the *Old Testament* of *The Bible*

Michelangelo - Italian. "Michael angel", referring to the archangel Michael; Notable Bearer: Renaissance painter and sculptor Michelangelo Buonarroti (1475-1564) was the man who created such great works of art as the statue of David and the mural on the ceiling of the Sistine Chapel

Michigan - Ojibwe. "Large water"; "large lake"

Midnight - Old English. "The middle of the night"; "the witching hour"

Mikado - Japanese. "Emperor of Japan"; "beautiful gate"

Mikaeus - *Magic: The Gathering* legendary zombie cleric

Mikoto - The Shinto god of sea and storms

Mikro/Micro - Greek. "Small"

Mila/Milla - Slavic. "Peace and love"; "the people's light"; Notable Bearers: Milla Jovovich and Mila Kunis are both American actresses

Milburn - Old English. "Mill stream"

Mildred - Old English. "Gentle strength"

Miles/Myles - Latin. "Soldier"; Notable Bearer: Myles Standish (1584–1656) was an English officer hired by the Pilgrims as military adviser for Plymouth Colony

Milena - Slavic. "Gracious present; dear"; Notable Bearer: Milena Markovna "Mila" Kunis is an American actress

Miletus - An ancient Greek city on the western coast of Anatolia, near the mouth of the Maeander River in ancient Caria

Milica - Slavic. "Kind and dear"; Notable Bearer: Milica "Milla" Bogdanovna Jovovich is an American actress

Milkyway - Latin. "The road of milk"; the Romans got the name from the Greeks, who called our galaxy "milky circle"

Millard - Old German. "Good; gracious"; "hardy, brave or strong"

Milledge - Old English. "Dairy farm"; "trading settlement"

Millenia/Melenia/Millennia - Latin. "Thousand"; the point at which one period of a thousand years ends and another begins

Miller - English, Scottish. "Mill keeper"

Millicent - Old English. "Work"; "strength"; the name was quite popular in the middle ages

Milton - English. "From the mill farm"; a fictional character in the cult film *Office Space* (1999); Notable Bearer: 17th century British poet, John Milton

Mima/Mimas - Hebrew. "Dove; little dove"; a short form of Jemima

Mimic - Greek. "Mime"; imitative of something, especially for amusement

Mimosa/Mimoso - Spanish. "Cuddly"; a genus of plants that are sensitive to touch

Mina - Dutch. "Protector"; the fictional heroine in Bram Stoker's horror novel *Dracula* (1897)

Minelauva - A star in the zodiac constellation of Virgo; it is also called Auva or Delta Virginis

Minerva - Latin. "Intellect"; Roman goddess of wisdom and war, equivalent to the Greek goddess Athena

Minetta - French. "Willing to protect"

Minnesota - Sioux. "Sky-tinted water"; "cloudy water"

Minos - In Greek mythology Minos was the first King of Crete, son of Zeus and Europa

Mira - Slavic. "Peace"

Mirabel/Mirabelle - Latin. "Wonderous"; "wondrous beauty"; it was unisex during the middle ages, but is now almost exclusively female

Miriam/Mirayam - Hebrew. "Sea of bitterness"; "mistress or lady of the sea"; a prophetess in the *Old Testament* of *The Bible*, the daughter of Amram and Yocheved, and the sister of Moses and Aaron

Mirkle - Scottish. "To grow dark"

Misha - Russian. "Bear"; a Russian short form of Mikhail

Mishra - [MEESH-ruh] Sanskrit. "Fixed"; "manifold"; later applied after a name as an epithet meaning "honorable"

Mississippi - Algonquin. "Great river"

Missouri - Native American. "Wooden canoe people"; "he of the big canoe"

Mist/Myst - Greek. "Fog"; a phenomenon caused by small droplets of water suspended in air

Mistrel - A medieval poet and musician who sang or recited while accompanying himself on a stringed instrument, either as a member of a noble household or as an itinerant troubadour

Mitchum - Scottish. "Who is like God"

Mizar - Biblical. "Little"; Mizar and Alcor are two stars forming a naked eye double in the handle of the Big Dipper asterism in the constellation of Ursa Major

Mizzix - *Magic: The Gathering* legendary goblin wizard

Moana - Maori. "Large body of water"; "lake"

Mochus - Phoenician proto-philosopher who allegedly wrote about atomic theory before the time of the Trojan War

Molokai - Hawaiian. "The friendly isle"

Monaco - Greek. "Monk"; "solitary"; Italian nickname for someone of Monkish habits or appearance, or an occupational name for a servant employed at a monastery

Monday - Latin. "Day of the moon"

Monet - From a French surname which was derived from either Hamon or Edmond; Notable Bearer: French impressionist painter Claude Monet (1840-1926)

Monoceros - Greek. "Unicorn"; a faint constellation on the celestial equator

Monsoon - Arabic. "Season"

Montague - French. "Pointed hill"; "steep mountain"; the House of Montague in William Shakespeare's *Romeo and Juliet* (1597) is one of fair Verona's two feuding families

Montana - Latin. "Mountain"

Montenegro - Spanish, Portuguese, Italian. "Black mountain"

Montgomery - French. "Mountain belonging to the ruler"; surname of numerous English and Scottish earls

Montu - Egyptian. "Nomad"; a falcon god of war in ancient Egyptian religion

Moon - Latin. "To measure" (the moon was archaically used to measure time); a celestial body that makes an orbit around a planet; a natural satellite

Moonless - A night of a new moon

Moonrise - The rising of the moon above the horizon

Moonstone - Considered a sacred healing crystal that manifests peace and harmony within the body and spirit

Morcant - Old Welsh form of Morgan

Mordecai - Hebrew. "Warrior"; a Babylonian deity

Mordin/Mordan/Morden/Mordon - English medieval surname; Mordin Solus is a fictional character in BioWare's *Mass Effect* franchise

Moriarty - Irish. "Navigator"; "sea worthy"

Moriz - Russian. "Moorish"

Morocco - Turkish. "Land of God"

Morpheus - Greek. "Shape", referring to the shapes seen in dreams; in Greek mythology, Morpheus was the god of dreams

Morrigan - In Irish mythology, the ancient goddess of war, often symbolised as a crow

Morris - Latin. "Moorish; dark-skinned; swarthy"

Morticia - Fictional character in the 1964 TV series *The Addams Family*

Mortimer - English, Welsh, Scottish, Irish. "Dead sea"

Mortis - In the *Star Wars* franchise, Mortis was an ethereal realm within the Force which was whispered over in legends and stories passed down through the millennia

Mosaic/Mosaique - Greek. "A muse"; decoration with small square stones; an individual composed of cells of two genetically different types

Mosca - Spanish. "Fly";

Moschus - Latin. "Musk deer"; Notable Bearers: 6th century Syrian writer Joannes Moschus; ancient Greek bucolic poet Moschus flourished about 150 BCE

Mose - [mo-ZAY] Italian; from the biblical name Moses

Moselle - Hebrew. "From the water"

Moses - Hebrew. "To pull/draw out of water"; a male given name, after the biblical figure Moses; according to *The Torah*, the infant Moses was given this name by Pharaoh's daughter after rescuing him from the Nile river

Moshe - (Moses) was a prophet in the Abrahamic religions; according to *The Bible*, he was adopted by an Egyptian princess, and later in life became the leader of the Israelites

Moss - Middle English vernacular form of the biblical name Moses; English and Scottish topographic name for someone who lived by a peat bog

Mountain - A large landform that stretches above the surrounding land in a limited area, usually in the form of a peak, formed through tectonic forces or volcanism

Mox - Dutch habitational name from Moxhe in the province of Liège

Mozambique - The country was named for Mussa Bin Bique, an Arab trader who first visited the island in the 14th century and later lived there

Mozart - Latin. "Love of God"; Notable Bearer: Austrian composer Wolfgang Amadeus Mozart (1756-1791) was actually born Wolfgang Theophilus Mozart but preferred the Latin translation of his Greek middle name

Mozza - Neapolitan. "To cut off"

Mu - Chinese. "Admired"

Mulder - German occupational name for a maker of wooden bowls; Fox William Mulder is a fictional character in the TV series *The X-Files*

Mumford - French. "Strong and impregnable hill"

Munda - Slovenian short form of the personal name Rajmund (Raymond); Turanga Munda is a fictional character in the animated series *Futurama*

Murdock - Scottish. "Protector of the sea"

Muriel - Celtic. "Sea"; "bright"

Murphy - Irish. "Sea warrior"

Murray - Scottish, Irish. "Settlement by the sea"; "seafarer"; extremely common name throughout Ireland

Muse/Muze - English. "A person or personified force who is the source of inspiration for a creative artist"; in Greco-Roman mythology, nine goddesses who preside over the arts and sciences

Mustang - English. "Wild horse"; "feral horse"

Myanmar - Burmese. "Fast and strong people"

Myr - Old Norse. "Bog; marsh; swamp"

Myra - Latin, Sanskrit, Slavic. "Wonder"; "peace and wonderful"; Latin. "Myrrh"

Myron - Greek. "Myrrh" (a fragrant resin used in making incense and perfume); the name was borne by a Greek sculptor of the 5th century BCE and is said to have been taken up by early Christians because of the gift of myrrh made to the Christ child

Myrrh - A fragrant gum resin obtained from certain trees and used in perfumery, medicines, and incense; one of the gifts bestowed upon the baby Jesus by the Magi

Myrtie/Myrtle - Greek. "Evergreen shrub"; first used as a given name in the 19th century, at the same time other plant and flower names were coined

N

Nabia - The goddess of rivers and water in Gallaecian and Lusitanian mythology

Nabu - The ancient Mesopotamian patron god of literacy, the rational arts, scribes and wisdom

Nachash - Hebrew. "Serpent"

Nachtigall - Old German, Jewish. "Sing at night"

Naenia - Latin. "Incantation"; the Roman goddess of funerals

Nahshon - Biblical. "That foretells"; "that conjectures"

Nakshatra - Sanskrit. "Lunar mansion"; "constellation"; a segment of the ecliptic through which the moon passes in its orbit around Earth, often used by ancient cultures as part of their calendar system

Namabia/Namibia/Namibie - A country in south west Africa on the Atlantic ocean

Namath - Hungarian. "German"

Nanaya - A Sumerian goddess who personified voluptuousness, sexuality and warfare

Nancy - Hebrew. "Grace"

Nanette - French. "Favor; grace"

Napoleon - Italian. "Lion of Naples"; Notable Bearer: Napoléon Bonaparte (1769–1821) was a French statesman and military leader who rose to prominence during the French Revolution

Narcissa - Greek. "Daffodil"; feminine of Narcisse, which comes from the legend of the beautiful Greek youth who became enamored with his own reflection

Narcissus - Greek. "Daffodil"; in Greek mythology, Narcissus was a beautiful young man who fell in love with his reflection and was transformed into the narcissus flower

Naret - Hindi. "Throat; gullet"

Narset - *Magic: The Gathering* legendary human cleric

Nash - English topographic name for someone who lived by an ash tree

Nashira - Arabic. "Bearer of good news"

Nath/Natha - Hindi from Sanskrit. "Lord"

Nathalie - French. "Birthday", especially the birthday of Jesus Christ

Natosi - Blackfoot. "Holy one"; Natosi was the god of the sun and the most important of the Blackfoot Sky People

Natrix - A genus of snakes known as grass snakes or water snakes

Nauru - Nauruan. "I go to the beach"

Nazareth - Biblical. "Separated"; "crowned"; "sanctified"

Nebraska - Chiwere. "Flat water"

Nebula - A beautiful, colorful cloud of dust and gas in space

Necco/Neco/Neko/Nico - English short name for Nicholas, after Nike, goddess of victory in Greek mythology; popular candy from 1847

Nectar/Nektar - Greek name for the drink of the gods; sweet liquid in flowers

Nefaria - Count Nefaria is a supervillain appearing in *Marvel Comics*

Nefarox - *Magic: The Gathering* legendary demon

Nefertari - Egyptian. "The most beautiful"; "beautiful companion"; Notable Bearer: Nefertari (died 1255 BCE) was an Egyptian queen of the New Kingdom and favourite wife of Rameses II

Nefertiti - Egyptian. "The beautiful one has come"; Nefertiti (1370-1330 BCE) was a powerful Egyptian queen and wife of Akhenaton, the pharaoh that briefly imposed a monotheistic religion centered around the sun god

Neith - The patron deity of Sais, an early goddess in the Egyptian pantheon, said to be the first and prime creator

Neitsyt - Finnish. "Virgin"; the constellation Virgo

Nekhbet - An early predynastic local goddess in Egyptian mythology, the patron deity of Nekheb

Nella - English. "Shining light"

Nelson - English. "Son of Neil"; Notable Bearers: British admiral Horatio Nelson (1758-1805); Nelson Rolihlahla Mandela (1918-2013) was a South African anti-apartheid revolutionary, political leader, and philanthropist, who served as President of South Africa from 1994 to 1999

Nemata - *Magic: The Gathering* legendary treefolk

Nembus - Nembus (Upsilon Persei) is an orange/red giant star that can be located in the constellation of Andromeda

Nepal - Sanskrit. "At the foot of the mountains"; Tibetan. "Holy land"

Neper/Nepra/Nepri - A child deity in ancient Egyptian mythology, Neper was the god of grain; his body was dotted to represent grains of corn

Nephthys - A member of the Great Ennead of Heliopolis in Egyptian mythology

Neptune - The farthest known planet from the sun in our solar system, named for the god of the sea in Roman mythology; similar to Poseidon of Greek mythology

Nergal - A deity worshipped throughout ancient Mesopotamia; hymns depict him as a god of pestilence, hunger, and devastation

Nerissa - Greek. "Sea nymph"; a fictional character in William Shakespeare's 1605 play *The Merchant of Venice*

Nero - Sabine. "Strong and energetic"; Italian. "Black"; Finnish. "Genius"; Notable Bearer: Nero was the last Roman emperor of the Julio-Claudian dynasty in the 1st century

Nerrick - A fictional dwarf character in the *Final Fantasy* franchise

Neruda - Pablo Neruda was the pen name and, later, legal name of the Chilean poet-diplomat and politician Ricardo Eliécer Neftalí Reyes Basoalto (1904–1973)

Neshmet - A blue subgiant star in the constellation of Lepus; the Neshmet bark was a vessel belonging to the god Egyptian god Nun

Nessa - Greek. "Poor; pure; chaste"; a nickname for Agnes

Nesta - Welsh. "Pure"

Nester/Nestor - Greek. "One who returns from travels"; in Greek mythology, Nestor of Gerenia was the wise King of Pylos described in Homer's *The Odyssey* (8th century BCE)

Nettie - Teutonic. "Clean"

Neva - Latin. "Snow"

Nevada - Spanish. "Snow-covered"

Neve/Nehv - Irish. "Dazzling; radiant"

Neville - French. "From the new village"

Nezumi - Japanese. "Rat" or "mouse"; Notable Bearers: Nezumi Kozo was nickname for 19th century thief; former name of Yukki Matsuda, a Japanese voice actor

Niagara - Iroquois. "The strait"; the Niagara Falls are three waterfalls that straddle the international border between Canada and The United States

Niall - Irish. "Champion; passionate; avid"; a dynasty of Irish kings was founded by Niall of the Nine Hostages, king of Ireland in the 5th century

Niamh - Irish. "Bright"; "radiant"; in Irish mythology Niamh was the daughter of the god of the sea and one of the queens of Tír na nÓg, the land of eternal youth; she was the lover of the poet hero Oisin

Nicarao - The indigenous group which inhabited the shores of Lake Nicaragua before the Spanish conquest of the Americas

Niccolo - Italian. "Victorious"; "conqueror of the people"

Nichelle - Hebrew. "Like God"; Notable Bearer: Nichelle Nichols was one of the first black actresses featured in a prominent role in a TV series (*Star Trek*)

Nicol - Scottish variant of the Italian Niccolo

Nicola - Latin. "Winner of the people"

Nicoline - Greek. "Victory of the people"

Nietzsche - German family name; Notable Bearer: Friedrich Wilhelm Nietzsche (1844–1900) was a German philosopher, cultural critic, composer, poet, philologist, and Latin and Greek scholar

Nigel - Gaelic. "Cloud; champion"

Nightingale - English. "To sing at night"; "to sing"

Nightshade - The name may come from a perceived resemblance of certain solanaceous flowers to the sun and its rays

Nihoa - Hawaiian. "Tooth"; the island is named so because of its jagged outline

Niihau - Hawaiian. "The forbidden isle"

Nika - Persian. "Good"; Greek. "Victory"

Nikita - Russian, Greek. "Victor"

Nikos/Niko/Neko - Greek. "Victory of the people"

Nimbus - A luminous cloud or a halo surrounding a supernatural being or a saint

Nimoy - Leonard Simon Nimoy (1931-2015) was an American actor, film director, photographer, author, singer and songwriter known best for his role as Spock in the *Star Trek* franchise

Ninurta - In ancient Mesopotamian religion, Ninurta was the farmer's version of the god of the thunder and rainstorms of the spring; he was also the power in the floods of spring and was god of the plow

Niobe - Greek. "Fern"; in Greek mythology, the daughter of Tantalos, a king of Asia Minor

Nirrti - Hindu. "Absence of"; the Hindu goddess of deathly hidden realms and sorrows, one of the dikpāla (guardians of the directions), representing the southwest

Nirvana - Hindu. "Ultimate bliss"

Nissa - Scandinavian. "Friendly elf"; *Magic: The Gathering* planeswalker

Nix/Nyx - Greek. "Night"; Latin. "Nox"; the Greek goddess of the night

Noble - Old English. "Belonging to a hereditary class with high social or political status"; "aristocratic"; "having or showing fine personal qualities or high moral principles and ideals"

Nocturne - A musical composition that is inspired by, or evocative of, the night

Noe/Noey - French, Spanish, Portuguese. "Rest; comfort"

Noesis - Greek. "Understanding"; "intellect"; a Greek word referring to perception of the mind

Noire/Noir - French. "Black"; having a bleak and darkly cynical quality

Nola - Gaelic. "Noble"; "fair"

Nomy - Hebrew. "Beautiful; pleasant"

Nonna - Latin. "Sage"

Norah - Italian, Irish, Arabic. "Honor"

Nori - Japanese. "Belief; doctrine"

Norin - *Magic: The Gathering* legendary human warrior

North - The direction in which a compass needle normally points; an English surname of antiquity and nobility; it is the hereditary surname of the Earls of Guildford, and during the 18th century was among the most prominent in the world's political circle

Northelle - English. "From the north"; used briefly in the late 1700s as a given name

Norway - Norse. "Land of the midnight sun"

Nosferatu - An archaic Hungarian-Romanian word, synonymous with "vampire"

Nova - Latin. "Chases butterflies"; a star showing a large, sudden increase in brightness and then slowly returning to its original state

Novalie - Swedish from Latin. "New"

Novella - Russian, Italian from Latin. "New"

November - From Latin "novem" (nine); November was originally the ninth month in the Roman calendar

Nox/Nyx - Latin. "Goddess of night"; Nyx is the Greek personification of the night

Noyan/Noyon/Nayan - Mongolian. "Mister; monsieur"; a title of authority in the Mongol Empire and later periods

Nu - The 13th letter of the Greek alphabet; the 13th star in a constellation; the symbol for "frequency"

Numida - A bird having dark plumage mottled with white, native to West Africa.

Numot - *Magic: The Gathering* legendary dragon

Nunilo - Gothic. "The martyr"; Notable Bearer: Nunilo, along with her sister, was a 9th century virgin child martyr later venerated as a saint

Nuoli - Finnish. "Arrow"; a variant of the constellation Sagitta

Nusakan - Latin. "Northern crown"; a binary star in the constellation Corona Borealis

Nusku - The name of the light and fire god in Babylonia and Assyria, indistinguishable from Girru; Nusku is the symbol of both the heavenly and the terrestrial fire

Nye - Welsh. "Gold"; Latin. "Man of honor"; Notable Bearer: William Sanford Nye is an American science communicator, television presenter, and mechanical engineer

Nykthos - *Magic: The Gathering* legendary land

Nylea - *Magic: The Gathering* legendary enchantment creature

Nyota - Swahili, Lingala. "Star"; Nyota Uhura is a fictional character in the *Star Trek* franchise

Nysa - Greek. "Goal"

Nyusha - Russian. "Pure"

O

Oahu - Hawaiian. "Gathering place"

Oak - Ancient Celts honored the oak tree for its endurance and noble presence

Obediah/Obadiah - Hebrew. "Servant or worshipper of the Lord"; Obadiah was a prophet in *The Bible*

Obi/Obie/Oby - African, Nigerian Ibo. "Heart"; Obi Wan Kenobi is a fictional character in the Star Wars franchise

Oblivion - The state of being unaware or unconscious of what is happening

Obsession - The domination of one's thoughts or feelings by a persistent idea, image, desire, etc.

Obsidian - Hard, dark, glass-like volcanic rock formed by the rapid solidification of lava without crystallization, named for its discoverer

Obsius/Obsidius - The Roman discoverer of obsidian

Ocarina - An ancient wind instrument, a type of vessel flute

Oceanus - A divine figure believed by the ancient Greeks and Romans to be the personification of the sea, an enormous river encircling the world

Octavia - Latin, Victorian. A name for the eighth child; Notable Bearer: Octavia the Younger (69-11 BCE) was the sister of first roman emperor Augustus and fourth wife of Marc Antony

Octavius/Octavian - Latin. "Born eighth"; Octavius was a Roman clan name, as well as the original name of Emperor Augustus (born 67 BCE)

October - Latin. "Eighth month" (of the old Roman calendar)

Octons - A type of eclipse in astronomy; a fictional creature in the *Dungeons & Dragons* universe

Oday/Uday/Odae - Indian. "Dawn; the rise"; Arabic. "To ascend; the first warrior in the battle"

Ode - Latin, Greek. "Song; sing"; "a poem meant to be sung"

Odelia - Hebrew. "I will praise the lord"

Odin - Old Norse. "Inspiration"; "rage"; "frenzy"; Odin was the highest of the gods, presiding over art, war, wisdom and death in Norse mythology

Odo/Oto/Otto - Old German. "Possessor of wealth"; a fictional character in the *Star Trek* franchise

Odric - *Magic: The Gathering* legendary human soldier

Odysseus - Greek. "To hate"; in Greek legend, Odysseus was one of the heroes who fought in the Trojan War; Homer relates Odysseus's misadventures on his way back to his kingdom in *The Odyssey* (8th century BCE)

Odyssey - *The Odyssey* is one of two major ancient Greek epic poems attributed to Homer; it is, in part, a sequel to *The Iliad*

Oedamsa - Persian. "White silk"

Oedipus - A mythical Greek king of Thebes; in Greek mythology, Oedipus accidentally fulfilled a prophecy that he would end up killing his father and marrying his mother, thereby bringing disaster to his city and family

Ogden - Old English. "Oak valley"; Notable Bearer: Frederic Ogden Nash (1902–1971) was an American poet well known for his light verse

Ogen /Ogenus - In Greco-Roman mythology, the god of the sea

Oger - Cornish. "Famous spear"

Ohio - Seneca. "Great river"; "large creek"

Oisin/Osian/Ossian/Osheen - Regarded in legend as the greatest poet in Ireland, and was a warrior in the Fenian Cycle of Irish mythology

Okami - Japanese. "Great god"; "wolf"

Oklahoma - Choctaw. "Red people"

Oksana/Oxzana/Aksana - Russian. "Praise be to God"

Oktant - An instrument for observing altitudes of a celestial body from a moving ship or aircraft; any of the eight parts into which a space is divided by three coordinate planes

Olean - The name of several municipalities in the USA

Oleana - Nordic. "Ancient Ana"; Hawaiian. "Oleander"; English. "Lily"

Oleander - Poisonous evergreen old world shrub grown for its clusters of flowers in white, red or pink.

Olga/Oleg - Old German. "Hale; hearty; blessed; holy"

Olive - Latin. "Peace"; the biblical olive tree symbolizes fruitfulness, beauty and dignity;
extending an olive branch signifies an offer of peace

Oliver - French. "Elf army"

Olivia - Latin. "Olive tree"; a character in William Shakespeare's 1601 comedy *Twelfth Night*

Oltar - Slavic. "Altar"

Olya - Russian. "Holy"

Olympia - Greek. "From the home of the gods"

Olwen/Olwyn - In Welsh mythology, Olwen is the daughter of the giant Ysbaddaden and cousin of Goreu

Om - ॐ A mystic syllable, considered the most sacred mantra in Hinduism and Tibetan Buddhism

Omaha - A member of an American Indian people of northeastern Nebraska; the Siouan language of the Omaha

Omari - African. "God the highest"

Omega - Ω The 24th letter of the Greek alphabet; the 24th star in a constellation

Omicron - The fifteenth letter of the Greek alphabet; the 15th star in a constellation

Omnath - *Magic: The Gathering* legendary elemental creature

Omphale - [oom-fale, OM-fa-lay, OM-fa-lee] In Greek mythology, Omphale was a daughter of Iardanus, river god and king of Lydia

Onasander/Onosander - A Greek philosopher; he was the author of *Strategikos*, one of the most important treatises on ancient military matters

Oney - Akan. "Honor"

Ontario - Wyandot (Huron). "Great lake; beautiful water"

Onyx - A semi precious variety of agate with different colors in layers

Oolong - Chinese. "Dark dragon tea"; a traditional Chinese tea

Oona - Gaelic, Finnish. "Lamb"

Oort - The Oort Cloud is a spherical shell of cometary bodies believed to surround the sun far beyond the orbits of the outermost planets

Opal - Sanskrit. "Jewel"; a popular name in Victorian times, along with other gemstones

Opalite - A rare stone that comes from opalized volcanic ash

Opera/Oprah - Italian. "Work"; first used in the modern musical and theatrical sense in 1639

Operetta - A genre of light opera, in terms of both music and subject matter

Ophelia - Greek. "Help"; "serpentine"; a fictional character in William Shakespeare's *The Tragedy of Hamlet, Prince of Denmark* (1609)

Ophiuchus - Latinized Greek. "Serpent-bearer"; an equatorial constellation that depicts the god Asclepius holding a snake

Oppian - Oppian of Anazarbus was a 2nd century Greco-Roman poet

Optimus - Latin. "The best"; Optimus Prime is a fictional alien robot in the *Transformers* franchise

Orbit - Latin. "Course, track"; "circular, ring"; the curved path of a celestial object or spacecraft around a star, planet, or moon, especially a periodic elliptical revolution

Orchid - A plant with complex flowers that are typically showy or bizarrely shaped; popular along with other flower names in the Victorian era

Orella - Latin. "Divine message"; "announcement from the gods"; "oracle"

Orenda - Iroquois name for a spiritual power inherent in people and their environment

Orenthal - Old Norse. "Eagle"; "dale, valley"; Notable Bearer: Orenthal James "O. J." Simpson is a former NFL running back, broadcaster, actor, advertising spokesman, and paroled armed robber and kidnapper

Oriel - Latin. "Golden"; Slavic. "Eagle"

Origin - Latin. "To rise"; the point or place where something begins, arises, or is derived

Orim - *Magic: The Gathering* legendary samite healer

Orinoco - Warao. "A place to paddle"; "a navigable place"

Orion - Greek. "Rising in the sky; dawning"; "son of fire"; mythological Orion was a mighty hunter and son of Poseidon; the constellation Orion contains three conspicuous stars

Oriss - Greek. "Son of fire"

Orist/Orest - Greek. "He who stands on the mountain"; "one who can conquer mountains"; Orestes is the son of Clytemnestra and Agamemnon in Greek mythology

Orla - Irish. "Golden princess"

Orlando - Italian. "Famous land"; "heroic"

Orleanna/Orlena - Finnish. "Gold"

Orodin - A fictional character in the game *Legend of the Cryptids*

Oros - Catalan. From an old personal name name, Orosius, which was borne by a 4th century theologian and disciple of Saint Augustine

Orpha - English. "Full head of hair"

Orpheus - Greek. "The darkness of night"; in Greek mythology, Orpheus was a poet and musician who went to the underworld to retrieve his wife Eurydice

Orson - French. "Bear cub"; Notable Bearer: George Orson Welles (1915-1985) was an American actor, director, writer, and producer

Orton - Old English. "Enclosure, settlement"; Notable Bearer: Randal Keith Orton is an American professional wrestler and actor

Orville - French. "Gold town"; Notable Bearer: aviator Orville Wright (1871-1948) who, along with his brother Wilbur, designed and built the first true airplane

Osanna - Hebrew. "Praise"

Osbern - Norman English. "God bear"

Osbert - English. "Divinely brilliant"; this name was borne by many kings and noblemen in the middle ages

Osburh/Osburga - The first wife of King Æthelwulf of Wessex and mother of Alfred the Great

Osburn/Osbeorn - Anglo-Saxon from Old Norse. "God warrior"

Oscar - English. "Divine spear"; "God's spear"; Notable Bearer: poet Oscar Wilde (1854-1900) was put on trial and imprisoned for homosexuality

Osip - Russian variant of Joseph

Osiris - In Egyptian mythology Osiris was the god of the dead and the judge of the underworld; he was slain by his brother Seth, but revived by his wife Isis

Ostara - One of eight neo-pagan sabbats (holidays) that make up the Wheel of the Year; the original "Easter"

Ostia - Latin. "Door"; "opening"

Oswain/Owain - Old Irish. "Born of the yew"

Oswald - Anglo-Saxon. "God"; "rule"; Oswald of Northumbria (604–642) was Bretwalda of the English and is venerated as saint

Oswyn - Old English. "God's friend"

Osya - Russian, Hebrew. "May god add/increase"

Othello - Italian diminutive of Otho; a fictional character in William Shakespeare's tragedy *Othello* (1603)

Otho - German. "Wealthy"

Otieno - African. "Born at night"

Otis - A variant of Otho

Ottante - Italian. "Octant"

Owen - Welsh. "Young warrior"; "well born"; "noble"

Oxford - English. "From the ox ford (river crossing)"

Oxmyx - A fictional character in the *Star Trek* franchise

Oxnard - Old English. "Herdsman"

Oxomo/Oxomoco - The goddess of the night, astrology and the calendar in Aztec religion

Oxton - English. "From the ox farm"

Ozella - Polish. "Great strength"

Ozema - Arabic. "Lion"

Ozias - Biblical. "Strength of the lord"

Ozioma - Igbo. "The message"

Ozzy - English. "Divine power"; Notable Bearer: John Michael "Ozzy" Osbourne is an English singer, songwriter and actor

P

Pabst - Old English. "One of papal character"; originated as a nickname for a person with an austere ecclesiastical appearance, or possibly for an actor, one who had played the part of the pope in the famous travelling pageants of the Middle Ages

Pace/Payce - Hebrew. "Passover"

Pacey - French locational origin surname derived from the Gallo-Roman Praenomen Paccius

Padraic - Irish - "Patrician; noble"

Pagan - Once a common given name, Pagan fell out of favor when it became a term used for an irreligious person or someone who believed in more than one god

Paisley - A distinctive, intricate pattern of curved, feather-shaped figures based on a pine cone design from India

Pakhet/Pehkhet - Egyptian. "She who scratches"; in Egyptian mythology, Pakhet was a lioness goddess of war

Palatina/Palatine - Any count or earl exercising certain royal powers within their own domains; a feudal lord in England or Ireland during the late Roman empire

Palau - An archipelago or more than 500 islands famous for its underwater wonders

Palestine - A geographic region in western Asia between the Mediterranean Sea and the Jordan River

Pallas - A crater on Earth's Moon; in Greco-Roman mythology, the daughter of Triton

Palmer - Old French. "Palm tree"; a nickname for someone who had been on a pilgrimage to the Holy Land

Palydovas - Lithuanian. "Attendant"; refers to moons as the attendants of planets

Pan/Pann - Middle High German. A topographic name for someone living in low lying terrain

Panama - Bokota. "Many butterflies"; "an abundance of fish"

Pandarus - Greek. "Killed for breaking a truce"; in Homer's *The Iliad* (BCE), Pandarus is a renowned archer and the son of Lycaon

Pandora - Greek. "All gifts"; in Greek mythology, Pandora was the first mortal woman; Zeus gave her a jar containing all of the ills and troubles mankind now knows and told her not to open it

Paradox - Latin, Greek. "Contrary opinion"; a situation, person, or thing that combines contradictory features or qualities

Parana - Guarani. "Wide river"

Parilee/Parlee/Paralee/Perlee - Old French. "To speak"

Parker - Old English. "Park keeper"

Parmelia/Permelia - Latin. "By sweetness"

Parthena - Old Greek. "Virgin"; "maiden"

Parysatis - Persian. "Like a fairy"; "angel"

Pasadena - Chippewa. "Crown of the valley"

Pascal - French, English from Greek. "Easter"; Hebrew. "Passover"

Pasha - Muslim. "A title"

Pasiphae - Greek. "All for all, of all" + "light"; in Greek mythology, Pasiphae was a queen of Crete; a category of Jupiter's many moons

Pastyr/Pastor - A minister in charge of a Christian church or congregation

Patience - Latin. "To suffer"; one of the virtue names coined by the Puritans of the 17th century

Patricia - Latin. "Noble"

Patron - Spanish. "Master"

Pavo - Latin. "Peacock"; a constellation in the southern sky

Paxton - Latin. "Peace town"

Peace - Latin. "Tranquil"

Peach - Latin. "Persian apple"; a particularly admirable or pleasing person or thing

Pearce - Irish form of Piers, from Peter

Pearl - A hard, lustrous spherical mass formed within the shell of a pearl oyster or other bivalve mollusk and highly prized as a gem; a precious thing; the finest example of something

Pegasus - A mythical winged divine stallion, and one of the most recognised creatures in Greek mythology

Penance - Latin. "Repentance of sins"

Pendente/Pendant - Latin, Old French. "To hang down"; loose-hanging piece of jewelry, generally attached by a small loop to a necklace

Penelope - Greek. "Bobbin"; faithful wife of Odysseus in Homer's *The Odyssey* (9th century BCE)

Pennylane - An alias one would use to hide their true identity; a song by The Beatles (1967)

Pennyrose - Norman Scottish. "Pin a rose on your nose"

Pennyroyal - Aromatic old world plant which yields an oil used in folk medicine

Peony - Latin, Greek. "Healing"; the flower was named after Paeon, the Greek physician of the gods

Pepper - English and North German occupational name for a spicer; Notable Bearer: Pepper J. Keenan is an American guitarist and vocalist

Peppermint - Mildly popular as a unisex name since the early 1900's; Peppermint Patty is one of Charlie Brown's friends in the famous *Peanuts* cartoons

Percival/Perceval/Percivale - English. "Pierces the valley"; one of King Arthur's legendary Knights of The Round Table

Perdita - Latin. "Lost"; the heroine of William Shakespeare's play *The Winter's Tale* (1623)

Peridot - A mix of Anglo-Norman and Arabic words meaning "gem"; a semi-precious green gem that is especially connected with ancient Egypt; some historians believe that the famous emeralds of Cleopatra were actually peridot gems

Perrin - Greek, Latin. "Rock"; "wanderer"

Perry - English, Welsh. "Pear tree"; "son of Herry"

Perselaine - Old French. "Bright, shining light"

Persephone - [pur-SEF-o-nee] In Greek mythology, the daughter of Demeter and Zeus; she was abducted to the underworld by Hades, but was eventually allowed to return to the surface for part of the year

Perseus - Greek. "To destroy"; in Greek mythology, the slayer of the gorgon Medusa and the rescuer of Andromeda from a sea monster; Perseus was the hero who was said to have founded the ancient city of Mycenae

Persistence - Middle English. "Constant"; "persevere"; "persist"; a virtue name used uncommonly by the Puritans

Peru - Greek. "Rock"

Petrichor - A pleasant smell that frequently accompanies the first rain after a long period of warm, dry weather

Petronilla - Latin. "Stone"; an ancient saint's name that relates to the Roman family name Petronius

Petrus - Greek. "Rock; rock oil"; a common name for people from antiquity through the medieval era

Petruvia - Latin, from Greek. "Rock"

Petula - Latin. "To seek"; "to attack"

Petunia - A plant of the nightshade family with brightly colored funnel-shaped flowers, native to tropical America; popular along with other flower names in the Victorian era

Phaethon - Greek. "Son of Helios"

Phaidra/Phaedra - Greek. "Bright"; in Greek mythology, the daughter of Minos and the wife of Theseus

Pharaoh - Egyptian. "Great house"; the name for a ruler in ancient Egypt

Pharika - Phoenician. "Land of fruit"; *Magic: The Gathering* legendary enchantment god

Phelan - Old Irish. "Wolf"

Phenax - *Magic: The Gathering* legendary enchantment god

Phi - The 21st letter of the Greek alphabet; the 21st star in a constellation

Philadelphia - Greek. "Brotherly love"; cities in Asia Minor and the US

Philemon - Greek. "Affectionate"; Philemon was the recipient of one of Paul's epistles in the *New Testament* of *The Bible*

Phillipa - Latin. "Lover of horses"

Philmore - Norman English. "Very famous"

Philomena - Old Roman representation of an ancient Greek word for "loved"; a Greek princess who was martyred in Rome in the 3rd century

Phineas/Fineas - Hebrew. "Oracle"; one of the two sons of the priest Eli in the *Old Testament* of *The Bible*

Phobos - The innermost and larger of the two natural satellites (moons) of Mars, the other being Deimos; in Greek mythology, Deimos and Phobos were the gods or personified spirits of fear

Phoenix - Greek. "A bird that built its own pyre and then was reborn from the ashes"

Phrixa/Phrixus/Phrixos - Latin. "Thrilling, causing shivers"; in Greek mythology, Phrixus was the son of Athamus and Nephele

Phylinda - An uncommon, yet steady, given and second name since the Colonial era

Phyllis - Greek. "Leafy foliage"; "green bough"; in Greek legend, Phyllis was changed to an almond tree after her death and bore no leaves until her love returned

Pi - Π The 16th letter of the Greek alphabet; the 16th star in a constellation

Pia - Latin, Swedish. "Pious"; "devout"; "prayerful"

Pianna - *Magic: The Gathering* creature

Picasso - Spanish. "Magpie"; Notable Bearer: painter and sculptor Pablo Picasso (1881-1973)

Pictor - Latin. "The painter's easel"; a constellation in the southern hemisphere

Pike/Pyke - Old English. "Point; hill"

Pilot - A pet form of the Old English personal name Pila; Notable Bearer: Pilot Inspektor, child of actor Jason Lee

Pippa - Greek. "To love horses"

Pippin - Latin. "Foreigner"; Notable Bearer: Pippin (or Pepin) the Short, first king of the Franks (752–768)

Pirate - Middle English. "Robber of the sea"

Piscine - Latin. "Fish"; of or relating to Pisces (astronomy, astrology)

Plateau - Old French. "Level"; an area of relatively level high ground

Plato - Greek. "Broad-shouldered"; Notable Bearer: Plato (4th century BCE) was one of the most important of the Greek philosophers; he was a pupil of Socrates and a teacher of Aristotle

Plaxico - Latin. "Peaceful"

Pleiades - [PLEE-ah-dees] A cluster of stars in the constellation Taurus; in Greek mythology, the seven daughters of Atlas became this group of stars

Pleione - A star in the Pleiades, from the Greek Pleo (to sail)

Pleo - Greek. "To sail"; Latin. "More"; "having more than the usual or expected number"

Plutarch - Greek. "Riches, wealth"; "master"; Notable Bearer: Plutarch was a 1st century Greek historian

Pluto - A dwarf planet, smaller than Earth's moon, with a heart-shaped glacier the size of Texas; the celestial body has blue skies, spinning moons, mountains and red snow

Pocahontas - Powhatan. "Playful one"; "spoiled child"; Notable Bearer: Pocahontas (1596-1617), born Matoaka and known as Amonute, was a Native American girl known for her association with the colonial settlement at Jamestown

Poe - Old Norse. "Peacock"; Notable Bearer: Edgar Allan Poe (1809-1849) was an American writer, editor, and literary critic

Poem - Latin, Greek. "Fiction"; "create"

Poetry - Literary work in which special intensity is given to the expression of feelings and ideas by the use of distinctive style and rhythm; something regarded as comparable to poetry in its beauty

Polaris - A star located at the end of the handle of the constellation Little Dipper; also called North Star

Pollux - An orange-hued evolved giant star in the northern constellation of Gemini; in Greek and Roman mythology, Castor and Pollux, or Kastor and Polydeuces, were twin brothers

Polina - A Russian feminine form of the Greek god Apollo

Polonia - A feminine form of the Greek Apollonios, of the same root as the name of the sun god Apollo

Polukranos - *Magic: The Gathering* legendary hydra

Polynices - Greek. "Manifold strife"; a character in Greek mythology

Polyxena - Latin from Greek. "Entertaining many guests, very hospitable"; in Greek mythology, the youngest daughter of the King Priam and Queen Hecuba; she was a Trojan princess who married Achilles to end the war between the Greeks and Trojans

Pompeii - An ancient Roman city near modern Naples; Pompeii, along with Herculaneum and many villas in the surrounding area, was mostly destroyed and buried under volcanic ash and pumice in the eruption of Mount Vesuvius in the 1st century

Poppy - In Greek and Roman myths, poppies were used as offerings to the dead, hence, poppies have long been used as a symbol of sleep, peace, and death

Porcelain - Middle French from Italian. "Cowrie shell"; synonymous with purity

Porter - Middle English. "Door keeper; gatekeeper"

Portia - Latin. "Offering"; a fictional character in William Shakespeare's play *The Merchant of Venice* (1605)

Portman - Dutch. "Gate man; man in charge of the gates"

Poseidon - Greek. "Husband"; "lord"; "earth"; in Greek mythology Poseidon was the unruly god of the sea and earthquakes, the brother of Zeus

Posey - French, English from Greek. "Brothers of Jesus"; a small flower bouquet usually tied with a colored ribbon

Potter - English and Dutch occupational name for a maker of drinking and storage vessels

Powel/Powell - Welsh. "Son of Hywel"

Prarie/Prairie - Old French from Latin. "Meadow"

Prashanta - Indian. "Quiet; tranquil"

Pray - Middle English. "Ask earnestly"; address a solemn request or expression of thanks to a deity or other object of worship

Prayer - Latin. "Obtained by entreaty"; an earnest hope or wish

Precious - Old French. "Of great value"; "greatly loved or treasured"

Primrose - Latin. "First rose"

Prisca - Biblical. "Ancient"; Notable Bearer: Saint Prisca was a 3rd century Roman woman allegedly tortured and executed for her Christian faith

Priscilla - Roman. "Venerable"; "ancient"; "classical"; "primordial"

Prism - A glass or other transparent object that separates white light into a spectrum of colors

Proteus - In Greek mythology, the prophetic old man of the sea and shepherd of the seals

Prudentia - Latin. "Good judgement"

Prue/Pru - Latin. "Prudence; good judgement"

Prunella - Latin. "Plum"; Spanish. "Brown"

Pryderi - A prominent figure in Welsh mythology, the son of Pwyll and Rhiannon, and king of Dyfed after his father's death

Psalm - Hebrew. "Song"

Psi - Ψ The 23rd letter of the Greek alphabet; the 23rd star in a constellation

Ptah - [pi-TAH, TAH] In Egyptian mythology, Ptah is the demiurge of Memphis, god of craftsmen and architects

Ptolemy - Greek. "Aggressive; warlike"; Ptolemy was the name of several Greco-Egyptian rulers of ancient Egypt

Pullman - German. "Bottle man"

Puma - A large brownish New World cat comparable in size to the jaguar; also called mountain lion, cougar, panther or catamount

Pure - Old French. "Wholesome and untainted by immorality"

Purity - Freedom from adulteration or contamination

Purje - Baltic. "Sail"

Pyrite - Greek. "Of fire"; a shiny yellow mineral consisting of iron disulfide and typically occurring as intersecting cubic crystals

Pyrrah/Pyrrha - In Greek mythology, the daughter of Epimetheus

Pythagoras - Greek. "Assembly; marketplace"; Notable Bearer: Pythagoras was a 6th century BCE Greek philosopher and mathematician

Pyxis - Latin. "Mariner's compass"; a small, faint constellation in the southern sky

Qais - Muslim. "Lover"

Qasar/Khasar - Mongolian. "Bravery"

Qatar - A peninsular Arab country whose terrain comprises arid desert and a long shoreline of beaches and dunes

Qatna - An archaeological site in the Wadi - il Aswad, a tributary of the Orontes; it comprises the largest Bronze Age town in Syria

Qaynan - A god of the smiths in pre-Islamic Arabia

Qetesh - Semitic goddess of Syrian or Sumerian origin who was assimilated into the Egyptian pantheon during 18th dynasty of the New Kingdom; she is the goddess of nature, beauty, sacred ecstasy and sexual pleasure

Qiturah - Arabic. "Incense; scent"

Qone - [kwo-NAY] In Chehalis mythology, the moon god Qone brought balance to the world by using his powers to change people, animals, and the landscape into the forms they have today

Quanah - Native American. "Sweet-smelling; fragrant"

Quark - Any of a number of subatomic particles carrying a fractional electric charge, postulated as building blocks of the hadrons

Quarri/Quarry - A place from which stones or other materials are extracted; an open-pit mine

Quartz - Greek. "Ice"; ancient Greeks and Romans believed that quartz was ice that never melted because it was formed by the gods

Queen - A female ruler of an independent state, especially one who inherits the position by right of birth

Quest/Questa - Latin. "Ask"; "seek"; "a long or arduous search for something"

Quill/Quille - Manx. "Hazel tree"; an ancient writing implement made from a moulted flight feather of a large bird

Quilla - English. "Quill; hollow stalk"; the Inca moon goddess

Quince - Pear shaped fruit used in preserves or as a flavoring

Quincey/Quincy - Latin. "From the place owned by the fifth son"

Quintessence - English. "The most perfect example of quality or class"

Quistis - Quistis Trepe is a fictional character in the *Final Fantasy* franchise

Quo - Old German. "Say; declare"

Quota - Latin. "How great"; "how many"

Quzah - The Arabic god of weather

R

Ra/Re - A major god in ancient Egyptian religion, identified primarily with the noon sun; in later Egyptian dynastic times, Ra was merged with the god Horus as Ra-Horakhty

Racida - A kind of plant used to reduce tumors; a grey/green color

Racinda - A popular name in the 1800's

Radkos - Slavic. "Happy; willing"

Ragna - Japanese anime criminal, Ragna the Bloodedge, from *Blazblue: Alter Memory*

Ragnar - Scandinavian. "Advice of the army"

Rahu - One of the nine major astronomical bodies (navagraha) in Indian texts

Raiden - Japanese. "Thunder"; "God; supreme being"; the typical English transcription of Raijin, the god of thunder and lightning in Japanese (Shinto) mythology

Raijin - 雷神 A god of lightning, thunder and storms in the Shinto religion and Japanese mythology

Rainbow - An arch of colors formed in the sky; symbol of promise and new life

Rajah - Hindi. "Indian king or prince"

Rajani - Hindi. "Night"; in mythology, another name for the goddess Kali

Rajka - Slavic. "Kind, dear, nice, pleasant, loving, gracious, gentle, or mild"

Rakdos - *Magic: The Gathering* legendary demon creature

Ral/Rall - Swabian. "To make noise"; "screech like a tomcat"

Raleigh - Old English. "Roe's deer meadow"

Rameses - Egyptian. "Born of Ra"; Rameses was the name of 11 Egyptian kings of the New Kingdom

Ramis - Of Norman origin, thought to be derived from the place name Rames in Seine-Inférieure, Normandy; Notable Bearer: Harold Allen Ramis (1944-2014) was an American actor, director, writer, and comedian

Ramona - Spanish. "Protecting hands"

Rana - Arabic, Persian. "Beautiful; eye-catching"; "to gaze at longingly"

Randolph/Randolf/Randulf - Old English. "Shield"; "wolf"

Ranger - Middle English occupational name for a gamekeeper or warden; a druid-type fighter class in the *Dungeons & Dragons* universe

Ranier/Rainier - French. "Strong counselor"

Ranulf - Old Norse. "Advice of the wolf gods"

Raphael/Rafael/Raffaello/Raffiel/Raffaele - Hebrew. "God is healer"; "God has healed"

Rare - Middle English. "Widely spaced"; "infrequent"; unusually good or remarkable

Rarity - Something that is valuable because there are few of its kind

Rashi - Hebrew. "Moon sign"; the sign in which the moon was placed at the time of your birth

Rashida - Egyptian. "Righteous"

Rashka - Form of Rachel (little lamb)

Raurica - Augusta Raurica is a Roman archaeological site in Switzerland

Raven - A glossy black color; a large, highly intelligent crow; the constellation Corvus

Razia - Arabic. "Happy; chosen; contented"

Razza - Arabic. "Servant of the provider"

Reality - The state of things as they really are

Rebel - Old German. "Raven"; someone who has taken part in a rebellion; the nickname of the members of the Confederate army

Redd/Red - English surname for someone with red hair, used often as a given name

Regina - Latin. "Queen"; used in the 2nd century and was revived twice, once in the middle ages and again in the 19th century; so fetch

Regor - A star in the constellation of Vela

Regulus - Latin. "Prince; little king"; the brightest star in the constellation of Leo; it was used by several 3rd century BCE consuls as well as many early saints

Reichert - Dutch. "Power"; "hardy"; "strong"

Rejoiner - Someone who joins again; used by western followers of religions that believe in reincarnation

Religa/Religo - Latin. "Scrupulous"; "conscience"; "exactness"; "to rely"

Rembrandt - From a Germanic name which was composed of the elements "ragin" (advice) and "brand" (sword); this name belonged to the 17th century Dutch painter Rembrandt van Rij

Remedy - Something that corrects, counteracts, relieves or cures

Remmy - French. "From Rheims"; a town in central France where champagne and fine brandies are made

Remon - French Gothic. "Council"

Rena - Greek. "Peaceful"

Renata/Renato - Latin. "Born again"

Renfry - The surname Renfrey was first found in Lincolnshire where they held a family seat as Lords of the Manor

Requiem - A token of remembrance

Retta - Latin. "Lover; beloved"; German. "House owner; lord of the manor"

Reuben - Hebrew. "Behold, a son"; in the *Old Testament* of *The Bible*, he is the eldest son of Jacob and Leah and the ancestor of one of the 12 tribes of Israel; it has been used as a Christian name in Britain since the Protestant Reformation

Reva - In Celtic mythology, Reva is the mother goddess of life and death who protects all men (mankind); she is the protector of all worlds

Revere - French. "To speak wildly"; "river bank"; Notable Bearer: Paul Revere (1735-1818) was an American silversmith, engraver, early industrialist, and patriot in the American Revolution

Reverie - Middle English. "Daydream"; "fanciful musing"

Reya - Spanish. "Queen"; "queen's advisor"; "a queenly woman"

Reyner/Rayner/Rainer - German. "Advice"; "army/council"; the Normans brought this name to England where it came into general use, though it was rare by the end of the Middle Ages

Rhea - In Greek mythology, the mother of the god Zeus and wife of Cronus; Notable Bearer: Rhea Jo Perlman is an American actress

Rhett - Welsh. "Ardent"; "fiery"; Rhett Butler was hero of Margaret Mitchell's *Gone With the Wind* (1936)

Rhiannon - The Celtic moon goddess Rhiannon was born at the first moon rise and is known as the "Divine Queen of Faeries"; she is the goddess of fertility, rebirth, wisdom, magic, transformation, beauty, artistic inspiration and poetry

Rhine/Rhein - Celtic. "To flow"

Rho - The 17th letter of the Greek alphabet; the 17th star in a constellation

Rhoda - Greek. "Rose"; in the *New Testament* of *The Bible*, this name was borne by a maid in the house of Mary; the name came into use in 17th century England

Rhode - The sea nymph and protector goddess of the island of Rhodes in Greek mythology; she was the daughter of the sea god Poseidon

Rhody/Rodi - Latin. "Rose"

Rhys/Reese/Reece/Rees - Welsh "Ardour"; "rashness"

Richmond - Old English, Old French. "Splendid hill"

Rickel - German. "Power"; "to rule"

Riclind/Riclynd - Old German. "Powerful"; "to rule"

Riddick - From the Anglo-Saxon, pre 9th century word "rudduc", an early name for the robin

Rigel - Arabic. "Foot"; Rigel is a blue star of the first magnitude that marks the hunter's left foot in the Orion constellation

Riot/Ryot/Ryatt - Hindi. "Flock"; "peasants"

Ripley - Old English. "Strip of land"; "wood"; "clearing"

Riven - English. "To tear apart into pieces"

Rocca - Italian. "Fortress"; "stronghold"

Rochelle - French. "Little rock"; a popular name in the 1930's; Notable Bearer: Rochelle Hudson (1914-1972) was an American film actress

Rochester - Old English. "Fortress"; "bridge"

Rock - The solid mineral material forming part of the surface of the earth and other similar planets; a genre of music; Notable Bearers: Rock Hudson (1925-1985) was an American actor; Dwayne Douglas "The Rock" Johnson is an American actor, producer, and semi-retired professional wrestler

Rockett - Old French. "Rook"; a family name used since very early times

Rockwell - Old English. "Rook woods"

Roderick - Middle Latin from Old High German. "Famous ruler"

Roe - Old Norse. "Clearing"; a habitational name for someone living on a farmstead in Norway; a nickname for a timid person

Rofellos - *Magic: The Gathering* elf legend

Rogue - Old English. "Scamp, knave, or mischievious person"; a character class in many role-playing games

Rohesia - Latin. "Rose"

Rohini - A lunar mansion in Indian astronomy corresponding to Aldebaran; a consort of Vasudeva and mother of Balarama and Subhadra in Hindu mythology; a series of Indian space satellites

Rolf/Rolph - Old Norse. "Renown wolf"

Roman - Latin. "Of Rome"

Romelia - Hebrew. "God's beloved one"

Romeo - Italian. "A pilgrim to Rome"; Romeo Montague is a fictional character in William Shakespeare's play *Romeo and Juliet* (1596)

Romilly - From Hebrew Romelia (God's beloved one)

Romulus - Latin. "Founder of Rome"

Romy - Latin. "Dew of the sea"

Rorik - Slavic. "Red"; a Danish Viking who ruled over parts of Friesland in the 9th century

Rorix - *Magic: The Gathering* legendary dragon

Rosaline/Rosalynd - Old French. "Tender horse"

Rosamonde - French. "Rose"; briefly popular in the early 1900's

Rosannah - Combination of Rosa (rose) and Anna (favor, grace, beautiful)

Roscoe - Norse. "From the deer forest"

Rosella/Roselle - Australian. "Rose of Gemini"; "little rose"; a type of colorful parakeet as well as a beautiful flower, both found in Australia

Rosemary - Latin. "Dew of the sea"

Rosetta - Italian. "Little rose"; "rose"; a name used by the French during the time of Napoleon Bonaparte's campaign in Egypt; the Rosetta Stone is a granodiorite stele inscribed with three versions of a decree issued at Memphis, Egypt in 196 BCE during the Ptolemaic dynasty on behalf of King Ptolemy V

Roswell - American. "Mighty horse"

Rotanev - A blue to white subgiant star that can be located in the constellation of Delphinus

Roth - German, Scottish. "Red"

Rousseau - Old French. "Red"; a nickname type of surname for a person with red hair or a ruddy complexion; Notable Bearer: Jean-Jacques Rousseau was a Francophone Genevan philosopher, writer, and composer of the 18th century

Roux - Latin. "Backward"; Old French. "Ruser"; Middle English. "A trick"

Rowan - Gaelic. "Little red one"

Rowena - Old German. "Fame"; "joy, bliss"; a daughter of 12th century Santon chief Hengist

Rowland - English, German. "Renown territory"; "bold"

Roxanna/Roxanne - Persian, American. "Dawn"; "bright"

Royal - Middle English. "Regal"; having the status of a king or queen or a member of their family

Royalty - Gaelic. "Red"; "of noble blood"; the status or power of a king or queen

Rubina - Arabic. "Ruby"

Rubix/Rubik - A Hungarian surname; Rubik's Cube is a 3D combination puzzle invented in 1974 by Hungarian sculptor and professor of architecture Ernő Rubik

Ruby - Latin. "Red"; birthstone of July, came into popularity as a given name in the late Victorian era

Rudolph/Rudolf - Old German. "Famous wolf"

Rudra - Sanskrit. "The roarer"; a Rigvedic deity associated with wind or storm and the hunt; Rudra has been praised as the "mightiest of the mighty"

Rufina - Latin, Greek, Italian, Russian, Spanish. "Red-haired female"

Rufus - Latin. "Red-haired"; a Roman cognomen and the name of several early saints, including one mentioned in the *New Testament* of *The Bible*

Ruhamah - Hebrew. "The one who has been spared"; in *The Bible*, Hosea is told by God to call his daughter Ruhamah

Ruhan - Arabic. "Spiritual"

Rune - Old Norse. "Secret"

Rupert - German variant of Robert; Notable Bearer: the military commander Prince Rupert of the Rhine, a nephew of Charles I, introduced this name to England in the 17th century

Ruric/Rurik - Russian. "Noted ruler"

Rush - A Middle English topographic name for someone who lived among rushes; an occupational name for someone who wove mats, baskets, and other articles out of rushes

Russel/Russell - Old French. "Red-haired"; "red-skinned"

Ruth - Hebrew. "Friend"; In the *Old Testament* of *The Bible*, Ruth was a Morobite woman who was the ancestor of King David; Ruth has been used as a Christian name since the Protestant Reformation; very popular in the United States following the birth of "baby" Ruth Cleveland (1891-1904), daughter of President Grover Cleveland

Ryby - Polish. "Fish"; the constellation Pisces

Rygar - A video game created by Tecmo in 1986 and originally released for arcades in Japan as *Warrior of Argus*

Ryu - Japanese. "Dragon"; a fictional character and the main protagonist of Capcom's *Street Fighter* series

S

Sabelina - Old English. "At the willows"

Sabra - Hebrew. "Opuntia fruit"

Sabratha - Berber. "Grain market"; "three cities"; a city in northwest Libya

Sacramento - Spanish. "Blessed sacrament"

Sadhbh (Saba) - Celtic. "The sweet and lovely lady"

Sadira - Persian. "Lotus tree"; "dreamy"; Arabic. "Star"; "ostrich returning from water"

Sacagawea - [sa-CAH-ga-wee-ah] Hidatsa. "Bird woman"; Shoshone. "Boat puller"; Notable Bearer: Sacagawea (1788-1812) was a Lemhi Shoshone woman who is known for her help to the Lewis and Clark Expedition

Safari - Swahili. "Expedition"; Arabic. "Journey"

Saffron - An Autumn-flowering crocus with reddish purple flowers prized for its color and flavor

Sage - Latin. "Be wise"; Middle English. "A profoundly wise (hu)man"; an aromatic plant with silvery green leaves

Sagitta - Latin. "Arrow"; a dim but distinctive constellation in the northern sky

Sagittarius - Latin. ♐ "Archer"; the ninth astorlogical sign; a constellation under the tropical zodiac

Said/Sa'id/Saeed/Saeid/Sayid - Arabic س"Happy"

Sailor - English. "One who sails"; *Sailor Moon* is a Japanese shōjo manga series

Saint - Latin. "Holy"; "consecrate"; a person acknowledged as holy or virtuous and typically regarded as being in heaven after death

Sakiko - Japanese. "Blossom child"

Salem - Hebrew. "Peace"; biblical name of an ancient city later identified with Jerusalem

Salinger - Norman English habitational name for someone living in a town dedicated to Saint Leger, the martyred 7th century bishop of Autun; Notable Bearer: Jerome David Salinger was an American writer known for his novel *The Catcher in the Rye* (1951)

Salix - Willows, also called sallows and osiers, form the genus Salix

Salvador - Latin. "Savior"; "to save"; Notable Bearer: Salvador Dali (1904-1989) was a prominent Spanish surrealist painter

Samar - Arabic. "Evening conversation"

Sampson - From the Hebrew name שִׁמְשׁוֹן (Shimshon) which meant "sun"; Samson was a hero granted exceptional strength by God in *The Bible*

Sanctuary - Latin. "Holy"; "a holy place"

Sanders - Greek. "Defender of men"

Sapphirah/Sapphira - Hebrew. "Beautiful gem"; wife of Ananias in *The Bible*

Sapphire - A beautiful blue gemstone; fancy sapphires also occur in yellow, purple, orange, and green colors; a popular name in Victorian times

Sappho - Greek. "Sapphire"; "lapis lazuli"; an ancient Greek poet from the island of Lesbos; Sappho (630-580 BCE) is known for her lyric poetry, written to be sung and accompanied by a lyre

Saqqara/Sakkara/Saccara - A vast, ancient burial ground in Egypt, serving as the necropolis for the ancient Egyptian capital, Memphis

Sardonyx - "Red Onyx"; a fictional character in the animated series *Steven Universe*

Sarek - A fictional Vulcan character in the *Star Trek* franchise

Sargas - Sumerian. "Seizer"; "smiter"; a binary star in the constellation Scorpius

Saria/Sariah - Hebrew. "Princess of Jehovah"; in *The Book of Mormon*, Sariah is the wife of Lehi who travels from Jerusalem to the promised land; a character in *Legend of Zelda: Ocarina of time*

Sarkhan - *Magic: The Gathering* planeswalker

Saturday - Latin. "Day of Saturn"

Saturn - Saturn was the Roman god of time and this is perhaps why the slowest (in orbit around the Sun) of the five bright planets was named after him; in legend, Saturn was the father of Jupiter

Saturnina - Latin. "Sowing"; "seed"; "birth"; "generation"

Savannah - Spanish. "Treeless plain"

Save/Sayve - English. "Keep safe"; "rescue"

Savior - Greek. "To save"

Saviti - Sanskrit. "Relating to the sun"

Savra - *Magic: The Gathering* legendary elf shaman

Sawyer - Celtic. "Cuts timber"; Tom Sawyer is the title character in a series of novels by Mark Twain (1835-1910)

Saxon - Teutonic. "Swordsman"; "knife"

Saxton - Gaelic. "Bodyguard"

Sayer - Welsh. "Carpenter, stonecutter or mason"

Sayne - French. An occupational name for someone who prepared cooked meats

Scarlet - English. "Red"; the heroine in Margaret Mitchell's *Gone With the Wind* (1939)

Sceptre/Scepter - A symbolic ornamental staff or wand held in the hand by a ruling monarch as an item of royal or imperial insignia

Scion - Old French. "Shoot; twig"; a descendant of a notable family

Scorch - Burn the surface of (something) with flame or heat

Scout - A solider or other person set out ahead of a main force so as to gather information about the enemy's strength, position of movements; Jean Louise "Scout" Finch is a fictional character in Harper Lee's novel *To Kill a Mockingbird* (1960)

Scribe - English. "Write"

Seattle - Chief Seattle (1786–1866) was a Suquamish chief noted for his accommodation to white settlers

Sedris - *Magic: The Gathering* legendary zombie warrior

Seer - A person who is supposed to be able to see what the future holds, through supernatural insight

Sefare - Native American. "Voyager"; "traveller of the stars"

Segal - Jewish acronym for the Hebrew phrase "SeGan Levia" (second rank Levite)

Segarus/Segaros/Seguros - A character in the *World Of Warcraft* franchise

Seger/Seager - Dutch. "Victory army"

Seinegal - Wolof. "Our Boat"

Seizan - Japanese 西山 A branch of Jōdo-shū Buddhism that was founded by Hōnen's disciple, Shōkū; Shōkū often went by the name Seizan as well, however the name derives from the western mountains of Kyoto where Shōkū often dwelt

Seker - A falcon god in Egyptian mythology; although the meaning of his name remains uncertain, the Egyptians in the *Pyramid Texts* (2400-2300 BCE) linked his name to the anguished cry of Osiris to Isis "sy-k-ri" (hurry to me); Seker is associated with two other gods, Ptah and Osiris

Selenia - *Magic: The Gathering* rare legendary angel

Selvala - *Magic: The Gathering* legendary elf scout

Semele - In Greek mythology, the mother of Dionysus

Seneca - Iroquois. "Place of stone"; a native american tribe that lived near the Great Lakes region of the USA

Sengir - *Magic: The Gathering* vampire lord

Senia - Variation of Xenia (hospitable)

Senna - Arabic. "Brilliance; radiance; splendor"

Sensei - Japanese. "Previous birth"; a martial arts teacher

Senua/Senuna - A goddess of rivers and springs in Celtic mythology

Sephira - In Kabbalah, each of the ten attributes or emanations; they are represented as spheres on the Tree of Life

Sephiroth - Plural of Sephira; the ten attributes or emanations surrounding the infinite and by means of which it relates to the finite in Cabalism

Sepia - Greek. "Cuttlefish"; a reddish-brown color associated particularly with early monochrome photographs; a brown pigment prepared from a black fluid secreted by cuttlefish, used in monochrome drawing and in watercolors

Septaria - Variant of Septarium; a concretionary nodule, typically of ironstone, having radical cracks filled with calcite or other minerals

September - Latin. "Seven"; the seventh month of the old Roman calendar

Seraphina - Hebrew. "Fiery-winged"

Serapis - A Greco-Egyptian god; the cult of Serapis was introduced during the 3rd century BCE on the orders of Ptolemy I of Egypt as a means to unify the Greeks and Egyptians in his realm

Serendipity - "Chance"; coined by Horace Walpole in *The Three Princes of Serendip* (1754), a fairy tale in which the heroes often made accidental discoveries of things they were not in search of

Serenity - French. "Serene, calm"

Sergeant - Middle English. "Attendant, servant"; "common soldier"; the term was later applied to specific official roles

Sergei/Sergi - Latin. "Servant, attendant"; an alternate form of Sergio and Sergeant

Serket - The goddess of fertility, nature, animals, medicine, magic, and healing venomous stings and bites in Egyptian mythology, originally the deification of the scorpion

Serpens - In Greek mythology, Serpens represents a snake held by the healer Asclepius

Serpent - Old French from Latin. "Creeping"; a dragon or other mythical snake-like reptile in medieval times

Serpentine - Old French. "Snake; snake-like"; "sly"; "deceptive"; a precious stone used archaically as an antidote for venomous snake bites

Serril - Greek. "Lordly"; "masterful"

Seuku - African. "Wise"; "educated"

Seward - Anglo-Saxon. "Sea guardian"; "guards the coast"

Sewell - Old English. "Seven springs"

Sextan - Gaelic. "Church warden"; "bodyguard"; "to resist or defend"

Seychelles/Seychelle - [SEY-shell] French. An archipelago of 115 islands in the Indian Ocean

Seymore/Seymour - From a Norman surname which originally belonged to a person coming from the French town of Saint Maur

Shade/Shayde - Celtic. "Defender"; a variation of the *Old Testament* name Shadrach; a fictional character in the *Doctor Who* universe

Shadow - Old English. "Screen or shield from attack"; Greek. "Darkness"; a shadow is a dark area where light from a light source is blocked by an opaque object; it occupies all of the three-dimensional volume behind an object with light in front of it

Shah - Persian. "King; ruler"; Sanskrit. "Honest"; "good"

Shai - Egyptian. "That which is ordained"; in Egyptian mythology, Shai was the god of fortune and is linked with the Greek god of fortune telling, Agathodaemon

Shakespeare - Old English. "To brandish a spear"; Notable Bearer: William "Bard of Avon" Shakespeare (1564-1616) was an English poet, playwright and actor, widely regarded as the greatest writer in the English language

Shala - An ancient Sumerian goddess of grain and the emotion of compassion

Shalom - Hebrew. "Peace, prosperity, harmony, wholeness, completeness, welfare and tranquility"; used as a greeting

Shanoa - The heroine of *Castlevania: Order of Ecclesia* (2008)

Shani - Irish. "God is gracious"; "gift from God"

Shara - In Sumerian mythology, Shara was a minor god of war, mainly identified with the city of Umma; he is noted in some texts as the son of Inanna (Ishtar)

Sharone - Hebrew. Referring to a fertile plain near the coast of Israel; a habitational name in the *Old Testament* of *The Bible*

Shasta - Sanskrit. "A teacher"; Native American Tribe of North California; Mount Shasta is the second highest peak in the Cascade mountain range

Shatura - [sha-TOO-rah, sha-TOR-ah] Town in Russia, east of Moscow

Shaula - A star on the raised tail of the scorpion in the constellation Lambda Scorpius

Shay/Shea - Irish. "Fine"; "fortunate"

Sheen - Gaelic. "Peaceful"

Shell/Shel - English diminutive form of Michelle or Sheldon

Shen - Chinese. "Deep thinker"; "deep thought"

Sheoldred - *Magic: The Gathering* legendary praetor

Sheri - French. "Darling"; "dear one"; "from the white meadow"; "beloved"

Sheriff - Old English contraction of the term "shire reeve"; a title designated a royal official responsible for keeping the peace throughout a shire or county on behalf of the king

Sherlock - Old English. "Bright hair"; Sherlock Holmes is a fictional character in a series of novels by Arthur Conan Doyle (1859-1930)

Sherman/Sharman - Anglo-Saxon. "Shearer of woolen garments"

Sherwood - Old English. "Bright wood"; Sherwood Forest is a royal forest in England, famous by its historic association with the legend of Robin Hood

Shiklah/Shikla - Transformation hero in Chinook mythology; often associated with Seuku and Qone

Shire - A county, especially in England

Shirina - Indian. "Night"

Shirley - English. "Bright wood"; "bright meadow"; "from the meadow"; Notable Bearer: Shirley Temple Black (1928-2014) was an American actress, singer and dancer

Shiva - Sanskrit. "The auspicious one"; the supreme god in Shivanism, one of the three most influential denominations of Hinduism

Shogun - Japanese from Chinese. "General"; a hereditary commander-in-chief in feudal Japan

Shoshannah - Hebrew. "Lily"

Shravishtha/Sravishta - The 23rd nakshatra (lunar mansion) in Hindu astronomy, corresponding to the constellation δ Delphinus

Shukra - Sanskrit. "Lucid; clear; bright"

Sia - The god of wisdom in ancient Egyptian mythology

Sibilla - Greek. "Prophetess"; "oracle"

Siculus - Diodorus Siculus (90-30 BCE) was a Greek historian known for writing the monumental universal history *Bibliotheca Historica*

Sidisi - *Magic: The Gathering* legendary naga shaman

Sidra - Urdu. "Of the stars"; "like a star"; also an Islamic name, short for Sidrat al-Muntaha, a holy tree at the end of the seventh heaven

Sierra - A long, jagged mountain chain

Sigarda - *Magic: The Gathering* legendary angel

Sigma - Greek. "Hissing"; "I hiss"

Sigmund - German. "Victorious defender"; "victory"; "protection"; Notable Bearer: psychiatrist Sigmund Freud (1856-1939)

Sigourney/Sigournay - French. "The Conqueror"; Notable Bearer: American actress Sigourney Weaver (originally Susan) took the stage name Sigourney from a character in *The Great Gatsby* (1925) by F. Scott Fitzgerald

Sigrid - Scandinavian from Old Norse. "Victory"; "wisdom"; "beautiful"

Sigurd - Old Norse. "Victory"; "guardian"; from Sigurðr, a legendary hero of Norse mythology and central character in the *Völsunga* saga (13th century)

Silas - Latin. "Of the forest"; "God of trees and forests"; in *The Bible*, Silas was a missionary companion of Paul and Timothy

Silik - A surname for one who worked or dealt in silk; a silk merchant

Silver - A soft, white, lustrous transition metal; it exhibits the highest electrical conductivity, thermal conductivity, and reflectivity of any metal

Silvester/Sylvester - Latin. "Wild wood"; "woodland"

Silvos - Nordic. "Wood"; *Magic: The Gathering* legendary rogue elemental

Simonette - Hebrew. "To listen"; "God has listened; a name given in gratitude by the parents who wished for a child and had their prayers answered

Simond/Simon/Symeon - Hebrew. "Listen"; also a classical Greek name, deriving from an adjective meaning "flat-nosed"

Sinclair - Norman Scottish. The name of a powerful Scottish clan; originally a habitational name for someone from places that dedicated their churches to Saint Clarus

Singapore - Sanskrit. "Lion city"; a Sumatran prince named Sang Nila Utama landed on Temasek (Singapore's former name) in the 14th century and saw a lion, which is called "singa" in Macay

Singer - Jewish occupational name for a cantor in a synagogue, from Yiddish "zinger"

Sinistra - Latin. "Sinister"; "left"; "with direction to the left"; a star in the constellation of Ophiuchus; a fictional character in J.K. Rowling's *Harry Potter* series

Sioux - Another term for the Dakota people or their language

Sir - Middle English. A reduced form of sire; used as a title before the given name of a knight or baronet

Sire - A respectful form of address for someone of high social status, especially a king

Sirius - Greek. "Glowing"; "scorching"; a star system and the brightest star in the constellation Canis Major and the Northern hemisphere; it was named after the ancient Egyptian god Osiris, who was represented as a dog, giving Sirius its more familiar name: the Dog Star

Sirona - A healing deity in Celtic mythology; she was associated with healing springs and her attributes were snakes and eggs

Sistine - An adjectival form of Sixtus, referring to Pope Sixtus, who commissioned the Sistine Chapel's famous frescoes

Situ - Chinese. The title of an official post, the minister of education, during the Zhou Dynasty

Situla - Latin. "Bucket"; "water jar"

Siva - Sanskrit. "The auspicious one"; in Hinduism, Siva is the destroyer and one of the three chief divinities of the later Hindu pantheon as well as the god presiding over personal destinies

Sixtus - Greek. "Polished"; five Popes of the Roman Catholic Church had this name

Skully/Scully - Irish. "High-ranking storyteller"; Old Irish. "Student"; Dana Katherine Scully is a fictional character in the TV series *The X-Files*

Skyla/Skylah - Dutch. "Sheltering"

Skylark - A common Eurasian and North African lark of farmland and open country, noted for its prolonged song during hovering flight

Skyler/Skylar - Anglicized spelling of the surname and given names Schuyler and Schuylar; introduced to America as a surname by 17th century Dutch settlers arriving in New York

Smoke - Once a popular nickname, it is now gaining popularity with boys as a given name

Snake - The snake is a legendary totem symbolizing transformation of energy from lower vibrations to higher aspects of mind, body and spirit

Snowbird - A northerner who relocates to a warmer southern location in the winter

Snowflake - A feathery ice crystal, typically displaying delicate symmetry; a white-flowered Eurasian plant related to and resembling the snowdrop

Sobek - In Egyptian mythology, Sobek was the ancient god of crocodiles; he is first mentioned in the *Pyramid Texts* (2400-2300 BCE) and his worship continued until the Roman period (27 BCE-1453)

Sochar - Irish. "Benefit"

Socrates - Greek philosopher who devised the Socratic method (469–399 BCE)

Soho - Derived from a former hunting cry; James Scott, first Duke of Monmouth, used "soho" as a rallying call for his men at the battle of Sedgemoor (1685)

Sojourner - Americanized form of French verb "so'journer" (to stay temporarily in one place); the name was created by African American abolitionist Isabella Baumfree in 1843 when she changed her name to Sojourner Truth

Solar - Latin. "Ancestral home"

Solaria/Solarium - Latin. "Light"

Soldier - Middle English. "Mercenary"; Old French. "Shilling's worth"; "wage"; Medieval Latin. "One having pay"

Soledad - Spanish name that refers to the Virgin Mary (our lady of solitude)

Solkanar - *Magic: The Gathering* legendary demon creature

Solomon - Hebrew. "Peace"; In *The Bible*, Solomon is the son of David and Bathsheba

Solstice - Old French, Latin. "The point at which the sun seems to stand still"; there are Pagan celebrations around the time of the winter and summer solstices, the shortest and longest days of the year

Solval - Spanish. "Solve"

Soma - Greek. "Body"; "the body as distinct from the soul, mind, or psyche"

Somalia - Arabic. "Wealthy"

Somerby - Middle English. "Summer village"

Sonata - A composition for an instrumental soloist, often with piano accompaniment

Sonder - German. "Special"

Song - A poem that is set to music or meant to be sung

Sonnet - A poem of 14 lines using any rhyme scheme, typically having 10 syllables per line

Sonorous - Latin. "Sound"

Sophitia - Fictional character in the *Soul* series of video games

Sophronia - Greek. "Prudent"; "of judicious mind"

Soprano - Italian. "Higher"; "situated above"

Sorcerer - Middle English from Latin. "A person who claims or is believed to have magic powers"; "a wizard"

Sorin - Romanian. "Sun"

Souhvezdi - Czech. "Constellation"

Southor - Of or from the south

Space/Spayce - The boundless three-dimensional extent in which objects and events have relative position and direction

Sparrow - Nickname from Middle English for a small, chirpy person, or for someone bearing some fancied physical resemblance to a sparrow; Notable Bearer: Sparrow James Midnight is a child of Nicole Richie and Joel Madden

Sparta - Greek. "Characterized by frugality or courage"; of or pertaining to the ancient Greek city of Sparta: famed for severity of its social order, the frugality of its people, the valor of its army, and the brevity of its speech

Sphene - Greek. "Wedge"; a very rare brilliant yellowish, green, orange or brown gemstone with a high luster, also known as "titanite" due to its titanium content; its Greek name alludes to the formation of its crystals

Spica - Latin. "The virgin's ear of wheat (grain)"; in Hindu astronomy, spica corresponds to the nakshatra Chitra

Spinoza - Hebrew, Portuguese. "Blessed"

Spiral/Spirel - Medieval Latin. In astronomy, it refers to a galaxy in which the stars and gas clouds are concentrated mainly in one or more spiral arms

Spock - Middle Dutch. "Spoke"; S'chn T'gai Spock is a famed vulcan/human Starfleet officer in the *Star Trek* franchise

Spokane - Native American. "Sun people"; "people of the sun"

Sravana - Hindu. "Star month"

Stanford - English. "Stony ford"; "stony meadow"; Stanford Blatch is a fictional character in the HBO series *Sex and the City*

Staniel - Middle English. "Bird of prey"

Stanton - Old English. "Stone enclosure"; "stone settlement"

Stark - Old English. "Unyielding"; "severe"; German, Dutch. "Strong"

Starla - American, Canadian. "Like a star"

Starling - Common name in the 1000's; the birds have strong feet, direct flight, and they are very gregarious

Starlite/Starlight - The light that comes from the stars

Starway - A tunnel through space; wormhole

Stella - Latin. "Star"; used by the 16th century poet Sir Philip Sidney for the subject of his collection of sonnets *Astrophel and Stella* (1591)

Stellar - English. "Like a star"; "otherworldly"

Sterling - English. "Of high quality"; "pure"

Stesha - Russian. "Crowned with laurels"

Stone - Stone Phillips is an American news anchor; Stone Gossard is a member of the rock band Pearl Jam

Storm/Stormy - Old Norse, Dutch. A name given to a child born at sea during a storm

Strabo - Greek geographer, philosopher, and historian who lived in Asia Minor during the transitional period of the Roman Republic into the Roman Empire

Straton/Stratton - English habitational name. "Roman road"; "enclosure"; "settlement"

Stratus - Latin. "Strewn"; a cloud forming a continuous horizontal gray sheet, often with rain or snow

Strick - Middle High German. "Cord"; "rope"; nickname for a ropemaker or for a rogue or prankster

Strickland - English. "Land (pasture) for young bullocks or heifers"

Strider - German, Dutch. "striving", "contest" or "quarrel"

Striker - Middle English. "To stroke"; "to smooth"; applied as an occupational name for someone whose job was to fill level measures of grain by passing a flat stick over the brim of the measure, thus removing any heaped excess

Strom - Swedish, Danish. "Current"; Old Norse. "Stream"; Notable Bearer: James Strom Thurmond (1902-2003) was an American politician

Stromkirk - *Magic: The Gathering* vampire soldier

Strong - Old English, German, Dutch. "Able to withstand great force or pressure"

Strummer - One who plays a stringed musical instrument

Suah - Biblical. "Speaking"; "entreating"; "ditch"

Suhaile/Suhaley - Arabic. Referring to a number of stars typically seen near the southern horizon from Arabia

Suijin - 水神 The Shinto god of water in Japan

Suky/Sookie - Hebrew. "Lily"

Sulis - A deity in Celtic mythology worshipped as a nourishing, life-giving mother goddess

Sullivan - Old Gaelic. "Eye"; the surname probably means either "one-eyed" or "hawk-eyed"

Sulu - Japanese. "Sea"; Hikaru Kato Sulu is a fictional character in the *Star Trek* franchise

Summit - English. "Peak of a mountain"

Summon - Latin. "Give a hint"; "call, evoke"; "secretly warn"

Summoner - One who summons or evokes

Sumter - The city and county of Sumter bear the name of General Thomas Sumter (1734-1832), the "Fighting Gamecock" of the American Revolutionary War

Sunastian - *Magic: The Gathering* legendary creature

Sundance - A dance performed by plains Indians in honor of the sun and to prove bravery by overcoming pain

Sundari - Indian. "Beautiful"

Sunday - Latin. "Sun's day"

Sunflower - The Native American flowers are named so because they turn toward the sky

Sunn/Sun/Sunny - The star at the center of our solar system, from Germanic languages that go back beyond recorded history

Sunrise - The aurora; the goddess of sunrise whose tears turned into dew

Sunrosa - Italian. "Rose of the sun"

Sunset/Sunsette - Greek. The name traditionally given to the repentant thief who was crucified beside Jesus Christ

Sunstorm - A disturbance or fluctuation in the Earth's outer magnetosphere, usually caused by streams of charged particles (plasma) given off by solar flares

Superior - Latin, Old French, Middle English. "Of high standard or quality"; "that which is above"

Surrak - *Magic: The Gathering* legendary human warrior

Surveyor - A person who investigates or examines something, especially boats for seaworthiness

Surya - Sanskrit. "Sun"

Susannah/Suzanne - From the Greek form of the Hebrew Shoshannah (lily); the name is mentioned in the biblical books of *Daniel* and *Luke*

Susquehanna - From earlier Sasquesahanough, the name of an Iroquoian people in an unidentified Eastern Algonquian language

Sutherland - Old Norse. "South land"; Notable Bearers: Donald McNichol Sutherland and his son Kiefer William Frederick Dempsey George Rufus Sutherland are Canadian actors

Suzette - French form of Susannah (lily)

Suzhou - The name Suzhou was first officially used for the city in 589 during the Sui dynasty

Sveta - Russian. "Saint"

Svetlana - Russian. "Northern star"; "light"; "luminescent"; "pure"; "blessed"; "holy"

Swait - Old English. "Sweet or gentle"

Swayze - Anglo-Saxon from German. "Swiss"; Notable Bearer: Patrick Swayze (1952-2009) was an American actor and singer

Sweet - Charming and endearing

Sweetpea - A climbing plant of the pea family, widely cultivated for its colorful fragrant flowers; a term of endearment

Sybil - Greek. "Prophetess"; in Greek and Roman legend, the sybils were ten female prophets who practiced at different holy sites in the ancient world

Sylvanas - Latin. "From the forest"; a popular girls name in the early 1900's

Sylvania - From Latin Sylvanas

Symmetry - Correct or pleasing proportions of the parts of a thing

Symphony - "Sounding together"; "harmony"

Syracuse - Biblical. "That draws violently"

Syrah - Also known as Shiraz, a dark-skinned grape variety grown throughout the world and used primarily to produce red wine

Syria/Siria - Spanish, Persian. "Associated with the sun"; "bright"

Syrma - Biblical. "Myrrh"

T

Tacoma - Latin. "To surpass"; "to go beyond"

Tahdisto - Finnish. "Constellation"

Tahngarth - *Magic: The Gathering* legendary minotaur

Taiwan - Formosan. "Sea people"; "island people"; an island off the coast of the Republic of China

Takei - Japanese. "Warrior"; "well"; Notable Bearer: George Hosato Takei is an American actor, director, author, and activist

Talania - A village in India

Talbot - A dog of an extinct light-colored breed of hound with large ears and a heavy jaw

Talcott - Middle English. "Tile cottage"; Talcott Hester is a character in *Final Fantasy XV*

Talina - Hebrew, German. "Tender morning dew"

Talinda - A derivative of the German Talina

Tallara - Aboriginal. "Rain"

Talon - English. "Claw"

Talrand - *Magic: The Gathering* legendary merfolk

Tallahassee - Apalachee. "Old town"; "abandoned fields"

Talon - English. "Claw"

Talulla/Tallulah - Irish. "Lady of abundance"; Native American. "Leaping water"

Tamar - Hebrew. "Date" (the fruit); "date palm"; "palm tree"; there are three characters in *The Bible* with this name

Tamesis - English. "Dark one"

Tamiyo - Japanese. "Moon sage"; *Magic: The Gathering* planeswalker

Tammuz - In Babylonia, the month Tammuz was established in honor of the eponymous god Tammuz, who originated as a Sumerian shepherd-god

Tampa - Believed to mean "sticks of fire" in the language of the Calusa, a Native American tribe that once lived south of the area

Tanaquille - Latin. "Worshipped in the home"

Tander - English, Irish. "One who sheared"

Tankard - Norman. "Hardy"; "brave"; "strong"

Tansy - Greek. "Immortality"; a flower

Tantalus/Tantalos - Tántalos was a Greek mythological figure, most famous for his eternal punishment in Tartarus

Tantrix - The rituals or practices outlined in the tantra

Tarantino - Italian. "Originating from Taranto"; Notable Bearer: Quentin Jerome Tarantino is an American film director, writer, and actor

Tarazed - An orange to red luminous giant star that can be located in the constellation Aquila

Tariel - *Magic: The Gathering* legendary angel

Taysa - Russian. "One who will be reborn"

Tatanka - Native American. "Short bull"

Tatenen/Tatenyn - Egyptian. "Risen land"; "exalter earth"; identified with creation, Tatenen was the god of the primordial mound in ancient Egyptian religion

Tatum - Old English. "Cheerful bringer of joy"

Tau - African. "Lion"

Taurik - Arabic. "Morning star"; Taurik is a fictional character in the *Star Trek* franchise

Taurus - Latin. "Bull-like"; a constellation picturing the forequarters of a bull and the second sign in the astrological Zodiac

Tawny - Irish. "A green field"; "the warm sandy color of a lion's coat"

Teague/Tighe - Irish. Cornish. Welsh. "Fair"; "beautiful"; a nickname for a handsome person

Teal - A bird; a blue-green color

Tekrick - A short-lived surname in Arkansas in the early 1900's

Temese - Temesa, later called Tempsa, was an ancient city of Magna Graecia on the shore of the Tyrrhenian Sea

Tempe - The Vale of Tempe is an important place in Greece and in Greek mythology; the modern cities in Arizona, USA and Australia are named after the Greek Tempe

Temperance - One of the qualities adopted as a first name by Puritans after the Reformation

Tempest/Tempestt - English. "Turbulent; stormy"; Notable Bearer: Tempestt Bledsoe is an American actress

Temple - Latin. "Open or consecrated place"; a building devoted to the worship, or regarded as the dwelling place, of a god or gods or other objects of religious reverence

Templeton - English. "Temple town"; this surname refers to medieval priories and settlements of the military religious order Knights-Templars

Tempo - Time; a musical term for the speed at which a piece of music is to be performed

Tennessee - Cherokee from Yuchi. "Meeting place"; "winding river"; "river of the great bend"

Teodora - Spanish feminine of Theodore (God given)

Teodosia - Russian. "God's gift"

Terric - A non-playable character in the *World Of Warcraft* universe

Tesla - Slavic. "Of the axe"; "harvester"; the name dates back to the 7th century when it was used to describe a tool used to harvest timber; Notable Bearer: Nikola Tesla (1856-1943) was a Serbian American inventor, electrical engineer, mechanical engineer, physicist, and futurist

Tester - German nickname for someone with a large or otherwise remarkable head; Bavarian topographic name for someone who lived at one end of a village or a row of fields

Texas - Caddo. "Friends"; "allies"; the name Texas was applied by the Spanish to the Caddo themselves and to the region of their settlement

Teysa - *Magic: The Gathering* legendary human advisor

Tezzeret - *Magic: The Gathering* planeswalker

Thabit/Thebit - Arabic. ثابت "The imperturbable one"

Thaddeus - Greek from Aramaic. "Courageous heart"

Thalia - Greek. "To flourish"; "to bloom"; in Greek mythology, Thalia was the muse of comedy and pastoral poetry

Thames - Celtic. "The dark one"; an ancient Celtic river

Thane - Old English. "Servant"; "soldier"; German. "Warrior"; Greek. "Child"; "parent"; a man who held land granted by the king or by a military nobleman, ranking between an ordinary freeman and a hereditary noble

Thassa - *Magic: The Gathering* legendary enchantment god

Thatcher - English. "Roofer"

Thea - Greek. "Goddess"; "godly"; the Greek goddess of light and the mother of the sun, moon and dawn

Theffania - Middle English. "Crown"

Thelma - Based on a Greek word for "will"; it was invented in 1887 by British writer Marie Corelli for the heroine in her novel *Thelma*

Thelon - *Magic: The Gathering* legendary elf druid

Thelonius/Thelonious - Latin. "One who plows the earth"

Themis - Greek. "Righteousness"

Theobald - German. "Bold person"

Theodocious/Theodosius - Greek. "Given by God"; Notable Bearer: Theodosius the Great was emperor of Rome in the 4th century

Theodora - Greek. "Gift"; "God's gift"

Theodore/Theodoros - Greek. "God given" the name was borne by several figures in ancient Greece, but later gained popularity due to the rise of Christianity

Theodosia - Feminine of Theodosius (given by God)

Theognis - Theognis of Megara was a Greek lyric poet active in the 6th century BCE

Theory - Latin from Greek. "Contemplation"; "speculation"; "spectator"; a mental scheme of something to be done

Therasia - Greek. "Reap"

Thergwen - Medieval variant of Gwendolyn; a unisex name at the time

Theron - Greek. "Hunter"; "untamed"

Theros - Greek. "Summer"; *Magic: The Gathering* plane of existence

Thersia/Therasia - Greek. "Summer"; "to harvest"; Notable Bearer: the Spanish wife of Saint Paulinus of Nola in the 4th century

Theseus - Greek. "To set, to place"; Theseus was a heroic king of Athens in Greek mythology

Theta - The eighth letter in the Greek alphabet; the eighth star in a constellation

Thethys/Tethys - In Greek mythology, Tethys was a Titan daughter of Uranus and Gaia, sister and wife of Titan-god Oceanus, mother of the Potamoi and the Oceanids

Thiago - Hebrew. "Yahweh may protect"; "holder of the heel"; "supplanter"

Thisalee - A druid in the *World Of Warcraft* universe

Thistle - Indo-European. "To prick"

Thoctar - *Magic: The Gathering* beast creature

Thor - Scandinavian. "Thunder"; Thor was the mythological Norse god of thunder and one of the sons of Odin; Thursday was named for Thor

Thora - Scandinavian feminine name honoring Thor, head of the Norse pantheon and god of thunder

Thorald - Norse. "Thor ruler"

Thorias - A fictional character in the animated series *Futurama*

Thorn - A stiff, sharp woody projection on the stem or other part of a plant

Thornton - Gaelic. "Town of thorns"; "Thorn" variants are English surnames occasionally used as given names

Thoth - The Egyptian god of writing, magic, wisdom, and the moon; he was one of the most important gods of ancient Egypt alternately said to be self-created or born of the seed of Horus from the forehead of Set

Thrace - Established by the Greeks for referring to the Thracian tribes

Thraix/Thraex - A gladiator fighting style representing the Thracian enemies of Rome

Thrake - A region and ancient country of the southeast Balkan Peninsula north of the Aegean Sea

Thunder - A loud rumbling or crashing noise heard after a lightning flash due to the expansion of rapidly heated air

Thurgood/Thurgod - Old Norse. "Thor god"; "completely good"; Notable Bearer: Thurgood Marshall (1908-1993) was the first Black American to be appointed to the Supreme Court

Thurman - Scandinavian. "Thunder"; Notable Bearer: Thurman Lee Thomas is a former American football player

Thursday - Old English. "Day of thunder"; named after Thor, the Norse god of thunder; Latin. "Day of Jupiter"; Thor was equated with the Roman god Jupiter

Thurstan/Thurston - Old Norse. "Thor stone"

Thyestes - In Greek mythology, Thyestes was a king of Olympia and the father of Pelopia and Aegisthus

Tibalt/Tybalt - Greek. "Prince of the people"; the main antagonist in William Shakespeare's play *Romeo and Juliet* (1597)

Tiberius/Tiberia - A Latin personal name used by both patrician and plebeian families throughout Roman history; Notable Bearer: Tiberius Claudius Nero (42 BCE-37 CE) was emperor of Rome; James Tiberius Kirk is a fictional character in the *Star Trek* franchise

Tiger - From the name of the large striped cat, ultimately of Iranian origin; Notable Bearer: American golfer Eldrick Tont "Tiger" Woods

Titan - The largest moon of Saturn; in Greek mythology, the Titans and Titanesses were members of the second generation of divine beings, descending from the primordial deities and preceding the Olympians

Titus - Biblical. "Pleasing"; Titus was Roman emperor from 79 to 81

Tobago - A southernmost island of the west Indian archipelago

Tobias - Greek. "The goodness of God"

Toci - The mother of the gods in Aztec mythology

Tolaria - *Magic: The Gathering* legendary land

Toledo - Spanish. "City of Spain"

Tonga - A light horse-drawn vehicle used in India; the Kingdom of Tonga is a Polynesian sovereign state and archipelago comprising 169 islands, of which 133 are uninhabited

Topaz - Latin. "Jewel"

Topeka - Native American. "A good place to dig potatoes"

Topper - An occupational name from a Middle English word for a tuft or handful of hair, wool or fibre, especially the portion of flax put on the distaff of a spinning wheel; Topper Harley is a fictional character in the movie parody *Hot Shots!* (1991)

Toral - Indian. "Folk heroine"; Toral is a fictional Klingon character in the *Star Trek* franchise

Tor/Torr/Tore - Scottish. "Watchtower"; "craggy hilltop"

Tornado - A rapidly rotating column of air that is in contact with both the surface of the Earth and a storm cloud; often referred to as a twister, whirlwind or cyclone; an altered form of the Spanish word "tronada" (thunderstorm) taken from the Latin "tonare" (to thunder)

Toro - Spanish. "Bull-like"; the constellation Taurus

Torrance - Scottish. "From the craggy hills"

Torsten/Thorstein/Torstein - Scandinavian. "Thor stone"

Torvil/Torvill - Old Norse. "Thunder weaver"

Tourmaline - Sinhalese. "Jewel"

Toviyah - Greek. "The goodness of God"

Train/Traine/Trayne - Old French. "Guile"; "snare"; "trap"; Middle English occupational name for a trapper or hunter

Tranquille - Peaceful; calm

Treasure - Middle English. "Value highly"; a quantity of precious metals, gems, or other valuable objects

Tremerig - A Welsh bishop tasked with looking after the duties of Æthelstan, a medieval Bishop; a common surname during the age of the vikings

Tremola - A valley in Switzerland

Tremolite - A mineral named for Tremola, the Swiss valley where it was found

Tressa - Greek. "Late summer"

Tresor - French. "Treasure"

Trinidad - Spanish. "Trinity"; an island in the West Indies

Trinity - Latin. "Triad"; refers to the holy trinity in the Christian faith, meaning "three in one: the father, son and holy spirit"; a Christian virtue name

Triton - The largest natural satellite of the planet Neptune; a mythological Greek god, the messenger of the sea

Trivia - Latin. "Diana"; details or pieces of information of little importance or value

Troilus - In Greek mythology, Troilus is a young Trojan prince, one of the sons of King Priam and a legendary character associated with the story of the Trojan War; the first surviving reference to him is in Homer's *The Iliad*, which some scholars theorize was composed by bards and sung in the late 9th or 8th century BCE

Trojan - Latin. "From Troy"; this was the name of a Roman emperor (53–117), who extended the Roman Empire east into Dacia (modern Romania); in early Slavic records the name is also borne by a mythical creature

Trooper - A private soldier in a cavalry, armored, or airborne unit

Truth - Old English. "Faithfulness; consistency"

Tucana - A constellation in the southern sky, named after the toucan, a South American bird

Tucson - Spanish. "At the base of the black hill"

Tuesday - Middle English. "Tyr's day"; named for the Norse god of war, Tyr; equivalent to the Roman Mars and the Greek Ares

Tulip - The flowers are originally from Turkey; the name comes from "tulbent" (turban), which is the shape some thought the flower to resemble

Turanga - Turanga Leela is a fictional character in the animated series *Futurama*

Turner - English and Scottish occupational name for a maker of objects of wood, metal, or bone by turning on a lathe

Turquoise - Turkish. "Turkish jewel"; a semiprecious stone, typically opaque and of a greenish-blue or sky-blue color

Tuvalu - A Polynesian island nation located in the Pacific ocean, midway between Hawaii and Australia; the name means "eight standing together"

Tuvoc/Tuvok - Tuvok is a fictional character in the *Star Trek* franchise

Tvastar - Sanskrit. "The visible form of creativity"; in historical Vedic religion, Tvastar is the artisan god or fashioner

Twilight - Old English. "Two light"; the soft glowing light from the sky when the sun is below the horizon, caused by the refraction and scattering of the sun's rays from the atmosphere

Twyla - Old English. "Two; double"; "woven of two threads"; "strength"

Tyche - Greek. "Luck"; the presiding tutelary deity in Greek mythology that governed the fortune and prosperity of a city, it's destiny; she is the daughter of Aphrodite and Zeus or Hermes; equivalent to the Roman Fortuna

Tycoon - Japanese. "Great lord"; a wealthy, powerful person in business or industry

Tymaret - *Magic: The Gathering* legendary zombie warrior

Tyrande - The chosen high priestess of the goddess Elune in *World Of Warcraft*

Tzar/Tsar - Russian. "Emperor"; refers to Julius Caesar

U

Uchtre - Gaelic. "A windy place"

Uganda - A landlocked country in East Africa

Ugo - Teutonic. "Spirit"

Ugutz - Basque. "John the Baptist"

Uhura - Swahili. "Freedom"; Nyota Uhura is a fictional character in the *Star Trek* franchise

Ukraine - Slavic. "Near the border"; "the borderlands"

Ukur - [OOH-koor] A god of the underworld in ancient Mesopotamian religion

Ulamog - *Magic: The Gathering* Eldrazi titan

Ulman - Arabic. "Scholar"; "the learned one"

Ulmer - German. "From Ulm"; Notable Bearers: Christian Ulmer, German ski jumper; Edgar G. Ulmer (1904–1972), Austrian American film director; Fran Ulmer, first woman elected as Lieutenant Governor of the state of Alaska

Ulrich - Old High German. "Powerful heritage"

Ulton/Ultan - Irish. "An Ulsterman"; there have been 18 saints named Ultan, the best-known being 7th century Saint Ultan of Ardbraccan

Ulysses - Greek. "Wrathful"; "hater"; Ulysses was the hero of Homer's *The Odyssey* (8th century BCE); Notable Bearer: American president Ulysses S. Grant (1822-1885)

Uma - Sanskrit. "Tranquility"; "splendor"; "fame"; "night"; the name of a Hindu goddess commonly known as Parvati; Notable Bearer: Uma Karuna Thurman is an American actress and model

Umaga - The name of the final and most painful part of the Samoan tattooing process, meaning "the end"

Umberto - Italian. "Renowned warrior"

Umbriel - Latin. "Shadow"; the "dusky melancholy sprite" in Alexander Pope's *The Rape of the Lock* (1712)

Umeko - Japanese. 梅子 "Plum tree child"

Umfrey - Old German. "Bear cub"; "peace"

Unah - Greek, Latin. "Pure; holy"; "one"

Unai - Basque. "A shepard"

Unega - Native American. "White"

Union - Latin. "Unity"; "one"; a state of harmony or agreement

Unity/Uniti - The state of being united or joined as a whole; a fictional hive-mind character in the animated series *Rick & Morty*

Universe - Late Middle English. "The whole world"; "cosmos"

Unut - [ooh-NUH] Egyptian. "The swift one"; in Egyptian mythology, Unut was a snake goddess; she was later depicted with a woman's body and a hare's head

Upshire - Anglo-Saxon. "Of Upshire"; refers to someone from the hamlet Upshire in county Essex

Upsilon - The 20th letter of the Greek alphabet; the 20th star in a constellation

Urania - Latin from Greek. "Heavenly"; "heaven"; in Greek mythology, the Muse of astronomy; another name of Aphrodite

Urborg - *Magic: The Gathering* legendary land

Uriah/Uriyah - Hebrew. "Yahweh is my light"; in the *Old Testament* of *The Bible*, this is the name of a Hittite warrior in King David's army; the first husband of Bathsheba

Uriel/Auriel/Oriel - Hebrew. "God is my light"; one of the archangels of post-exilic rabbinic tradition

Uril - *Magic: The Gathering* legendary beast

Urilda - A popular unisex name in the 1800's which is of uncertain ancient etymology

Urika - Omaha. "Useful to everyone"

Urna - Sanskrit. "Warm"

Ursa - Latin. "Bear"; Ursa Minor (Little Dipper) and Ursa Major (Big Dipper) are constellations in the northern sky

Ursley - Scandinavian. "Little bear"

Ursula - Latin. "Little she bear"; Notable Bearer: Saint Ursula was a legendary virgin princess of the 4th century who was martyred by the Huns while returning from a pilgrimage

Urthelmine - Popular female name in the 1700's and 1800's; German variant of Latin Ursula

Urthula/Urtula - Popular female name in the 1500's; Greek variant of Latin Ursula

Urtzi - Basque. "Sky"; an ancient sky god in Basque mythology

Uruguay - Guarani. "River of the painted birds"; "river of the shells"

Usoa - Spanish. "Dove"

Utah/Uta/Yutta - Shoshone. "People of the mountains"; Navajo. "Upper"; "higher up" applied to a Shoshone tribe called Ute

Utina/Utinah - Native American. "Woman of my country"

Utrilla - A common surname in Peru and used uncommonly as a given name in Italy, Mexico and Spain

Utu - Akkadian. "Sun"; the ancient Sumerian god of the sun, justice, morality, and truth; the twin brother of the goddess Inanna, the queen of heaven

Uxmal - An ancient Mayan city of the classical period in present-day Mexico; it is considered one of the most important archaeological sites of Mayan culture

Uzumati - Native American. "Bear"

Uzume - The goddess of dawn, mirth and revelry in the Shinto religion of Japan, and the wife of fellow-god Sarutahiko Ōkami; she famously relates to the tale of the missing sun deity Amaterasu Omikami

V

Vabiana - Latin. "Bean grower"; "bean seller"

Vada/Vayda - English. "Famous ruler"; Norwegian. "One who wades on water"; Vada Margaret Sultenfuss is a fictional character in the 1991 film *My Girl*

Vader - Dutch. "Father"; Darth Vader is a fictional character in the *Star Wars* franchise

Vahy - ♎ Czech. "Scales"; the constellation Libra

Valaskala - Finnish. "Dolphin"; the equatorial constellation Delphinus

Valdemar/Vladimir - German, Slavic. "Famous ruler"; it was introduced into Scandinavia by the 12th-century Danish king Waldemar (or Valdemar) who was named after a royal ancestor of his Ukrainian mother

Valdez - German. "Brave"; "son of Baldo"; Baldo is a shortened form of Baltazar, one of the three magi

Valdis - Icelandic from Old Norse. "Goddess of the dead"

Valentine/Valentino - Latin. "Strong"; "vigorous"; "healthy"; Notable Bearer: Saint Valentine was a 3rd century martyr; his feast day was the same as the Roman fertility festival of Lupercalia, which resulted in the association between Valentine's day and love

Valhalla - In Norse mythology, Valhalla is a majestic, enormous hall located in Asgard, ruled over by the god Odin; equatable to heaven in modern religions

Valiant - Middle English. "Robust"; "well-built"; Latin. "Be strong"; possessing or showing courage or determination

Valinda - Thought to be a variant of Linda (pretty); very popular in the USA in the 1950's

Valerian - Latin. "Strength"; "health"

Valkyrie - Old Norse. "Chooser of the slain"; in Norse mythology, the Valkyries were maidens who led heroes killed in battle to Valhalla

Valor - Middle English. "Brave"; "bold"; "courage"; "value"

Valya - Russian. "Strong, vigorous or powerful"

Van - Dutch. "Of"; Van was sometimes converted from a surname prefix to a given name by early immigrants to America; Notable Bearer: Sir George Ivan "Van" Morrison is an Irish singer-songwriter

Vana/Vanna - Variant of nirvana (bliss)

Vander - Greek. "Good man"; "family of good man"

Vanilla - Spanish. "Little pod"; a flavoring derived from orchids

Vanya/Vanja - Russian. "Gracious gift of God"; a diminutive of the Slavic Ivan

Vanzo - Notable Bearers: Alain Vanzo (1928–2002), French opera singer and composer; Fred Vanzo (1916–1976), American football player; Julio Vanzo (1901–1984), Argentine artist

Varanetta - A name lost to time, once popular in the middle ages; it is a variant of French "little Vera"

Varily/Verily - Middle English from Old French. "Truly"; "certainly"

Varnum - Southwestern English variant of the habitational name Farnham, reflecting the voicing of "f" that was characteristic of southwestern dialects of Middle English

Varolz - *Magic: The Gathering* legendary troll warrior

Varya - Russian, Greek, Czech. "Strongest in the world"

Vash - Old Persian. "Beautiful"

Vatican - Latin. "Characteristic of a prophet"; "oracular"; the Imperial Seat of the Roman caesars; the home of the Pope

Vaughn/Vaughan - Welsh. "Small"; often used as a variant of the Irish surname McMahon

Vayce/Vayse - Fictional character in the *World Of Warcraft* universe

Vaysa - Russian. "Royal"

Vedder/Vetter - Middle Low German. "Cousin"; also used to denote any male relative; Notable Bearer: Eddie Vedder is an American musician

Vega - Latin. "Star"; a Spanish surname for a person who lives in the open plains or meadow lands

Vegas - Spanish. "Meadows"

Vela - Spanish, Portuguese. "Sail"; "watchman"

Velania/Velanie - Old Greek. "Dark"

Velleron - Originally a Gallo-Roman oppidum (a large fortified Iron Age settlement) which became a fortified village in the Middle Ages

Vellichor - The strange wistfulness of used book stores

Velma - Old German. "Determined protector"; Velma Dinkley is a fictional character in the *Scooby Doo* franchise

Velryba - Czech. "Whale"; the constellation Cetus, which is named after a sea monster in Greek mythology

Velvette/Velvet - English. "Soft"

Venezuela - Spanish. "Little Venice"

Venser - *Magic: The Gathering* planeswalker

Ventura - Italian, Spanish, Catalan, Portuguese, Jewish. "Good fortune"; "luck"

Venuatu/Vanuatu - Melanesian. "Our land forever"

Venus - The Roman goddess of love and beauty, associated with the Greek goddess Aphrodite; the planet Venus spins in the opposite direction of most planets and has no moons

Venusia - Of or relating to the planet Venus

Vera - Latin, Russian. "Truth"

Veracruz - Latin. "True cross"

Verde - Spanish. "Green"

Verdelite - Italian. "Green stone"; the green variety of tourmaline

Verdie - Russian, Slavic. "Faith; hope"

Verdite - A gem with a rich green color often with a sparkling shine from small crystals

Verity - Late Middle English. "True"; a true principle or belief, especially one of fundamental importance

Verlene - Slavic. "Faith"

Verlin - Irish. "The farthing coin"

Verlinda - A variant of Verlene (faith)

Vermeer - Dutch. "From the lake"; Notable Bearer: Dutch genre painter Johannes Vermeer (1632–1675)

Vermont - French. "Green mountain"; named by French explorer Samuel de Champlain; on his 1647 map Vermont's nickname is "The Green Mountain State"

Verna - Latin. "Born in the spring"; "spring time"

Vernal - Latin. "Of the spring"; "spring (season)"

Vernon - Gaulish. "Alder tree"; "springlike"; "flourishing"; "full of life"

Verona - From Latin Vera (truth); fair Verona is the setting of William Shakespeare's play *Romeo and Juliet* (1597)

Veronese - Medieval Italian. "From Verona"; Notable Bearer: Veronese della Scala, daughter of Mastino II della Scala, a 14th century lord of Verona

Vertigo - A sensation of whirling and loss of balance; giddiness

Vertiline - A Victorian-era name that relates to the Latin Vera (truth)

Veruca - Derived from Veruschca; a fictional character in Roald Dahl's *Charlie and the Chocolate Factory* (1964)

Veruschca/Verushka - Slavic. "True"; "honest"; "faith"

Vesimies - Finnish. "Aquarius"

Vespa - Italian. "Wasp"; Princess Vespa is a fictional character in Mel Brook's 1987 spoof *Spaceballs*

Vesta - In Roman mythology, the virgin goddess of the hearth, home, and family

Vesuvius - An alternate name for Hercules, the son of the god Zeus and Alcmene; Zeus was also known as Ves in his aspect as the god of rains and dews; Hercules was thus alternatively known as Vesouvios (son of Ves); this name was then corrupted into "Vesuvius" from an Oscan word meaning "smoke"

Vibri - A fictional character in the game *Vib-Ribbon*

Victoria - Very rare in the English-speaking world until the 19th century, when Queen Victoria began her long rule of Britain; she was named after her mother, who was of German royalty

Victorine - French. "Victory"

Vienna - Dutch. "Forest stream"; the capital city of Austria, nicknamed the "City of Music" and the "City of Dreams"

Vietnam - Chinese. "Far off"; "beyond"; "to cross over; to go beyond"

Vigga - Scandinavian. "War"; "battle"

Vigilance - Latin. "Wakefulness"

Vignette - French. "Little vine"

Vigo/Vego/Vygo - Latin. "Small village"

Vikenti - Russian version of Vincent (conquering)

Vikesh/Vikesha - Hindu, Russian. "The moon"

Viletta - French. "From the country estate"

Vinz - Sumerian. "Conqueror"; Vinz Clortho is a fictional character in the *Ghostbusters* franchise

Viola - Italian. "Violet"; "violin"; a fictional character in *Twelfth Night* (1602), a comedy by William Shakespeare

Violet/Violette - Old French name for the flower; the name has been in use since the Middle Ages but did not become common until the Victorian era when flower names came into vogue

Viper - Any one of numerous species of Old World venomous snakes belonging to the family Viperidæ

Virgil/Vergil - Latin. "Vigil"; a given name made popular by Roman poet Publius Vergilius Maro (70–19 BCE)

Virginia - Latin. "Maiden"; "virgin"; a feminine given name derived from the ancient Roman family name Virginius (an homage to Virgo)

Virgo - Latin. "Virgin"; Virgo is the sixth astrological sign in the Zodiac and the second largest constellation

Virgon - Virgon is one of the three planets in the Trojan orbit in the *Battlestar Galactica* franchise

Viridis - Latin. "Green"

Virtue - Middle English from Latin. "Valor, merit or moral perfection"; behavior showing high moral standards

Visalia - Spanish from Latin. "Precious angel from the heavens"

Visara - *Magic: The Gathering* rare flying gorgon

Vishnu - Sanskrit. "All-pervasive"; the Hindu god Vishnu is the protector and preserver of the universe, usually depicted as four-armed and blue-skinned

Visma - A character in *Mahabharata* (9th century BCE), one of two major Sanskrit epics of ancient Hindu culture

Vito/Vita - Italian. "Life"

Vitolf - Old English variant of Vito

Vitus - Latin. "Life-giver"; Saint Vitus is the patron saint of dogs and a heroic figure in southern Italian folklore

Vitya - Russian variant of Victor

Vividine/Vivid - "Strikingly bright or intense"; "lively animated and strong"

Vivien - Latin. "Alive"; Saint Vivian was a French Bishop who provided protection during the Visigoth invasion

Vizzini - Habitational name from a place so named in Catania, Sicily; a fictional character in *The Princess Bride* (1973) by William Goldman

Vlad - Slavic. "Rule"

Vladimir - Slavic. "Universal ruler"

Vladya - Slavic. "Wreath of glory"

Vocatus - Latin. "One who is called or appointed"

Vodnar - Czech. "Aquarius"

Vogg - Wacław "Vogg" Kiełtyka is a Polish musician and composer

Vogul/Vogel - A hunting and herding tribe of the northern Ural mountains of western Russia

Voight - From the Latin Vocatus (one who is appointed)

Volans - Latin. "To fly"; the Flying Fish, a southern constellation between Carina and Hydrus

Volcana - Latin. "Vulcan"; feminine variant of the Roman mythological god of fire

Volcoff/Volkoff - Russian. "Wolf"

Volga - The longest river in Europe; a dragon knight warrior character in *The Legend of Zelda* franchise

Volodya - Slavic. "Universal ruler"

Volpetta - Italian. "Little fox"; a faint constellation in the northern sky known in English as Vulpecula

Volrath/Vollrath - Old German. "Council of people"; *Magic: The Gathering* legendary creature

Volsunga - Late 13th century legendary Icelandic saga of the origin and decline of the Völsung clan

Voltaire - The pseudonym of French writer, playwright and poet François-Marie Aroue (1694–1778)

Volya - Russian. "Freedom"; "will"

Vonda - Polish. "True image"; "wanderer"

Vondra - Czech. "Womanly"; "brave"

Vordus - The god of thunder, lightning and storms in Celtic mythology

Vorel - Czech. "Eagle"; a habitational name for someone who lived at a house distinguished by the sign of an eagle

Vorian - Vorian Dayne is a fictional character in *The World of Ice and Fire* (2014) by George R. R. Martin

Vosegus - A name used in the Roman Empire for a Celtic god of hunting and forestation

Vova - Russian diminutive of Vladimir (universal ruler)

Voyager - Someone who goes on a long trip, especially if they travel in a ship and explore

Vozka - Czech. "Charioteer"

Vraska - Gothic. "Fruit which is hewn or plucked off"; *Magic: The Gathering* planeswalker

Vulcan - The god of fire including the fire of volcanoes, metalworking, and the forge in ancient Roman religion and myth; his Greek counterpart is Hephaestus, the god of fire and smithery; a fictional planet in the *Star Trek* franchise

Vulpecula - Latin. "Little fox"; a faint constellation in the northern sky

Vyasa - Sanskrit. "Compiler"; Vyasa was one of the seven immortals in Hindu tradition

Vyveva - The Czech variant of the constellation Antlia

W

Wade/Wayde - English. "Ford"; "river crossing"; "advancer"; medieval given name from Scandinavian mythology

Waclaw - Polish. "Great fame"

Waldo - German "Powerful"; "ruler"; Notable Bearer: philosopher Ralph Waldo Emerson (1803-1832)

Waldorf - Old High German. "Forest" + "village; settlement"; habitational name from any of at least three places so called

Walken - Aboriginal. "Rainbow"; Notable Bearer: Christopher Walken is an American actor

Walker - Old English. "To walk; to tread"; this was the regular term for the occupation of a fuller during the Middle Ages

Wallace - Scottish. "Foreigner"; "Welshman"

Wallflower - A southern European plant of the cabbage family with fragrant flowers of yellow, orange-red, dark red or brown

Walter - Old German. "Ruler of the army"; Notable Bearer: Sir Walter Scott (1771-1832), a Scottish novelist who wrote *Ivanhoe* (1820) and other notable works

Waltz - An Anglo hereditary surname; a name for a man who was a young ruler

Wander - Old English; "To meander"; "to move casually or aimlessly"

Ward - Gaelic. "Son of the poet"; Old English. "Watchman"; "guard"

Warden - English. "Guard"

Warhol - Polish. "Squabbler"; Notable Bearer: Andy Warhol (1928-1987) was an American artist who was a leading figure in a movement known as pop art

Warlord - A military commander, especially an aggressive regional commander with individual autonomy

Warner - Norman English. "Army guard"

Warren - Old French. "Game preserve"; "dweller at or keeper of a game preserve"

Warrior - Middle English. "Brave or experienced soldier or fighter"

Washington - English. "From the intelligent one's farm"; "from the town of Wassa's people"; Notable Bearer: founding father and first president of the USA George Washington (1732-1799); because of his celebrity, the name became popular for baby boys at the time

Watkyn/Watkin - English pet form of Watt, a short form of Walter

Watson - A patronymic surname of English and Scottish origin meaning "son of Walter"; the popular Old English given names Wat or Watt were pet forms of the name Walter

Watt/Wat - An extremely common Middle English personal name; a short form of Walter

Wave/Wayve - The sea; a sudden occurrence of, or increase in, a specified phenomenon, feeling or emotion

Weather - The state of the atmosphere at a place and time as regards heat, dryness, sunshine, wind, rain, etc.

Weatherly - Old English. "Woodland clearing"; Notable Bearer: Michael Manning Weatherly, Jr. is an American actor

Weaver - Old English. "To weave"; an occupational name for a weaver

Webster - Old English female version of a weaver

Wednesday - The Old English word for Wednesday indicates that the day was named for the Germanic god Woden; in romance languages, the name is derived from the Roman god Mercury

Wei - Chinese. 威 "Power"; 薇 "fern"

Welles - English. "Lives by the spring"

Wellington - Anglo-Saxon. "From the wealthy estate"

Wendell - German. "Wanderer"; Notable Bearer: American writer Sir Oliver Wendell Holmes (1809-1894)

Werlanda - Old Dutch. "Wetlands"

Wernstrom - Professor Ogden Wernstrom is a fictional character in the animated series *Futurama*

West - Latin. "Evening"; the direction toward the point of the horizon where the sun sets at the equinoxes

Westell - Anglo-Saxon surname that was common before the 8th century

Westelle/Westella - A genus of green algae

Westley - English. "From the west meadow"; Westley "The Dread Pirate Roberts" is a fictional character in the novel *The Princess Bride* (1973) by William Goldman

Westor/Weston - Old English. "West town"

Wheeler - Middle English occupational name for a maker of wheels

Whimsy/Wimsie - Middle English. "Playfully quaint or fanciful behavior or humor"; "a thing that is fanciful or odd"

Whisper - Old English. "A soft rustling or murmuring sound"

Whitman - Middle English. "White man"; an occupational name for a servant of a bearer of the name White

Wichita - Choctaw. "Big arbor"

Wilde/Wild/Wyld/Wylde - Middle Dutch. "Wild man"; "savage"

Wilder/Wylder - German. "Hunter"

Wilfred/Wilfrid - Old English. "Desiring peace"; Notable Bearer: Saint Wilfrid was a 7th century Anglo-Saxon bishop; the name was rarely used after the Norman conquest until it was revived in the 19th century

Willa - Old German. "Will"; "desire"; English feminine form of William

Willamina - Old Dutch. "Desire protection"

Willow - English. "Slender"; "graceful"; from the willow tree which is noted for slender, graceful branches and leaves

Wilma - Dutch. "Resolute protector"

Wilmetta - Old German. "Determined protector"

Wilmot - German. "Resolute spirit"

Wilton - Old English. "Willow town"; "well town"; "town on the River Wylye"; Celtic. "Tricky"

Winder - Old English. "Windan"; "to wind"; occupational name for a maker of baskets, etc.

Windsong - A name denoting the musical sound created by the wind

Winfield - Old English. "Meadow"; "pasture"; "open country"

Winifred/Wynifrid - Welsh. "Reconciled"; "blessed"; Notable Bearer: Winifred was a martyred Welsh princess, traditionally the patron saint of virgins

Winslet/Winslette - English surname gaining popularity as a given name; Notable Bearer: Kate Elizabeth Winslet is an English actor

Winston - English. "From Wine's town"; "from a friend's town"; Notable Bearer: Sir Winston Leonard Spencer-Churchill (1874-1965) was Prime Minister of the United Kingdom

Winthorpe/Winthrop - English. "Friend's village"; "friend's farm"

Wisconsin - Algonquin. "It lies red"

Wisdom - Old English. "The quality of having experience, knowledge, and good judgment"; "the quality of being wise"

Wizard - Late Middle English. "A being who has magical powers", especially in legends and fairy tales

Woden - Anglo-Saxon. "King of the gods"

Wolf - A canine native to the wilderness and remote areas of Eurasia and North America

Wolfgang - Old High German. "Path of the wolf"; Notable Bearer: Wolfgang Amadeus Mozart (1756-1791) was a prolific and influential composer of the classical era

Wonder - Old English. "A feeling of surprise mingled with admiration, caused by something beautiful, unexpected, unfamiliar, or inexplicable"; "desire or be curious to know something"

Woodrow - Originally an Old English surname which may originally derive from a toponym meaning "row of houses by a wood"; Notable Bearers: Thomas Woodrow Wilson (1856-1924) was 28th president of the USA; Woodrow Tracy Harrelson is an American actor; Woodrow Wilson Guthrie is an American folk singer

World - The world is the planet Earth and all life upon it, including human civilization

Wosret - Egyptian. "The powerful"; Wosret was an Egyptian goddess with a cult center at Thebes

Wray - Norse. "From the corner property"

Wren - Welsh. "Ruler"; a small passerine bird

Writer/Riter - A person who uses written words in various styles and techniques to communicate ideas

Wyck - English. "Village"

Wymar/Weimar - Old German. "Magnificent"

Wymarc - Popular name in England and Ireland; a fictional character in the *World Of Warcraft* universe

Wymond - Medieval English. "Battle protector"

Wyoming - Munsee. "At the big river flat"

X

Xabat - Spanish. "Savior"

Xabier/Xavier - Basque. "New house; new home"

Xalbador - Spanish. "Savior"; a variant of Salvador

Xander/Zander - Greek. "Defender of men"

Xandra - [ZAHN-druh, SHAN-druh] Feminine of Xander

Xanten - A tourist town in Germany

Xanthe - Greek. "Yellow"; "blonde-haired"

Xanthus - In Greek mythology, Xanthos was the king of Thebes and the son of Ptolemy

Xapa - Greek. "Joy"

Xara - American. "Princess"

Xariffa/Xarifa - [zah-REE-fah or sha-REE-fa] Pen name of 19th century poet Mary Ashley Townsend; Beatrix Potter, writer of *Peter Rabbit*, had a pet mouse with this name

Xarissa - [za-RISS-ah or sha-riss-AH] American from Greek. "Very dear"; "beloved"; "being close to perfection"

Xarles - French. "Manly"

Xarus - [ZUH-ris or SHA-rus] A fictional son of Dracula in the *Marvel* Universe

Xaymaca - [yi-MAKE-ah] Arawak. "Land of wood and water"; also known as Jamaica

Xenagos - [ZEN-ah-gos] The Spartan commander of the several contingents in the Peloponnesian League; *Magic: The Gathering* legendary enchantment god

Xenia - Greek. "Welcoming; hospitable"

Xenovia/Zenovia - Greek. "Life of Zeus"

Xerxes - [ZIRK-cees] Greek. "Leaving"; the fourth king of kings of the Achaemenid dynasty of Persia

Xi - [SHE or ZEE] Chinese. "Hope"; "wish"; "rare"; the 14th letter of Greek alphabet; the 14th star in a constellation

Ximen/Ximon/Ximun - Hebrew. "God has heard"

Xin - Chinese. "Beautiful"; "elegant"

Xing - Chinese. "Star"

Xinthea - Variant of Greek Kynthia, from Mount Cynthus, where Greek moon goddess Artemis and her twin brother Apollo were born

Xu - Chinese. "Brilliant rising sun"

Xuxa - [shoo-SHUH] Latin. "Lily"

Xystus - The Greek architectural term for the covered portico of the gymnasium, in which the exercises took place during the winter or in rainy weather, etc.

Y

Yagul - Latin. "Old stick"; "old tree"; one of the most studied archaeological sites in the Valley of Oaxaca

Yahto - Lakota. "The color blue"; most often used as a boy's name

Yakobe - Basque. "Young; youthful"

Yama - Sanskrit. "Twin"; a god of death, the south direction, and the underworld, belonging to an early stratum of Rigvedic Hindu deities

Yamanaka - Japanese. "In the middle of the mountain"

Yamka - Native American. "Blossom"

Yamoria/Yamozha - The benevolent culture hero of the Dene tribes; he is generally portrayed as a heroic monster-slayer and friend to mankind

Yanaba/Yanabah - Navajo. "She meets the enemy"

Yanamara - Basque. "Memory"

Yancy - Native American. "Englishman"

Yandel - Hebrew. "God is merciful"

Yang - The active male principle of the universe, characterized as male and creative and associated with heaven, heat, and light in Chinese philosophy; Yin is its counterpart

Yankee - An inhabitant of New England or one of the northern states; a Union soldier in the Civil War

Yannena/Yanninah - The goddess Ioannina is often called Yannena within Greece; the capital and largest city of Epirus

Yarrow - A Eurasian plant of the daisy family with feathery leaves and tiny flowers of white, yellow or pink

Yasmin/Yasmine - Arabic. "Jasmine flower"

Yatha - Arabic يثع "Savior"; a pre-Islamic god worshiped by the Sabaeans and Himyarites of Yemen

Yatokya - Native American. "Sun"

Yawgmoth - *Magic: The Gathering* human spirit god

Yaxha - Spanish. "Green water"; an ancient city of the Mayan culture

Yeare/Year - Old English. The length of time it takes for a planet to make full trip around its sun

Yemen - An Arab country in western Asia

Yemima/Yemina - Hebrew. "Right hand"

Yenene - Native American. "Wizard poisoning a sleeping person"

Yepa - Native American. "Snow woman"

Yera - Basque. "The virgin Mary"

Yesterday - Old English. "The day before; the recent past"

Yeva - Ukrainian. "Life"

Yin - In Chinese philosophy, the passive female principle of the universe associated with earth, dark, and cold; its counterpart is Yang

Yiska - Navajo. "The night has passed"

Yitro - Hebrew. "Plenty"; "bounty"

Yoki - Hopi. "Rain"

Yoko - Japanese. "Child of the ocean"; "child of the sun"; a very common female name in Japan; Notable Bearer: Yoko Ono was the wife of John Lennon of The Beatles

Yolanda - Greek. "Violet"

Yon/Yona - Hebrew. "Dove"

Yordana - Hebrew. "Descended from"

York - Old English. "Yew"; "pig farm"

Yoseba - Hebrew. "God will multiply"

Yosei - [yo-SAY] Japanese. "Fairy"; this word usually refers to spirits from western legends, but occasionally it may also denote a creature from native Japanese folklore

Yosemite - Miwok. "Those who kill"; originally referred to the native tribe that lived in Yosemite Valley

Yoshe/Yoshi - Japanese. "A beauty; lovely"; a fictional character in the *Super Mario Bros.* franchise

Yossarian - John Yossarian is a fictional character in Joseph Heller's satirical novel *Catch-22* (1961)

Yowah - A small town in outback Australia; home of the Yowah opal

Yuki - Japanese. 幸 "Happiness"; 雪 "snow"

Yuko - Japanese. 優子 "Gentle child"; 裕子 "fertile child"; 祐子 "helpful child"; 夕子 "evening child"

Yulene - Latin. "Young"

Yuli - Basque. "Youthful"

Yulia/Yuliya/Yulya - Russian. "Young"

Yuma - Native American. "Chief's son"

Yuna - Brazilian. "Dark river"; "black water"; a female given name in Chinese, Malaysian, Japanese, Korean, Breton and Brazilian cultures

Yutu - Native American. "To claw"

Yves - Celtic. "Yew"

Yvette - French. "Yew"; "archer"; feminine of Yves

Yvonne/Yvon - French. "Archer"

Z

Zada - Arabic. "Huntress"; "fortunate"

Zadoc - Hebrew. "Just"; "righteous"; the name of several biblical figures

Zadornin - Basque. "Saturn"

Zahra - Arabic. "Flower of the world"; "sparkling, bright and beautiful"

Zajic - Slavic. "Hare"

Zaidelle - [ZY-dell] Argentinian and Polish surname; a fictional character in the *Final Fantasy* universe

Zaire - Congo. "River that swallows all rivers"

Zakhar - Russian. "Remembrance of God"

Zala - Ancient Slavic. "Beautiful girl"

Zaltana - Native American. "High mountain"

Zambia - A landlocked country in Southern Africa

Zana - Kurdish. "Wise"; "knowing"; "learned"; "smart"; "astute"

Zane - Hebrew. "Gift from god"

Zaniah - Arabic. "Corner"

Zaphod - A fictional character in *The Hitchhiker's Guide to the Galaxy* (1979) by Douglas Adams

Zapp/Zap - To strike (an object or target) with a beam of energy, an electric current, or supernatural power; Zapp Brannigan is a fictional character in the animated sitcom *Futurama*

Zaqar/Zakar - The messenger of the god Sin in Mesopotamian mythology; he relays these messages to mortals through his power over their dreams and nightmares

Zarek - Polish. "Baal protect the king"; the last king of Babylon in *The Bible*

Zaurak - A red pulsating giant star that can be located in the constellation Eridanus

Zay/Zayin/Zain/Zayn - The seventh letter of the Semitic abjads

Zealand - Māori. "Land of the long white cloud"

Zeb/Zebby - Pet form of the Hebrew Zebulon

Zebulon/Zebulun - Hebrew. "Dwelling place"; "exalted, honored" the tenth son of Jacob in the *Old Testament* of *The Bible*

Zedaron - A star in the constellation Cassiopeia

Zedock - Hebrew. "Fair"; "righteous"; a biblical name that was used in colonial times

Zedruu - *Magic: The Gathering* legendary minotaur monk

Zeek/Zeke - Hebrew. "God strengthens"; "may God strengthen"

Zegana - *Magic: The Gathering* merfolk

Zeger - Dutch. "Victorious"

Zelda - German. "Dark battle"; Yiddish. "Blessed"; "happy"; a fictional character in *The Legend of Zelda* franchise

Zell/Zelle/Zeller - Dutch. "Hermit's cell"

Zella - African-Bobangi. "Lacking nothing"; "one who knows the path"

Zeta - ζ The sixth letter of the Greek alphabet; the sixth star in a constellation

Zen - 禅 Sanskrit. "Absorption"; "meditative state"

Zenith - Arabic. "Over the head"; the time at which something is most powerful or successful; the point in the sky or celestial sphere directly above an observer

Zeno - Zeno of Elea was a pre-Socratic Greek philosopher of Magna Graecia and a member of the Eleatic School founded by Parmenides

Zenobia/Xenobia - Greek. "The life of Zeus"; Notable Bearers: Saint Zenobia of Aegae was the 3rd century patron saint of those with breast cancer; Queen Zenobia was third century ruler of the wealthy Arabian desert city of Palmyra

Zenon - Greek. "Friendly"

Zenya/Zhenya - Greek. "Guest; stranger"

Zephoria - An obscure name that gained mild popularity in the early 1700's

Zephyr - Old English. "A soft gentle breeze"; "west wind"

Zephyrin - French variant of Zephyr (west wind)

Zephyrus/Zephuros - The Greek god of the west wind; Zephyrus is known as the fructifying wind and the messenger of spring

Zeppelin - A large German dirigible airship of the early 20th century, long and cylindrical in shape and with a rigid framework; zeppelins were used during World War I for reconnaissance and bombing, and after the war as passenger transports until the 1930s

Zepto - From Italian "sette" (seven)

Zeta - The sixth letter of the Greek alphabet, derived from the Phoenician letter zayin; the sixth star in a constellation

Zetta - Italian. "Seven"

Zeus - Greek. "Shine"; "sky"; in Greek mythology he was the highest of the gods

Zhang - Chinese. "Archer"

Zhen - Chinese. 珍 "Precious; rare"; 真 "real; genuine"; 贞 "virtuous; chaste; loyal"

Zi - Chinese. "Graceful"; "beautiful"; "saint"

Ziggy - English. "Victory and protection"

Zigmin - Related to Sigmund (victorious defender)

Zigor - Basque. "Punishes"

Zihna - Native American. "Spins"

Zilpah - Hebrew. "Frailty"; in the *Old Testament* of *The Bible*, this is the name of the handmaid who was given to Jacob by Leah

Zimmer - Old German. "Room"; "a chamber within a structure"

Zinaida - Spanish, Russian. "Of Zeus"

Zinc/Zink - A silvery-white metal that is a constituent of brass and is used for coating (galvanizing) iron and steel to protect against corrosion

Zinnia - A flower from the aster family that symbolises remembrance

Zippora/Zipporah - Hebrew. "Beauty"

Ziracuny - Native American. "From the water"

Zirafa - Arabic. "One who is graceful"

Zircon/Zirkon - A mineral occurring as prismatic crystals, typically brown but sometimes in translucent varieties of gem quality

Zirconium - Modern Latin, from Zircon

Ziva/Zivah/Zhiva - Hebrew. "Radiance"; "brilliance"; "light"; "God"; "brightness"

Zizilia - In Polish mythology, the goddess of love and sexuality

Zoelae - An ancient Celtic tribe of Gallaecia, living in the north of modern Portugal

Zoelle/Zoella - Greek. "Alive"

Zoisite - A mineral with gem varieties which is related to the heart chakra and said to alleviate grief, anger, despair and defeat

Zona - Latin. "The zone"; a very famous name in Serbian culture

Zonta - Sioux. "Honest and trustworthy"

Zora/Zorah - Slavic. "Dawn"

Zoreal - [zo-RAIL] A fictional character in the *World Of Warcraft* universe

Zorel - A fictional character in *DC Comics*

Zorg - A character in the film *Betty Blue* (1986); a character in the film *The Fifth Element* (1997)

Zoriah - Slavic. "Star"; "strong-willed"; "independent"

Zorian/Zorion/Zoriona - Latin. "Happy"

Zory/Zorie - Russian. "Farmer"

Zosma - A star with two names, one Greek, the other Arabic; Zosma rides the back of Leo the Lion in the constellation

Zotheca/Zotheke - Latin. "Closet"

Zothecula - Diminutive of Zōthēca

Zuben - The brightest star in the constellation Libra

Zultanite - Greek. "To scatter"; Zultanite is an extremely rare gemstone that, despite its beauty and suitability for jewelry, was previously plagued by scant availability

Zuma - Arabic. "Peace"

Zuri/Zuria - Swahili. "Beautiful"

Zurine - Spanish. "White"

Zuul/Zule - A fictional Sumerian demigod and minion of Gozer in the 1984 film *Ghostbusters*